A. QUINN STANLEY, PHD

Coherent
CHAOS

THE UNITY PARADOX...

innovo
PUBLISHING
innovopublishing.com

Published by Innovo Publishing, LLC
www.innovopublishing.com
1-888-546-2111

innovo
PUBLISHING
innovopublishing.com

Innovo Publishing LLC is a Christ-centered publisher located near Memphis, TN. Since 2008, Innovo has published quality books, eBooks, audiobooks, music, screenplays, and online and physical curricula that support the Great Commission, equip believers, and help create a positive Christian worldview. Innovo's capabilities and global reach provide Christian authors, artists, and ministries access to the world for Christ. To learn more about Innovo Publishing, visit our website at innovopublishing.com. To connect with other Christian creatives and to learn best practices for creating, publishing, marketing, and selling Christian titles, visit the Christian Publishing Portal at cpportal.com.

COHERENT CHAOS
The Unity Paradox . . .

Names marked with an "" have been changed to protect the privacy of the individuals.*

All scripture was taken from the King James Version of the Bible. Public domain.

Library of Congress Control Number: 2025915009
ISBN: 979-8-88928-095-8

Cover Design & Interior Layout: Innovo Publishing, LLC

Printed in the United States of America
U.S. Printing History
First Edition: 2025

To Amy: You bring harmony to a life filled with paradoxes, embodying the profound connection this book explores.
You are my most cherished connection.

· · ·

To Kevin Reeves: You remain a life-long friend.
1964–2023

Acknowledgments

I would like to extend a heartfelt "thank-you" to my wonderful editor and interior layout designer, Rachael Carrington, and cover designer, Yvonne Parks.

CONTENTS

Runway to Revelation
··· 202 ···

Embracing the Embarrassing
··· 239 ···

PREFACE

This book is about *chaos* and its smaller cousins *conflict* and *confusion*. It's also about *connection* and *peace* and their larger cousin *unity*. Specifically, it's about how chaos can promote and improve connections. Yes, disputes often drive people apart, and for good reasons. However, when handled well, conflicts can also provide opportunities for healing.

Conflicts have been part of human history since the very beginning. Humanity has been shaped by *survival of the fittest*, while Christianity is based on two conflicting elements: salvation (life) through willing crucifixion (death). And on a smaller, more personal scale, we learn from our daily struggles with others and with ourselves.

Of course learning is always easier through hindsight, but being aware of how we can learn while we're in the middle of a situation is much more difficult—especially since large-scale and personal conflicts often give rise to increased societal, mental, and physical health problems. As a result, conflicts with others increase, which further increases societal and health problems. It's a vicious cycle that only continues to worsen.

Through these pages, allow me to provide some clarity and promote some harmony by demonstrating how to turn conflict into a chance for growth. Along the way, we will unpack some data on various controversial topics from two areas that often needlessly oppose each other: science and religion. I'm not trying to affirm nor denigrate; I only want to show how facing a possible conflict while respecting both sides can lead to honest conversations with positive outcomes.

I will also share some personal and professional experiences that show how conflict can end in healing cooperation. I hope that as you see how these conflicts have played out in my own life and in the lives of others, you'll gain a sense of how disputes can harmonize into something stronger than either side alone can produce.

AN INTRODUCTION, KINDA
Kickoff Contrasts

Connections

Opposites attract. We've all witnessed life-long relationships between seemingly unsuitable individuals. Rivals in sports are often friends before and after the game. Even some soldiers at war have enjoyed socializing with the enemy. Some even played games such as soccer and only returned to fighting when their superiors forced them to. Even then, there's evidence that some combatants purposely missed when shooting at their newfound friends.

I do not mean to say that relationships involving people with similar interests can't be wonderful as well. I know people who don't have many conflicts. Several times I've seen one spouse pass away, leaving a healthy surviving spouse who ultimately dies not long after; they literally could not live without their spouse. For the purpose of this book, however, it's much harder to see the positives that can result from *conflicts*. That's why I want to focus on those oft-maligned contentious relationships.

I've long been drawn to apparent discord. Sometimes this magnetism leads me to people I have never met before, usually because of perceived personality similarities or a shared quirkiness. I often relate to people whose lives exhibit contrasts, as my life has been full of them. I'm one of those oddballs who is happy with very little social interaction, yet I've been curiously labeled a *talker*. I've spent some periods of my life in the blue-collar world, but I also enjoyed reading Shakespeare and John Bunyan's *Pilgrim's Progress*. I might swing a hammer during the day and then spend the night drawing. I could jump out of an airplane on a Sunday morning and then go to Sunday school. At other times I would play a rugby match and then go minister to abused children. Moving from one world to another would cause some people a lot of stress, but for me, those contrasts are what make life interesting, and they teach me to find peace, even during the melee.

There are two people I feel a connection with because we seem to share lives of contrasting quirks: the biblical David and the philosopher William James. I don't claim to be at David's spiritual level or James's intellectual level, but I relate to the contrasts within their lives that I recognize when reading their writings. David was a shepherd who, through no personal ambition of his own, became a king. He was a poet and great musician who could calm others' moods, but he was also a skilled warrior. He was the great leader of a nation but failed as a father. He was a murderer and adulterer but one of God's greatest worshippers. David was far from perfect, but it is hard to deny that his varied experiences led to an interesting life. I think his full life is one reason David was able to peacefully pass into the next one.

William James first trained to be an artist but ultimately became a scientist. He defended the value of individual opinions and explored such mental states with the use of physiology. He was a pessimist who struggled with severe bouts of depression and suicidal thoughts, and he was fascinated by spiritual experiences. He earned a medical degree but never practiced medicine. He moved from teaching physiology to teaching psychology and, later, to teaching philosophy. At the age of thirty-four, he was living in his parents' home, unemployed and bedridden. Yet James went on to open the first psychology lab in North America and wrote *The Principles of Psychology*.[1] *The Varieties of Religious Experience: A Study in Human Nature* resulted from a series of lectures he was invited to give in 1901 and 1902.[2] It is such a monumental work that it remains in print to this day.

> **❝ From an educational viewpoint, I sometimes refer to myself as a redneck who wasn't smart enough to stop going to school, so I ended up with a PhD. ❞**

The contrasts found within David and James are why I feel a connection with them. It's a sort of familiarity related to emotional ups and downs and learning from our experiences. One of the most intriguing parts of their lives is how their contrasts converged to create legacies that continue to connect with people long after they have passed on. As I said, I am not at their level—I feel, as C. S. Lewis once put it, that I don't even feel worthy to sit on the back pew of the church. From an educational viewpoint, I sometimes refer to myself as a "redneck who *wasn't* smart enough to stop going to school, so I ended up with a PhD."

How Did I Get Here?

I often add, "but I *was* smart enough to drop out of high school." I called my old public high school and asked if I could get a copy of my transcripts to make sure I got my facts correct. I vaguely remembered my grades were not good, and when I went to pick up my records, I was curious to see just how bad they were. As I walked to the desk, I commented to a girl sitting outside the principal's office that I had spent a lot of time there and that "it will get better." The office worker was smiling and laughing as she handed me the envelope, and it looked and sounded like she was embarrassed for me. I knew she had looked at them. We chatted and laughed for a while.

I opened the envelope on the way back to my truck. In my freshman year, I had passed two—count 'em, *two*—classes. One of them was physical education (PE). In my second year, I failed *every* class, including PE. In my third year, I passed one semester of PE and failed everything else. So to sum it up, when I dropped out of high school during my senior year, I had passed a total of two and a half classes instead of the eighteen to twenty-one I needed to graduate.

When I had left the house that morning to get my transcripts, I was in such a rush that I didn't think to change into nicer clothes. I must have looked rather odd as I walked down the school hallway wearing an old frayed and stretched t-shirt, sweatpants, and flip-flops, with the little hair I have pointing in all directions and me laughing to myself. I wasn't laughing at my grades; I was laughing at the contrast between my high school grades and my PhD.

How had I had such a dismal high school career? During my teenage years, I became very hardheaded and rebellious and began to get into fights. I skipped school and often slept through classes, even when I was there. In the religious environment of my youth, I'd often heard comments that devalued education, implying that it would raise questions and cause confusion that would just mess up my theology. School tended to be my only secular social setting, and even though religious themes were more prevalent in schools than they are now, school still presented scientific ideas that drove a wedge between what I believed and what I was expected to learn. I may not have passed many classes, but that doesn't mean something wasn't sinking in between (or during?) naps—enough that I became increasingly suspicious and angry at the school that was, I believed, corrupting my faith, and that caused me to doubt this faith could hold up to even the most basic scientific knowledge.

My mother attended Bible college when I was young, but her studies were focused on religious music so she couldn't help me negotiate the divide. So given my hardheaded and rebellious nature, I took matters into my own hands, dropped out, and joined the U.S. Army at the age of seventeen. It seemed like a logical choice for me. If education was useless, why waste time on it? If religion could not stand up against scientific concepts, then the Bible must not be true, so it, too, was useless. Why should I waste time on either? I would get started on a career.

I realize that not everyone my age share my experiences. Some of my friends grew up in settings that supported both religion and science. Others grew up in settings that were even more isolating and divisive than mine—Christian schools, Christian colleges, hothouses that never exposed them to anything that might challenge their faith. Later in life, I learned that, when I was growing up, large factions of both religious and secular forces were purposely working to pull the two worlds further apart, while the factions trying to reunite the two were too weak. Some blame religion for being shortsighted and non-inclusive, and they're right. Others blame science for being shortsighted and non-inclusive, and they're right too. Hindsight makes it clear that the fault for the divide and the animosity between the two groups lies with both. Maybe if, at a younger age, I had heard some of the ways that the two areas supported each other, I would have taken a very different journey through life. I certainly would have had a better-looking high school transcript.

Don't misunderstand. I wouldn't trade my path for any other. I don't harbor ill feelings for either group. My rebellion led me to have experiences that the vast majority of the world's population will never get to enjoy. Most of my family was blue-collar, and that taught me the value of hard work. When it was time for my grandfather to go to bed, it didn't matter who was around or what was going on—he was going to sleep. As he walked down the hallway, his standard goodnight was, "I don't know 'bout the rest o' y'all, but I gotta get up 'n go t' work in t' morning." We used to joke with him that after he died, he'd just keep working until we put him in the ground. I still treasure his memory, in part, because of the motivation and direction he provided throughout my life.

At the same time, I've always had an inquisitive mind. Many years after dropping out of high school, I decided to revisit the whole battle between religion and science. I thought the intellectual journey might at least be interesting, even if my first impressions were right and both were false. If I found that one or the other was true, then I would support it. I decided to start with religion.

I began with the thought that *if* there is a God, I wanted to know which religion was true, so I began to study all the religions I could find. I visited different churches and talked with attendees and ministers. I participated in the rituals of some. I lived among some groups for a time. I was even honored to be invited to participate in some Native-American rituals, such as the Creation Dance. Once I settled on the religion I felt most closely followed biblical teachings, I still needed to decide if the Bible was true. I know, some of you will think I should have started with verifying the Bible, but my response is that not all religions are based on the Bible. So beginning with the Bible would have limited my options.

The Bible guides how humans should live, and it uses combinations of both physical and spiritual worlds to present its lessons. Though it begins with a very broad description of the physical world's creation, it's not a scientific document. After Creation, the Bible presents stories that often use the material world to provide direction. There are lots of examples of spiritual beings entering the physical realm for a specific purpose, and vice versa. There are definite interactions between the two worlds, and it is clear that each can affect the other. That much I knew from childhood.

That left me with the thought that *if* there is a God, and *if* the Bible is true, then it would be a bit hypocritical of Him to prohibit the exploration of the world He created for us to inhabit. After all, the Bible says that creation shows His glory, and it instructs us to seek to know Him. That left me with the thought that one of the ways to get to know God better is to study His creation. Therefore, in my mind, there needed to be some level of unity between religion and science. Could the two harmonize?

Why Did I Decide to Write This?

Basically there are four reasons.

First, if we are to effectively connect with people we disagree with, we need conversations where we simply learn about each other. No arguing, no pushing our ideals, no trying to convert. We just need to visit. The intrigue and joy of learning about the other person should be the purpose.

" One of the ways to get to know God better is to study His creation. "

Second, most of my professional life has been spent in the field of education, with some shorter stints in other areas like construction, church ministry, the military, and law enforcement. Most of those fields involved working with people who typically engaged in unproductive or violent behaviors. In the field of education, I was a special educator who studied and worked with special needs children, including gifted and talented ones, but students labeled as severely emotionally/behaviorally disturbed became my specialty. Though I worked with people ranging in age from kindergarteners to prison-lifers, the bulk were in high school. At times, talking was enough to manage my clients, but some situations required *physical counseling*, such as manual restraints or physical confrontations. When I talked to people after a physical intervention, most of them could not explain why they'd done what they did. One reason is that the subconscious affects human behavior much more than the conscious. Sure, to some extent, the cause could be traced back to the environment, genetics, and one's age, but we're also responsible for our actions. Working with people so out of control, unaware, unwilling, and/or unable to change helped me learn that strong relationships can result from contentious interactions. I know, it seems counterintuitive.

Third, I put this book together because people asked me to. Shortly before I graduated with my bachelor's degree, one of my English professors offered to ensure I received a graduate assistantship if I applied for the Master of Fine Arts program. The only stipulation was that he wanted my graduation project to be an autobiography. I was surprised and honored at the same time. However, I politely declined with the excuse that I was only in my mid-twenties and hadn't done anything worth writing about. (Ironic, right? Since this work uses some autobiographical experiences.) Later, some friends, family, and students made similar requests, but I always shrugged off their suggestions for the same reason. In all honesty, I still feel the same as I did with my English professor. I'm just Quinn—a high school dropout.

Finally, I decided to begin this book out of a growing compulsion. Maybe it's because I'm getting older, and I hope that someone else might find something useful in my struggles and ramblings. I eventually told myself that, if an idea just happened to pop into my head that might be useful to others, then I might give it a shot, but I was not going to work at it. So here I am. For clarity and brevity, I will make a few more short statements. Each will be explained further later on in the book.

What Is This Book About?

In the broadest sense, this book is about *connecting* despite and because of contentious situations. One way we explore this idea is by looking at some ways that data enters our brains and, in turn, influences our behaviors. It's a general principle of neurological processing that good information results in good communication and positive connections: *good in = good out*. The process works the other way too: *bad in = bad out*. Honest and respectful socialization is one of the best tools we have for increasing the flow of good information, but it requires us to show respect for ourselves and others. I'm hoping you might learn from some of my experiences as I intertwine some personal and professional stories, academic information, and ministerial experiences. At the very least, I hope you find something interesting or helpful.

Though I draw from both secular and theistic settings, this is not intended to be either an agnostic or an atheistic work. Nor is it intended to be a religious tract. While I can see how it might be used in multiple settings—ministry training, university classrooms, social work, to name a few—I only intend it to be a conversation about finding coherence. I hope that readers of all belief systems will find something useful to promote positive connections within themselves and with others. Simple conversations in which you feel free to talk about your beliefs are sorely missed.

I expect that the conversational language, real-life experiences, and associated research I bring to this work may unsettle some of you. There is plenty to offend deistic and atheistic minds alike. While I don't want to offend, I won't dilute the information so much that it won't move you to reconsider your thoughts. However, I do try to soften the blow of some sections, such as the section where I discuss medications and spiritual experiences. Honestly, some of the information unsettles even me, including some of my personal experiences. I could have done better, but you can't learn from them as I did if I don't share them. Mistakes can be great teachers if we allow them to be.

> **" Offenses in which people learn to effectively settle differences produce long-term positive results. To improve as humans, we need to learn to listen to opposing views and find common ground. "**

Additionally, I expect some of you will be offended by what looks like an attempt to reduce highly spiritual experiences to amoral, neurological functions. My intention is the opposite—to add to the significance of those intense experiences by providing an understanding of some physical processes that underlie them. For some people, their faith is increased when they understand the scientific processes. I am not a highly spiritual person. At times I wish I were, but I have had to accept that, for whatever reason, my station in life is as a *normal* spiritual person. I have come to embrace this role because I have learned that my way of viewing spirituality is a benefit to some. Hopefully, if you are a *normal* like me, this work will help you be more at ease with your role. If you are highly spiritual but you don't find it easy to understand those who are not, I hope that this will help you be more understanding.

I've long taken the stance, both in my professional and my personal life, that avoiding offenses leads to a long-term inability to deal with conflict. The result is much of the chaos we see in *civilized* (i.e., conflict-avoiding) societies around the world. Offenses in which people learn to effectively settle differences produce long-term positive results. To improve as humans, we need to learn to listen to opposing views and find common ground. Of course, some people only want to drain our energy through argument. I call them *energy suckers*. We should simply leave them alone until they want to engage in productive conversations—if they ever do. When we do have conversations, we should be wary of becoming energy suckers ourselves by trying to change or manipulate whomever we're talking to. We should simply enjoy learning about another human.

Some sections of this book may have been written decades ago, while others were written within the last few years. Various purposes of these writings will provide different *feels* for you. I could have rewritten each section, worked better on the literary flow, and updated old academic references, but I decided to change as little as possible so that you might gain a better understanding of my perspective, and the research, at the time of the writing. Sort of a growth process. This is also a good representation of life; it is not easy and requires some humility.

Hopefully It's Positive

I want this book to be a positive experience. A little tricky since some of the topics explored may be hard for you to consider. I certainly don't want to offend any belief system; as I've aged and gained more wisdom, I've learned to try to avoid needlessly inflaming people's emotions. Unfortunately some others are not so concerned with that. I recently began reading a book written by an atheist, but I stopped before I'd finished the first chapter because of the gratuitous negativity. The author used words like *ignorance, superstition,* and *intellectual ruins* to refer to theism. There were even some obscenities. Definitely not a way to win people over. And this was from an academic with multiple PhDs who teaches at a university that supposedly promotes the free expression of ideas.

While reading those few pages, I thought many times that I could just as easily refer to the author's atheistic beliefs as *ignorance, superstition,* and *intellectual ruins.* I also made note of how I felt about the author's negative word choices (later we'll get into how words affect us on a neurological level). In short, they made me want to enroll in one of the author's classes just so I could give him my opinion in front of other students. But, alas, unfortunately I am struggling to mature.

One thing I find amusing about works by militant atheists is that, if I ignore their atheism, their writings sound oddly similar to religious sermons. On the other hand, and to be fair, if I ignore that some religious writings or sermons are presented by believers, they sound awfully secular. I hope that, as we learn to have respectful conversations, rather than trading *sermons* we can begin to learn more about each other, and that will lead to healthier relationships and connections with others.

Understand, I have read other works written by atheist scholars who used less biased words to present their views, and I've learned things that

I'm grateful for. That's the kind of reaction I'm hoping for with this book. Some of what I write about may be difficult for you to read, but if you see anything that seems disrespectful, I promise you, that wasn't my intention. I even refrain from using some of the more offensive authors on both sides of the argument. Some of my most treasured conversations have been with people who held vastly different points of view from me, but we genuinely listened, didn't try to change each other, wanted to learn about the other's views, didn't use inflammatory language, and showed respect for the other's views. I hope to demonstrate those qualities here.

Prism

William James used a prism to explain some functions of the brain, but I use it here to share a few of the colors (lenses) I used to write this book. A prism allows us to see the different colors included in light. Similarly, some of my *colors* act as guidelines for this work.

My normal inclination is to look for answers in the physical world, even in ministerial settings. If you're like me, you find that a little odd. It used to bother me. Why does my mind automatically begin to search for advice from secular information when a youth group student asks for counseling? Why do I not think of theological or biblical advice first? I have become more accepting of my natural thought processes because I have found that they are beneficial for some. After all, we do not get to live in church settings all of the time, so it can help to see applications of secular data by a church leader. That is why I rely heavily on a secular lens to explore spirituality.

You may be wondering why I have used spirituality and connection interchangeably. What is the relation? As you will see throughout this book, healthy spirituality leads to more, and better, relationships. It is a pathway to close relationships with animate and inanimate objects and beings. So I rely heavily on spirituality to explore the concept of connection. And, for those who may be wondering if spirituality applies to secular settings—yes, it does. More later.

The majority of my teaching occupation involved working with students who were labeled *severely emotionally/behaviorally disturbed*. When I moved into the university setting, I helped prepare future educators to work with these types of individuals. And, from the beginning of this chapter, you can probably see that I had my own behavioral issues. So I am heavily *colored* by behaviorism. Our behavior is important because it is our greatest communication method, and things like the environment, genetics, internal processes, and our histories can affect our actions. Simple behavior modification techniques like rewards and punishments—a behaviorist's bread and butter—can be used to train earthworms, while more sophisticated methods can be used to change the behaviors of whole societies.

As a new educator, I could see *what* my students did, and I knew on a psychological level *why* they did those things, but I couldn't answer *how*

> **" Our behavior is important because it is our greatest communication method. "**

from a physiological perspective. The physical mechanics behind our behaviors are important to me and is some of what I'm trying to share here. The Bible leans heavily on behavioral examples to instruct, and it includes several references to science, so I turned to science for answers. After all, if God truly made us to exist in this world, and if we are to seek to know

Him, then surely science could provide some clues about human mechanical workings. So I urge you to keep an open mind, not only about each other, but also about what science can teach us about our spirituality and what's going on inside of us.

The subconscious and its influence on our behaviors intrigues me. While in various jobs, I often had to make decisions without immediately knowing why I made them. For example, sitting in a meeting and *knowing* a parent was abusing a child even though I could not immediately say *how* I knew. A student trying to assault me didn't allow me time to consciously consider options; I just reacted. With Bill* I stepped closer so that his punch went behind my head, and I could take him to the floor and control his movements. That was the last time I had a physical confrontation with him, and years after his graduation, we stood in a department store, shook hands, and laughed about it. As Hillary* returned to her seat, I saw her reflection in a window as she raised her hand as if to stab me in the back with her newly sharpened pencil. I simply said, "Make it count," and continued teaching. She paused, sat down, and later became my classroom artist.

Why had I reacted differently to those students? Naturally I understood that I had reacted to protect myself and manage their behaviors, but why had I chosen those specific responses? I now know that such varied decisions were the result of my subconscious mind processing millions of bits of information without my consciousness being aware of it. It might be days before I could put into words why I had reacted a certain way because my slower, conscious mind took quite a while to catch up. While this book looks at some conscious mental processes, the focus is on the subconscious because it has a much greater influence on our behavior.

My life-prism also includes *colors* created by stints in the military and law enforcement. So I use those lenses too, and I share some experiences and research data from them. All of this combines to create the prism that is my life.

Autoethnography

To help intertwine such varied experiences and data fields, I use a method known as *autoethnography* (*auto* = self, *ethno* = people, *graphy* = writing). Granted, I use the method somewhat loosely. In simple terms, it is a qualitative research method that provides some academic structure but still allows me to share and evaluate some of my experiences so that I, and you, can learn from them. It's kind of like I learn as I write, and you learn as you read about some of my experiences. The processes and struggles I experienced are important. Balancing memories, emotions, and academics is tricky, and while there are some drawbacks (as with any research method), the benefits of connecting personal experiences with cultural issues and data outweigh the negatives. Most of the information is not new except for my experiences, how the information is organized, and my comments.

My initial intention was to write without using scholarly references because I understand that some will simply not read a book with academic information. Honestly, at times, I am part of that group. Just tell me some stories, and let's see what I can glean. But after some consideration, I decided to include some data for multiple reasons, including the following two: (1) academics play a part in my life, and (2) I want you to see there is support for the arguments that I make; they are not just ramblings from my head.

In support of the autoethnographic method, I begin each chapter with a personal experience, and I occasionally include others within the chapters. Sometimes I share a story as a transitional piece, while other times I engage in a little analysis. Sometimes I string together multiple stories so that you can see how my learning progressed along with my experiences. The research that I use is limited to areas that have helped me to understand something within the story, that I've used in secular and ministerial settings, or that may provide you with some insight into how I sometimes mentally process data. However, I do try to keep the academics to a minimum. If you would like to study the topic further, the references will help get you started. As you read and reflect on my experiences, I ask that you also reflect on your own.

Brief Explanation of the Title (Part 1)

Finding *coherence* within *dissonance* is what this book is about. Many people are puzzled (*paradox*) by the fact that struggles can promote close relationships (*unity*). Throughout the book I use many different words like *chaos, stress, disagreement, dissociation, struggle, conflict, animosity*, and so on to represent *dissonance*. *Coherent* may use synonyms like *unity, harmony, relationship, connection*, and *association*, and it is the central idea that this book explores—connections between religion and science, person to person, and person to something. The brain is the common element between all of these connections, so we'll be looking at how what we see and hear are cognitively processed and then how they affect our experiences and behaviors.

The ellipsis (. . .) at the end of the title is as important as any of the words. Ellipses can be used to indicate the trailing off of a thought, to show something isn't quite complete, or to show that a process is continuing. That continuing process may be represented by synonyms like *journey* or *voyage* or terms like *personal evolutionary growth*. And if you are reading this, you are still on your *expedition*. All of these apply to this book. Additionally, I end the book with an ellipsis as a way to indicate that there is much more we could have talked about and to show that our belief *odysseys* are not yet complete.

In Summary

In this introduction, we laid the foundation for the book's core theme: finding positive connections despite, and often because of, contrasts and contentious situations. I argued that difficult relationships actually offer unique opportunities for growth. Early on, we looked at David, a shepherd-king and poet-warrior, and William James, an artist-scientist who grappled with depression and spirituality. My own experiences, which have been marked by significant contrasts (e.g., high school dropout to PhD; blue-collar work, academia, military, ministry; science and faith), served as an example of how differences can harmonize. As we continue, autoethnography will be used to blend personal stories with research to explore this theme by examining areas like the subconscious mind's influence on behavior; the importance of learning-focused dialogue; insights gained from working with difficult individuals; and viewing life through multiple perspectives (*prisms*). This is done with the goal of fostering understanding and connections across different belief systems and experiences. One way I suggested for doing that is with talks focused on learning, not arguing, avoiding "energy suckers," and just learning about the other.

Introspective Questions for Introduction

? **Internal Contrasts and Relationships:** What contradictory traits define your personality (like the author's solitude/talkativeness)? How do these tensions shape your connections with others?

? **Personal Growth:** How have your views on education, science, or faith evolved since youth, and what experiences prompted these changes (similar to the author's journey from dropout to PhD)?

? **Connection Through Difference:** Reflect on a relationship that thrives despite significant differences or conflict. How have these challenges actually strengthened the bond, aligning with the author's idea of finding connection *through* contrast?

? **Dialogue Across Disagreement:** Think of someone you strongly disagree with. How could you structure a conversation focused solely on *understanding their perspective* without debating or trying to persuade them? How does the author's belief that "focusing on difficulties obscures positives" apply to this experience?

? **Navigating Worlds:** When have you moved between contrasting environments (e.g., academic, cultural, or professional), and how did this shape your ability to connect with others?

? **Spirituality and Science:** How does the author's idea that exploring the world scientifically can deepen spiritual connection sit with you? What natural or scientific phenomenon inspires awe for you, and why?

? **Subconscious Influences:** Recall a time you acted instinctively in a challenging situation. What might your subconscious have been processing? How does the author's focus on subconscious drivers inform your understanding? How aware are you generally of subconscious influences on your daily reactions?

? **Critical Self-Examination:** How comfortable are you with your level of spirituality (or lack thereof)? How does the author's acceptance of being a "normal" spiritual person influence your self-view?

? **Your Interpretive "Lenses":** What primary perspectives or "lenses" (e.g., logical, emotional, relational, scientific) do you typically use to make sense of the world? How might consciously adopting a different lens change your view of a current challenge or relationship?

? **Engaging with the Author's Story:** How does hearing the author's personal struggles and background influence your receptiveness to his ideas? Does his vulnerability make the concepts more relatable or impactful?

CHAPTER 1

Sanctuary Siestas and Synaptic Secrets

Sleeping Under Church Pews

Sleeping under a church pew during the sermon is awesome. Trust me, I know. I have a lot of experience.

I was born into a conservative religious family and spent many of my adolescent years attending a church founded by Reverend D. L. Welch. In most of those services, I would watch my elders raise their hands in worship, dance in the spirit, run around in excitement, speak in tongues, laugh in the spirit, and yell "Amen!" "Hallelujah!" and "Preach it!" back at the fiery preacher. Energy, sweat, and noise were staples. Of course, I also spent time playing with my G. I. Joe or scribbling rudimentary pictures of race cars on scrap paper. Since this all took place in hot and humid Florida, one of the coolest places was on the hard tile floor under the wooden pews. I usually found my way down there for a good nap within the first few minutes of the sermon, and it was not uncommon for my mother to have to carry me to the car for the trip home. Sometimes I faked being asleep. I just didn't want to walk.

I don't mean to give the impression that I was simply an observer of those services. Even though I was too young to understand what was happening or to participate without possibly getting injured by the adult worshippers, I did experience what was happening *around* me. I could feel *something* during those services. I didn't know what it was, but I knew I didn't feel it anywhere else. I also felt a special something while with my grandparents, and I could locate the source of that something with them.

However, I could not locate the source at church, and it had a different *feel* to me. The something seemed to be coming from everywhere rather than one particular place, though it could feel more concentrated in some areas. I learned that if someone were having a particularly deep spiritual experience, the closer I got to that person, the more strongly I could feel the *something*, but even then I knew that the person was not the source. Though I couldn't identify the source, I knew that I enjoyed it. It was not uncommon for me to stop shooting my G. I. Joe with my fingers and just sit on the pew and focus on that feeling.

It was not until much later in life that I was able to mentally relive those experiences and apply some academic information. From a behaviorist perspective, I now know that each time I went under the pew to catch a nap, I caused those in the vicinity to change their behaviors. Let me try and paint a picture.

Our spot in the sanctuary was relatively consistent: looking from back to front, the left-hand row of pews, a few rows from the front, on the long, squeaky, unpadded wooden benches. Specifically, the fifth pew, notorious for a small crack that demanded careful sitting was the desired one. My mother liked to sit near the center aisle but not quite on the end, ensuring we were enveloped by the community.

When I slipped under the pew to sleep, an unspoken coordination began. Those sharing our bench, except for my persistently kicking sister, became mindful of their feet and created a living barrier with their legs that shielded me from dropped Bibles or purses.

That awareness extended to those on the pew behind. Occupants consciously avoided stretching their legs forward into my space. Even amidst fervent "Hallelujahs!" and rising to their feet, they navigated carefully to avoid disturbing me. A quiet rearrangement of items occurred below the bench: any objects like purses or suit coats (never Bibles, which were never on the floor) under our pew were moved to accommodate me. After the repositioning they formed a secondary protective wall behind my sleeping nook. It wasn't uncommon for a woman from the back pew to fold her husband's coat and offer it as a pillow. Thus a temporary, protected space was collectively created—walled by legs in front and belongings behind, furnished with a coat pillow, grounded by the cool floor—a testament to the quiet community of care within the congregation.

I also learned physiology to gain a deeper understanding of some unseen actions. For example, my sleeping under pews caused chemical reactions in the brains of those in the vicinity: some parts of our brains experienced an increase in blood flow, while blood flow reduced in other areas; neurochemicals began to affect things like mood, sleep, and relationships; acetylcholine (helps with muscle movements) decreased in me, while it increased in others so that movements like moving purses could be performed.

I came to understand that when I decided to nap under a pew, I created behavioral, physiological, and emotional changes in myself and others within my vicinity. We even created some basic neurological bonds, though they were not nearly as strong as the neurological bonds I now have with my wife and kids. Even this simple task of writing about sleeping under pews gives me a sense of peace and calm; a release of serotonin helps to produce a positive mood, and oxytocin strengthens those mental memories and relationships. Those individuals still hold a special place in my heart, and I enjoy laughing with them about how small and cute I was.

Science-Religion Relationship

While I often think of events in terms of science, I realize that science cannot fully explain spiritual events. Neither can spirituality fully explain science. Neither does one need the other to survive or prosper. However, at times, they can provide a better understanding of one another and can help correct some bad behaviors of the other—science balancing religion's capacity for self-delusion, and religion balancing science's tendency toward reductionism, for instance. Both have existed in some form in all known civilizations, and both have had tremendous influence on humanity. At times they've worked together; at other times they've fought each other. Let's look at a very broad history about this relationship.

" Science cannot fully explain spiritual events. Neither can spirituality fully explain science. Neither does one need the other to survive or prosper. However, at times, they can provide a better understanding of one another. "

The Greek philosopher Heraclitus suggested that humans were made of both a body and a soul, with the soul being responsible for thoughts and emotions. Plato proposed a more strictly *dualistic* view that confined the soul to the brain; it was physically located within the body. Democritus, apparently not comfortable with some of the supernatural parts of those philosophies, proposed that everything is composed of only matter, no soul; everything is physical. When we die, we simply cease to exist. Hippocrates (of Hippocratic Oath fame) argued that, since a brain injury can impair mental processing, it must be the seat of conscious thoughts. A few centuries later, Galen also postulated that thoughts are limited to the brain.

During the Middle Ages, the church was so forceful in its attempts to control science that the Renaissance saw a growing interest in separating religious influence from scientific exploration. This movement led to the Age of Reason, which began around the time Francis Bacon published *Novum Organum* in the early 1600s, spelling out how to use theory and experiment to advance knowledge—what we now know as the scientific method. During the Scientific Revolution, the separation between science and religion grew as Galileo and Kepler dislodged the earth from the center of the solar system and Newton showed how the universe worked without theology. Calculus allowed for the measurement of the world and the larger universe, while the microscope allowed for the discovery of much smaller worlds. With all this new information, who needed religion?

Descartes revived the mind and body dualism presented by Plato. He approached his philosophy by rejecting anything that could be doubted. This allowed him to reach his understanding of what was fundamentally real—"I think, therefore I am." The realization that thinking could prove, and maybe even cause, existence was an important moment in philosophy. He viewed humans as a mixture of material bodies and immaterial minds, both of which were from God. The body was confined to functioning within the laws of physics, but the mind was exempt from those laws because it was not physical. His theory might have been adopted more widely if it hadn't had one clear weakness: if the brain were subject to the laws of physics but the mind was not, how could they influence each other?

Following the Scientific Revolution, scientific discoveries during the second half of the Age of Reason—the Enlightenment Period—caused further separation. Rationality was advocated as the only process for understanding the world, and religious revelations were increasingly challenged and belittled. After all, who needed a god when scientists could look at substances like bacteria and viruses to find the causes of diseases? Or when they explained elemental processes like gravity, light, electricity, and magnetism? Spiritual elements were not needed. The progression is understandable because it is easier to believe in observable things. This period reached its height with Immanuel Kant's *Critique of Pure Reason*.[3]

The Industrial Revolution followed, and as machinery became more common, humans began to be thought of as nothing more than biological machines. Medicine became purely materialistic—a mechanical tool to repair a mechanical body. Around the same time, astronomers began to develop new philosophies that said the entire universe was nothing more than a machine composed of mindless bits of matter obeying natural laws. Darwin caused some to wonder if humans were nothing more than a chance creation within the evolutionary process. Nietzsche proclaimed that God was dead, and other philosophers posited that the spirit world was only a religious fantasy. In the latter part of the nineteenth century, studies regarding the negative impact of brain damage on mental functions furthered the idea that the mind was nothing more than physical. In 1876, Thomas Huxley wrote that humans were only biological machines, and the illusion of consciousness was nothing more than a side effect of physical processes—no more important than a steam whistle was to making a train move down the track.

By the beginning of the twentieth century, this materialist view of humanity dominated science. However, some philosophers and scientists were still trying to find a way to understand the mind. In 1891, Ferdinand Schiller postulated that matter does not create consciousness but represses consciousness.[4] Powerful. Then, in 1898, William James argued that an injured brain causing mental changes was not proof that the brain created consciousness, and he used a brilliantly simple example to explain.[5] He showed that as light passes through a prism, it is separated into different colors. The prism is not the source of the light, but it allows us to see the light in multiple ways. He extended this to the brain. The brain processes information it receives, and we see that information represented in different behaviors (colors). An injured brain simply represents the processed information in different ways.

As the twentieth century continued, there was a quiet, slow return of dualism, often urged along, ironically, by science. Wilder Penfield conducted experiments that were influential in promoting the reunion, though he began his career intending to further support the materialist theory. Penfield developed a surgical procedure to remove brain parts thought to cause severe epileptic seizures, and since brain tissue is not sensitive to pain, Penfield worked with fully conscious patients. He would stimulate different parts of the brain and then chart the brain functions by observing the resulting behavior of the patients.

Penfield performed the procedure on more than a thousand patients. He discovered that electric stimulation caused only basic sensations or motor responses, with rare hallucinations. He also found that patients could tell the difference between movements caused by his electrical stimulation and movements that they (the patients) caused. For example, if a patient's body part moved while he was working, the patient would say something like, "You made me do it," or "I did it."[6] By the end of his career, Penfield was teaching that higher-level mental functions such as consciousness, imagination, will, and reasoning are not produced in the brain; rather, they are produced in the non-physical mind.

Another scientist who furthered this discussion was John Eccles, who, in 1963, was awarded the Nobel Prize in Physiology or Medicine (he shared the prize with Alan Lloyd Hodgkin and Andrew Huxley) for his study of the synapse. The synapse is a very small space between neurons over which nerve impulses flow. Later, in 1994, Eccles wrote that humanity was demeaned by science if it reduced humans to chemical processes alone.[7] He argued that humans have both a mind and a brain. The mind functions in the non-physical world, while the brain functions in the physical world, and both influence each other. However, in opposition to Descartes, Eccles argued that the mind is not a substance like the brain. Though influential, Penfield and Eccles were not part of the dominant trend at that time. Materialists continued to defend their philosophies, but, like Descartes, they still could not solve the problem of the mind and brain interactions.

" Religion without science produces blind belief because theists begin to focus only on spiritual values and slowly lose all understanding of secular environments. "

The 1960s saw increasing interest in how to combine religion and science. In 1959, during a lecture series, C. P. Snow discussed the divide that existed between science and the humanities.[8] Like many before him, he argued that the two areas should work to build bridges because the joining would benefit both human knowledge and human society. Around the same time, A. H. Maslow was also writing about the need for science and religion to reunite.[9] Religion without science produces blind belief because theists begin to focus only on spiritual values and slowly lose all understanding of secular environments. They become the embodiment of the saying, "Too heavenly-minded to be any earthly good." In effect, they abandon the biblical charge to have dominion over the earth, and that abandonment produces twisted or evil religions and beliefs. On the other hand, science without religion focuses on raw facts, and values are thrown out the window. This result is a science that is amoral, anti-moral, or even anti-human. Religion and science are both needed to keep each other in check.

I have often run into Christians who struggle to understand how to relate biblical teachings to scientific knowledge. This struggle usually begins around the time youth enter middle school. That's when science classes begin to conduct experiments, dissect animals, and teach evolution. Science becomes something students can see, hear, smell, touch, manipulate, and experience in the physical world. On the other hand, Sunday school classes are places that tell stories of ancient people and historical events. As such, a divide is created, and it is cultivated by both sides. Attending college often widens the gap exponentially. The result is that many students forsake religion for science when they become adults, while others forsake science and cling to their faith alone.

However, some within the religious community believe in the value of exploring scientific findings, even if we don't understand how they fit with theological teachings. After all, past philosophers, scientists, and religious thinkers came to their conclusions based on the knowledge available at the time. They did their best with what they knew. Those who followed them discovered that their predecessors' limited knowledge sometimes led them astray, so they added their new findings to the conversation, adjusted, and the process of discovery continued. As it should.

Unfortunately this process can develop *hiccups* when scientists know that their conclusions are wrong, yet they continue to promote them as truth. Or worse yet, they make small, hard-to-spot changes so that their results fit a particular purpose. Albert Einstein did just that. He wrote an equation that showed the universe was still expanding, but he had a difficult time comprehending the answer because, at the time, the universe was thought to be static. So he made a slight change in the equation so that it fit his idea of a static universe. Einstein later called that his "biggest blunder" because it led to someone else making one of the most popular scientific arguments of all time—the Big Bang. As I write this, I visualize the atheists clapping and the theists booing. But there will be some from both camps who understand that the Big Bang and Creation are not mutually exclusive; they are mutually supportive.

When people realize how important it is for both sides to cooperate, both may begin to reap greater benefits because of deeper understanding. There seems to be an increase in momentum in this direction. In 2008, *Science, Evolution, and Creationism* was published by the National Academy of Sciences to explain some differences and similarities between religion and science.[10] The publication argues that accepting God does not keep one from believing in scientific theories like evolution. Likewise, believing in scientific theories does not keep one from believing in God. The key is to understand how they fit. And this integration of religion and science is central to the relatively new field of *neurotheology*.

Neurotheology

Much of what I share falls within neurotheology because it tries to understand the relationship between spirituality and science, with the brain as the connecting element. This is not a religious study of neuroscience, nor is it a neuroscientific study of religious experiences (though it is sometimes called *neuroscience of religion* or *spiritual neuroscience).* However, I do try to incorporate information from soft sciences (e.g., education, sociology, psychology, anthropology, theology) and hard sciences (e.g., physics, chemistry, astronomy, geology, biology) to increase our understanding of spiritual experiences.

I understand that some Christians might be uncomfortable with the evolutionarily-infused term *neuro,* and some atheists might be uncomfortable with the theologically-infused term *theology.* Therein lies part of the problem with discussions like this. Trying to answer questions with biases imposes limitations on our minds' abilities to understand the other. Science is not able to explain our subjective experiences of the physical world, and religion is not able to explain the physical processes that accompany our spiritual experiences. However, the brain applies meaning to both and is essential for both. The brain is the focal point.

While the term *neurotheology* is relatively new, its beginnings can be found in some texts from thousands of years ago. Hindu and Buddhist writings contain many references to evaluating oneself and changing our mental states through meditation and other practices. The Upanishads (the oldest Hindu scriptures) discuss some of the workings of the mind and how it affects our perceptions of reality. They also discuss some of the problems that the limitations of the human mind can cause and try to explain some of its workings.

Unlike Hindu and Buddhist writings, the Bible does not spend much time on consciousness or thought processes, but that does not mean such teachings are entirely missing. The first humans are a good example. Adam named the animals (used language) shortly after he was created—a process that used many cognitive processes. Adam was lonely, so God created Eve to ease his mental anguish. For some time they did not know evil, but when they did, their new knowledge engaged their limbic systems, and they experienced embarrassment. So they made coverings. Another sign they'd learned about evil was when they blamed someone else for their behaviors. They knew they had done wrong and didn't want to pay the consequences.

Later, Cain killed Abel and then lied about it. He had to have some mental concept of what killing was, how to accomplish it, and the future result—he wouldn't have to put up with Abel being God's favorite anymore.

This indicates that Cain's prefrontal cortex was operational because he could understand the future consequences of his current behavior. He also had the mental processes necessary to understand the procedure of lying to try and keep from paying the consequences for his bad behavior. He had to understand that others had mental processes as well and that they would react to Abel's death based on his (Cain's) behaviors. Thus he hid the body to cover his actions.

There are other biblical references to human mental functions. The Ten Commandments are a good example. We can decide to perform or not perform behaviors like adultery, revenge, idol-making, theft, and honor, but not one of the Commandments refers to behaviors that we cannot control—"Thou shalt stop the hurricane from reaching thy house." The commandments are limited to behaviors that we can choose to accept or reject.

> **" We can never be sure that our understanding of reality is true because our understanding is produced by the very thing (the brain) that we're trying to evaluate. "**

Confined

Though the brain is the essential connection between science and religion, it creates a philosophical problem. Our brain gives meaning to the information our senses gather from the world. The meaning then affects our behaviors. But how do we know for certain that the world we experience is the world as it really is? We can never be sure that our understanding of reality is true because our understanding is produced by the very thing (the brain) that we're trying to evaluate. We are not able to escape our brains and make truly objective observations of the world because there would be nothing with which to experience the world. Even if we could somehow observe the world while in a brainless state, we would not have a *control group*, to use a scientific term, with which to compare our brainless observations. The result would be that what we observe while outside of our brain would still be our *true* reality. This puts us back where we began this argument—we are limited in our understanding of reality, no matter how hard we try.

However, there is a bright side to this mental confinement. The brain helps us to be relatively satisfied with our imprisonment. I often think of this as the *institutionalized brain*. I worked in a literal prison, and the patients I found the most difficult were the ones who were institutionalized. They were comfortable in prison and didn't want to leave. I often laughed with an elderly inmate who joked that prison was his retirement plan. Free housing, free food, and lots of friends. Similarly, many humans are happy to go through life without thinking of anything beyond what they experience. On the other hand, some want to explore what may lie beyond the prison walls of the brain. The character of Neo in *The Matrix* thought he was living in reality only to learn that he was dreaming and being used as an energy source.[11] Once he awakened to the true reality (*red pilled*), he did not want to return to the dream state.

For the most part, we are happy with our confinement. Another way the brain makes us happy with our confinement is by making us feel happy about being wrong. Jokes are a good example. Expecting one result only to find another when the joke hits the punch line is what makes us laugh. Also, magicians trick or confuse us, and our brains make us happy about being tricked or confused. We are intrigued. Unexpected notes in music can cause us to pay more attention. We listen more closely as we try to understand why *that* note is *there*. It is processes like these that help make us content to remain confined within our institutionalized brains.

Black-Clothed Man

Whatever your views are regarding the topic of this book, please try to understand what I'm about to say from a different perspective. Let me give you a quick example of what I mean.

While in graduate school I managed to afford a ticket to hear the Russian Symphony Orchestra. The floor and the bottom half of the balcony were packed. I was a few rows from the very top of the back of the balcony— the *nosebleed* seats. There were few others up there, and we had enough space to keep a few empty seats between us. I was playing the part of a studious classical concert attendee. I took a shower beforehand and put on a suit. People around me were also classical concert attendees—stuffily polite, quiet, sitting down, giving the symphony their full attention. I closed my own eyes when the overture started, focusing on the Tchaikovsky and enjoying the contrast between rock and classical concerts.

At one point I opened my eyes, and my peripheral vision caught unusual movement to my right. A young man had sat down while my eyes were closed. He was wearing a frayed, black t-shirt, black jeans, and black Converse shoes, and he had *long*, thick dreadlocks.

Black-clothed man was sitting, but I could tell he wanted to stand. He was leaning forward in his seat, his elbows were on the armrests, and his hands grasped the ends so tightly I could see in the dim light that his fingers were white. During the faster parts of the music, he did a subdued, classical-

34

concert version of head-banging, and his dreads would slap the back of the empty seat in front of him. But during the slower parts of the music, his body continued to rock forward and back while his head movements switched to side-to-side in time with the music. The dreads would fan out then slap him on the side of the face before doing the same on the other side. The dreads got confused whenever he shifted from front-to-back movements to side-to-side movements, or vice versa. But after a few head shakes, they were back in time with his head movements.

At that point, I was fighting to contain my laughter. Not at him but at the contrast he provided for the rest of us. We were all enjoying the concert in our own ways, but he was the only one rockin' out to Tchaikovsky—though he was trying to be respectful of others. I tried to pay attention to the concert after that, but I had to close my eyes to concentrate. Even then, I occasionally took a peek. Yep, still at it. Each time I looked I smiled and began to silently chuckle again. I laughed out loud when I suddenly thought it would be funny if he started running around the concert hall like some of the church members I described at the beginning of this chapter. If we had been sitting on pews, I might have taken a nap as the orchestra played and he ran around.

I thought it would be cool to talk to him afterward, but as we were giving the ovation he hurried out of the auditorium. I assumed he worked there, which would explain why he came in late and didn't dress the part of a classical concertgoer. Or he could have just been enjoying the concert in his own way, comfortable in his own skin. Either way, I was glad he was there. His enjoyment was infectious, and he provided some welcome humor, even if he wasn't aware of it. He left such an impression on me that I can still recall him and the contrast he made with the rest of us. He clearly viewed his experience from a different side.

And that's what I'd like you to do.

I use science to look at spiritual practices, so it's appropriate that I rely heavily on secular writings, but not completely. For large sections of this book, I've purposely adopted an agnostic or atheistic point of view, similar to what I might use while working in a secular job. I use words like *evolution*, which some believers might feel is a *degradation* (to use James's word) of their beliefs. At other times I write from the stance of a believer. During those parts, I use words like *God*, which non-believers might feel is a *degradation* of their beliefs. I'm not trying to degrade anyone's beliefs; I'm simply using the terminology that fits the writing perspective of the time. So I'm asking you to set aside your prejudices and accept the writings in the spirit with which they're intended—to provide information that has been filtered through my experiences and that I feel you might find useful.

In Summary

I began this chapter by recounting some childhood experiences of sleeping under church pews and feeling a unique spiritual presence. That was followed with a brief demonstration of how I sometimes combine those youthful memories with data learned later in life. Scientific perspectives (behavioral, physiological) provide greater depth of understanding as I consider those memories of a "protective wall" of legs, purses, and coats created by others. We then traced, broadly, the historical science-religion divide before I argued for the importance of integrating science and religion. Neurotheology was introduced as a framework for using the brain to bridge science and spiritual understanding. However, the philosophical problem of our objectivity being limited because we can only experience reality through our brains (*confinement*) was presented. Therefore we cannot be truly objective, but open-mindedness and mutual respect for both science and religion can help us to realize the complementary roles of both in understanding the human experience so that we are better able to build relationships. We concluded the chapter with an anecdote about an instance that led me to approach some life events with more openness.

My sanctuary siestas occurred among loud worship, music, dancing in the Spirit, speaking in tongues, and call-and-response behaviors. Some people believe those excited behaviors spring from mental pathologies, and we'll explore the validity of such claims later. On the other hand, some within my chosen belief system may take offense at looking at such highly spiritual and personally meaningful behaviors from a secular viewpoint. I don't mean to offend either—and to be fair, I put some of my own religious behaviors on display and analyze them with scientific research, particularly in the last few chapters. Instead, I hope that through this process both sides will gain a better understanding of the psychological and physiological foundations of some practices. But why even worry about the natural side of things?

Introspective Questions for Chapter 1

? **Personal Connection:** The author vividly describes feeling an undefined "something" in church as a child. Can you recall any experiences from your own life (spiritual, emotional, or otherwise) that felt powerful but difficult to pinpoint or explain rationally? How do you make sense of such experiences now?

? **Childhood Memories and Meaning:** The author's childhood memories of church services shaped his later reflections on science and spirituality.

What childhood experiences (religious, cultural, or otherwise) have influenced your current beliefs or questions about life's big questions?

? **Impact of Small Actions:** The author reflects on how napping under pews influenced others' behaviors and physiology. Can you think of a time when a seemingly small action of yours (or someone else's) had a ripple effect on those around you? How might this relate to the idea that our actions are interconnected?

? **Science and Spirituality:** How do you feel about applying scientific lenses (like behaviorism or physiology) to analyze personal or spiritual moments, as the author did with his napping experience? Does it enrich your understanding, or does it feel like it diminishes the experience?

? **Role of the Brain In Perception:** The author likens the brain to an "institutionalized prison" that shapes and limits our understanding of reality. How does this idea resonate with you? Have you ever questioned whether your perception of the world is true? How might this influence your beliefs or actions?

? **Perspective and Bias:** Consider the *black-clothed man* anecdote. Can you recall a time when someone's unique way of experiencing or expressing something challenged or enriched your own perspective? How might this apply to bridging science and religion?

? **Integration or Conflict:** The author argues that science and religion can be mutually supportive and act as checks on each other. Based on your own knowledge and experiences, where do you see the biggest potential for synergy between them? Where do you see the most significant conflicts?

? **Neurotheology:** What is your initial reaction to the field of neurotheology—studying the brain's connection to spiritual experience? Does it seem like a promising field for understanding, or does it risk reducing complex beliefs to mere brain chemistry?

? **Comfort with Ambiguity:** The author suggests that science and religion don't need to fully explain each other to be valuable. How comfortable are you with ambiguity or unanswered questions in your own beliefs or knowledge? How do you approach areas where science and spirituality seem to diverge?

? **Language:** The author notes that terms like *evolution* or *God* can be challenging, depending on one's background. How sensitive are you to the language used when discussing science and religion? How can language hinder or help bridge understanding between different viewpoints?

CHAPTER 2

Provoked to Harmony

Creation and Evolution

Late in my academic career, I was invited to join a committee that was preparing to launch a new educational initiative. All of us were from different universities, and one of our first meetings was to take place during a national conference. I didn't have anything scheduled before the meeting, so I arrived at the room quite early. I selected a *non-power position* seat at the large table and after organizing my items on the table took a closer look around the room. One wall contained a magazine rack, and a magazine found at most store checkout lines caught my attention. The cover featured a large photo of a prominent person who was known to support biblical creationism along with a sarcastic caption that informed readers of that fact.

I retrieved the magazine and began flipping through it. When the meeting started I laid the magazine down. After the meeting we had some time, so we just sat around making small talk. I began to fidget with the magazine, and after a few minutes one of my colleagues said, "That crazy [person's name] believes the world was created in six days."

We all chuckled a little. What a ludicrous idea.

As the comments relating to the craziness of the thought died down, I said something like, "Well, you know, if you take Einstein's Time Dilation Theory and the billions of years that NASA says have passed since the Big Bang and work through the math, you get about 5.7 days. That rounds to six, and the Bible says God chilled on the seventh day."

The room got really quiet. After a few moments someone said, "You know, there's a professor in our science department who's taught that biblical Creation is an option. I never paid him much attention. I always thought he was crazy."

Someone else was a mathematician, and our conversation flowed into a very broad discussion of math and spirituality. That was out of my area, so I sat and listened. Before that discussion, I had not made the connection between the two. I jotted some unorganized notes on a conference schedule so I could jog my memory later.

One of the oldest records of connecting spirituality and math can be found in Hindu religious texts written between 800–300 BC. But there is some evidence that they may be based on traditions from thousands of years earlier. Many of us in the Western culture may not be familiar with the Upanishads, but most of us have at least heard the names Pythagoras and Plato. In general, both found spiritual significance in math. Pythagoras (570–510 BC) thought that studying math was actually studying God, while Plato (428–348 BC) thought math prepared one to experience God. One *was* God and the other got you *to* God. They talked about some mathematicians through the centuries who connected math and spirituality. They even talked about some of the sacred numbers of the indigenous tribes of the Americas, like the Maya, Inka, Sioux, Hopi, and others. They also went down other interesting rabbit holes along the way. I found the idea of linking spirituality and math interesting but didn't think about it too much—only when it popped into my head. But a few years later I started giving the idea more thought.

66 Not only do some find that math is a way to study spirituality, some have spiritual experiences because of math. 99

The university courses I taught related to education, so all of the subject areas (e.g., English, math, science, counseling, social work) were in my courses. One of the undergraduate courses required students to give a final presentation about their subject matter that intertwined certain educational practices. Building relationships with students was one practice that needed to be included. One semester a group of math majors gave a presentation and used words like *beautiful, organized, epiphany, wow,* and so on. One of them referenced a book by Zee titled *Fearful Symmetry: The Search for Beauty in Modern Physics*.[12] As I listened and graded and jotted down the Zee title, that conference meeting popped into my head, and I had an epiphany of my own: not only do some find that math is a way to study spirituality, some have spiritual experiences *because of* math.

As I continued to read on this topic, I ran across a quote by Sarvepalli Radhakrishnan, former President of India, academic, philosopher, and one of the most influential Indian thinkers of the twentieth century: "A little bit of science takes you away from religion—but a little bit more of it will bring you right back."[13] I have found that general concept to be true in my life. When I was young and nonchalantly *scratched* the surface of science, it created a divide with religion, but, later in life, the more science I learned, the more it drew me back.

There are several reasons why I made the statement that started the discussion in the committee meeting. To be candid, one reason is that I just felt a little rambunctious. You know what I mean. We've all had those moments when we felt like *getting something going* to liven things up. Another reason is that, by that time in my life, I was in the early stages of an old-guy attitude—not caring as much about what other people thought about my beliefs. Though my reasons for making the comment may not have been entirely pure, I'm glad that I did because otherwise I may not have made the connection between math causing spiritual experiences in some people. After that, I began to study that connection, and along the way I found a wealth of data.

Another reason I made the comment is because I believe we need to be able to laugh, not mock, at ourselves and some of our beliefs. Let's be real—the entire universe being created in only six days is a ridiculous idea. It is such a preposterous theory that we can't wrap our minds around it. We often chuckle about it because we don't know how else to respond to such an absurd thought. It was youthful thoughts like that combined with a lack of knowledge that initially led me to consider atheism. Other less humorous thoughts related to human suffering also contributed to my walk down the atheistic and agnostic philosophical paths. To give you a little better understanding of my path, let's return to my youth.

Theism, Agnosticism, Atheism, then Back to Theism, then Mix It All Together . . .

My earliest memories include attending church at least three times a week— twice on Sunday, once on Wednesday evenings, and more during revivals. When I became a teenager, I threw in Friday night youth services. Bibles were everywhere I looked. I had no problems with biblical teachings or our particular religious practices. Like most children, my main question about anything was, *Why?* The adults around me could generally give me reasonable answers. The hiccups came when, at a rather young age, I switched to, *How?* and *What? How* was the universe created? *What* were the mechanics that allowed me to speak? *What* were the mechanics that allowed me to hear what others said? *How* did I process what I heard or saw? I knew it was all my thoughts, but *what* allowed me to even have the ability to think? It was those types of questions that I could not answer, and it was that inability that prompted me to flow between religion, agnosticism, and atheism.

Which camp I flowed into usually depended on which questions were running around in my head at the time. When my time in the military made human suffering real, I might flow toward agnosticism. After all, how could a loving God who was supposedly interested in the well-being of His creation allow such things? When I saw a child with mom's eye color and dad's hair color or heard about breeding pink flowers, fat cattle, or faster horses, I might flow to atheism. If humans could manipulate some aspects of evolution, who needed God? If there was no need for God, then maybe the universe did come into being by random chance. But when I went to church and felt the *something,* those *how* and *what* questions seemed less important. God was beyond our explanation, so those questions didn't really matter. Then I might flow back to theism.

66 I've met others who became believers by studying non-religious material. Some others have remained Christian because of secular study. 99

Such fluidness between belief systems had both negatives and positives. At times I created tension between and within the groups because of my flowing in and out. While I was with one group, I asked questions about their thoughts regarding the others. They'd become frustrated with me because I wouldn't make up my mind.

Strangely, it was the study of secular data that had the greatest influence on my return to theism. Or maybe not so strangely. Since then I've met others who also became believers by studying non-religious material. Some others have remained Christian because of secular study. All of this led to my realization that religious materials are not always necessary for someone to become, or remain, a theist. In the sections that follow, I'll give you three examples of relatively well-known individuals who were atheists but became theists through the influence of secular study.

I suspect that some theists will read the following sections and think something like, *Yep, those atheists really needed to change what they believed in.* But in true hypocritical style, they (theists) will not stop to consider their own theistic beliefs in relation to secular data. Theologically, that unwillingness to consider alternatives weakens theists' foundations. One of the broad concepts taught in the Bible is to live by example, and I've heard from many atheists who have felt frustrated by Christians who expected them to have an open mind without returning the favor.

On a side note, I've noticed that many who become, or remain, theists because of scientific information may not be super spiritual—full of public, emotional expressions of belief. But neither do they slide into the dumps without justifiable reasons. Their moods and behaviors tend to be more constant. In most cases, they are steady, faithful, and trustworthy church members. They are not manipulated by emotions or new ideas, and they often use new ideas as opportunities to reconsider (not simply reaffirm) their belief system. Just as a house's foundation needs to be checked occasionally, so do our foundational beliefs.

C. S. Lewis

C. S. Lewis was raised in a Christian family and was baptized into the Church of Ireland. He turned to atheism at the age of fifteen. At seventeen, he shared with a friend his disbelief in any religion, explaining that he saw no evidence for them and that, from a philosophical standpoint, Christianity didn't present the strongest case.[14] After a decade and a half of pursuing atheism through logical rigor, Lewis wrote to his friend that Christianity provides the framework through which God communicates His presence via the material world. He recognized his earlier rejection of faith as philosophically narrow and underdeveloped. Currently, people of all belief systems recognize Lewis as one of the greatest Christian apologists of the twentieth century and possibly one of the greatest philosophers of all time. We'll return to Lewis a little later.

Antony Flew

If we were to place Antony Flew on an atheism/theism continuum, he would be somewhere on the opposite side from C. S. Lewis. Though his father was a Methodist minister, Flew is recognized as one of the most influential atheists of the last hundred years. Like Lewis, he is also recognized as one of the great philosophers of the twentieth century. That recognition is deserved. During that time, no other philosopher developed and presented such comprehensive, original, and systematic anti-theological arguments. Lewis and Flew engaged in some rather legendary debates. His first paper supporting atheism, "Theology and Falsification,"[15] was presented in 1950 at a forum presided over by C. S. Lewis. Its first printed publication was in Oxford University's *University* and has become the most widely reprinted philosophical publication in the last century.[16]

We take a brief look at what made Flew so different because it's important to our discussion of turning conflict into connection. Three of Flew's writings found particular influence. The question of how theology can make any meaningful claims was raised in "Theology and Falsification." His most compelling argument was that theology's perceived substance could be systematically dismantled. The argument hinged on the idea that by *chipping away at its foundation until nothing is left*, one could meticulously deconstruct its doctrines, challenge its historical assertions, and expose its logical fissures. This process of intellectual attrition aimed not to engage theology on its own terms but to reduce it piece by piece, ultimately revealing a void where its authority and relevance were once presumed to stand, thereby rendering it irrelevant.

Later, in "God and Philosophy," he explained that his initial intention was to present and examine the case for theism.[17] But he abandoned that goal because he was not able to find sufficient theological and philosophical arguments because theists did not have any at the time. In the end, Flew used theists' lack of viable arguments to contend that theists must first establish a coherent concept of an omniscient and omnipresent spirit before they could begin discussing God's existence. I respect the fact that Flew urged theists to produce some viable arguments—he wanted a genuine discussion.

Still later, "The Presumption of Atheism" argued that a discussion about God's existence should begin with a presumption of atheism, not a presumption of theism as was the standard.[18] Atheism should be everyone's *default* philosophical position, and the burden of proof for a theistic position should rest with theists. During this time, many other atheists made arguments against theism, but what made Flew so special was the way he reframed the arguments against theism.

Honestly, I'm surprised that an atheist did not present such a reframing before Flew. Religiously and professionally I'm comfortable with Flew's arguments and criticisms. Let me explain.

Before Flew, theists had become comfortable with their strategies and abilities while constantly playing on their home turf. Academic laziness ensued. Suddenly, after Flew's publications, they needed to function on someone else's turf. It took some time for theists to adjust. One such adjustment was to spend time studying atheists' positions. And in the end, Flew's challenge caused theists to develop more sophisticated arguments. They learned to be successful while operating at *away games*, so much so that theists are currently recognized as having the superior and most easily defensible philosophies. Atheists continue to refine their arguments, and the pendulum may swing back to their side. That is the nature of honest debate.

Some thinkers have based their life's work on Flew's anti-God arguments. As such, his 2004 announcement that he now believed in the existence of a universal designer threw a wrench into some peoples' thinking. Flew had come to believe in an Aristotelian-type god who was responsible for the workings of the universe but was not involved with humanity. He had arrived at deism because of his lifelong commitment to follow the evidence where it led him.

Some atheists' responses to his announcement were less than respectful (I refrain from naming any). Some claimed that Flew's mind was failing him because of his advanced age, while others said that he had never been a good philosopher. Some even called him an atheistic "apostate." While acknowledging the surrounding negativity, Flew affirmed that his evolving beliefs were met with the same intellectual vigor and ethical steadfastness that marked his earlier years.[19] He still wanted open, respectful debate.

Francis Collins

Francis Collins was the leader of the International Human Genome Project, which revealed the magnitude of the deciphered human genome. Collins characterized the human genome as a vast, three-billion-letter blueprint; its immensity is such that reading three letters a second aloud nonstop would require thirty-one years, or if printed, it would form a stack as high as the Washington Monument, granting humanity its first-ever access to the complete instructions for building a human being.[20]

> **He began to wonder how he could draw conclusions without considering the data and still consider himself a scientist.**

Collins was moderately aware of God in his youth. Later in life, he didn't want to have to choose between atheism or theism, so he became an agnostic. From there he gradually shifted to atheism. Then, in his third year of medical school, he was struck by the spirituality of many of his patients. Despite great suffering, their faith gave them peace. One elderly woman who suffered from an untreatable condition asked him what he believed in. He hesitated, then admitted that he didn't really know. He began to wonder how he could draw conclusions without considering the data and still consider himself a scientist.

He began his investigation with confidence that atheism would win. His first step was to survey all of the major religions, but they left him mystified. A local minister gave him a copy of C. S. Lewis's *Mere Christianity*. Lewis's own foray into atheism addressed Collins' questions. One of his arguments that had a great effect on Collins was philosophical, not scientific—the Moral Law argument.

Lewis's Moral Law argument was that, in daily disagreements, people unknowingly refer to an unstated standard that humans have. We often hear someone who is treated unfairly say, "That's not right." Disagreements between spouses occur because of a perceived wrong done by the other. The wrong could be as simple as not starting the dishwasher, but still, "You should have started it!" I recently watched a US Congressional debate. Each speaker made comments showing they thought that they, and their political party, were right and the other party was wrong. Such appeals to a *law of right behavior* are present in all cultures.

A fundamental question arises: *What is the source of this law?* Skeptics might argue that without knowing its source, its reality cannot be confirmed. C. S. Lewis addressed this by reasoning that a power beyond the universe couldn't be just another object within it, similar to how an architect is separate from the house he or she creates. He proposed that such an external authority would instead reveal itself internally, through a sense of duty or an intuitive urge guiding our actions. This commonly felt internal experience, Lewis highlighted, should prompt us to explore the possibility of an external, guiding intelligence.[21]

I know there was a builder for my house because my house exists. I don't know who built my truck, but I know someone did. Lewis's argument has caused many to consider that the unseen, universal Moral Law must have been put in place by something. How else could it be so universal?

Philosophical reflections and deeper exploration of scientific disciplines guided Collins toward theism. In 2000, Collins stood beside President Clinton at the White House during the announcement of the completion of the human DNA sequencing. In his remarks, Clinton stated that this achievement was undoubtedly the most significant and remarkable blueprint ever discovered by humanity, emphasizing that it revealed the code through which Divine creation was expressed, deepening our reverence for the intricate, beautiful, and wondrous nature of life's sacred endowment.[22]

Collins' speech, following Clinton's, echoed similar sentiments. He described it as a joyous moment for the world, expressing humility and awe at having glimpsed the blueprint of human creation, a mystery once known only to the Divine.

Gerald Schroeder

The physicist Gerald Schroeder argued for theism by considering the likelihood that the universe could have occurred by chance alone. This argument has affected many, including Flew. So I share it here by walking us through some of Schroeder's argument in *God According to God*. There's a teensy-weensy bit of math, but stick with it.

Stephen Hawking, in his bestselling science book *A Brief History of Time*, suggested that random events, when given enough time and opportunities, can create useful order—using the example of monkeys randomly hitting typewriter keys eventually typing a Shakespearean sonnet. He admitted that most of what they wrote would be trash, but eventually, a sonnet would be produced.[23] This concept, while thought-provoking and widely embraced, including on the 2002 Christmas and New Year's cover of *The New Yorker*, falls apart under closer scrutiny.

Shakespearean sonnets are typically fourteen lines long. In his analysis, Schroeder uses the first line of a sonnet to illustrate his point: "Shall I compare thee to a summer's day?" That particular sonnet has just fewer than five hundred letters, so Schroeder asks readers to imagine five hundred bags, each holding the twenty-six letters of the English alphabet. The chance of randomly drawing the *s* for *Shall* from the first bag is one in twenty-six. The probability of then correctly drawing an *h* for the second letter from another bag (we can't reuse a bag after a letter is drawn from it because the complete alphabet needs to be in the bag), thus getting the first two letters *Sh* in sequence, is 1 in 26×26. Continuing this process for all five hundred letters, and getting the correct letter on each draw, while not taking the empty spaces between words into account, the probability of randomly producing a sonnet is twenty-six multiplied by itself five hundred times—resulting in a figure equivalent to a 1 followed by 700 zeros (or 10^{700}). Compare that number to the known universe's weight (approximately 10^{56} grams), its known particles (around 10^{80}), and its age (roughly 10^{18} seconds). In short, meaningful structure like a sonnet doesn't arise from randomness in any realistic scenario.

> **" Meaningful structure like a sonnet doesn't arise from randomness in any realistic scenario. "**

Schroeder used an actual experiment—six monkeys typing randomly for a month without forming any English words—to further illustrate probability. While one might expect single-letter words like *a* or *I* to appear, Schroeder noted that forming a one-letter word requires a *space-letter-space* sequence. For a keyboard with approximately 100 keys, the chance of this specific three-character sequence occurring randomly is 1 in 100^3, or 1 in 1,000,000. This calculation reveals the immense unlikelihood of meaningful text arising from random keystrokes, even for the shortest words.[24]

Schroeder's numbers are truly astronomical as they are written. But they become exponentially more astronomical when we add other needed elements, such as environmental necessities like technology, mental processes, understanding, motor abilities, genetics, biology, and so on. Whatever those numbers would be if someone could even do the math would be far beyond the number of basic particles that make up the known universe. And those numbers would apply to only one sonnet.

Now extend that argument to one of the most basic species on our planet, which is far more complex than a sonnet. The development of one species by chance would far outweigh the requirements for one sonnet. And like the doubling of the numbers for the sonnet, the same numerical doubling would be required for the evolution of another species. (The number wouldn't be an exact doubling because more than one species could develop within an environment, but the probabilities are still astronomical.) The sizes of the animals and needed adaptations would also affect the numbers, but you get the point. The likelihood that the most basic lifeforms could develop strictly by chance is far less likely than it is for those monkeys to accidentally type a comprehensible sonnet. If I were a betting man who was forced to make such a bet, and if Vegas gave such odds, I would put every penny I had on the monkeys.

In Summary

Chapter 2 began with a humorous committee meeting in which I purposely made a provocative comment about biblical Creation aligning with the Big Bang through Einstein's time dilation theory. That led to broad comments from others about math and spiritual experiences, which led me later to recognize spiritual references to math as a group of students gave a class presentation. My youth produced fluid beliefs—suffering and "How?" questions that led to atheism/agnosticism/theology. Examples of thinkers who took broadly similar paths were presented: C.S. Lewis and his philosophical Moral Law, Antony Flew's turn to deism because of scientific discoveries, Francis Collins's awe at human DNA, and Gerald Schroeder's challenge to the probability of life arising by chance. I consistently advocated for intellectual honesty through "belief checks" and emphasized the importance of respectful dialogue, as demonstrated by the Lewis-Flew debates. Furthermore, I argued that reason and science can be sources of faith-affirming insights. Ultimately, I hope to encourage you to reflect on how secular knowledge influences your beliefs. So if you are, like the varied thinkers above, willing to engage in an open-minded consideration of matters involving God, let's consider the spiritual nature of what it means to be human.

Introspective Questions for Chapter 2

? **Fluidity and Doubt:** The author "flowed" between theism, agnosticism, and atheism, driven by questions about human suffering and life's mechanics. Have you experienced shifts or uncertainty in your beliefs about God or existence? What intellectual, emotional, or experiential factors influenced these changes? How did they shape your worldview?

? **Big Questions:** The author moved from asking "Why?" as a child to "How?" and "What?" about existence (e.g., thought, Creation). Which type of question—why, how, or what—resonates most with you now? How do you grapple with unanswered questions about life? What impact do they have on your beliefs?

? **Science and Religion:** Sarvepalli Radhakrishnan's quote, "A little bit of science takes you away from religion—but a little bit more of it will bring you right back," reflects the author's journey. Has deeper engagement with science (e.g., biology, cosmology) ever challenged or reinforced your spiritual beliefs? Why or why not?

? **Secular Paths to Belief:** C. S. Lewis, Antony Flew, and Francis Collins embraced theism or deism through logic, philosophy, or science (e.g., DNA's complexity, Moral Law). Do you find their reasoning compelling? Has secular knowledge ever unexpectedly shaped your views on a higher power? How?

? **Mathematics and Spirituality:** The author's epiphany that mathematics can evoke spiritual experiences broadened his view of spirituality. Have you found beauty or transcendence in intellectual fields like math or science? How might such experiences influence your sense of meaning?

? **Probability and Design:** Gerald Schroeder's argument that life's complexity is too improbable to arise by chance supports intelligent design. How convincing is this idea to you? How does it shape your view of life's origins as random or purposeful?

? **Belief Checks:** The author's "belief checks" involve examining beliefs to maintain intellectual honesty. How willing are you to critically test your core beliefs, whether theist, atheist, or agnostic? What might prompt you to refine your worldview?

? **Motives In Discussion:** The author's "rambunctious" comment about creationism sparked meaningful dialogue. How do motives (e.g., curiosity, provocation) affect discussions about religion or science? Have you sparked a conversation with mixed intentions, and what did you learn?

? **Engaging Criticism:** Antony Flew's challenge to theists strengthened their arguments, showing criticism's value. Do you agree that engaging opposing views can enhance your beliefs? How has respectful disagreement deepened your understanding?

? **Conversations Across Beliefs:** The chapter's emphasis on dialogue (e.g., Lewis-Flew debates) highlights engaging diverse perspectives. How might these ideas influence your approach to discussing God, Creation, or science with others? What makes such conversations productive?

CHAPTER 3

Mountain Dances, Altered States, and Whispers of the Unseen

Nature and Spirituality

I had a rather broad view of spirituality when I arrived in Alaska, but an experience soon broadened my view even more. I'll try to share it briefly but with some depth because it figures into the discussion that follows. One of the other teachers (Jay*) and I decided to take a climbing trip over a three-day weekend. The goal was to leave Friday after work and take a skiff out to spend the night on the northern tip of Khantaak Island. On Saturday morning we'd cross Yakutat Bay, enter Disenchantment Bay, and spend Saturday night on Haenke Island, which lies close to the base of Hubbard Glacier. On Sunday morning we would squeeze between Hubbard Glacier and the mainland and enter Russell Fjord. Once in the fjord, we would spend some time climbing, then make camp. On Monday, we would make the entire trip back to Yakutat.

But as many other adventurous souls know, plans change.

We could have taken an easier way into Russell Fjord by driving a few miles on Dangerous River Road and then carrying kayaks to the southern end of the fjord, but where's the adventure in that? We loaded our camping and climbing gear into the skiff on Friday afternoon. The boat was loaded with two men weighing over two hundred pounds each, camping gear, climbing gear, food, fuel, guns, and so on. We were riding low in the water. We joked about the low-riders in Los Angeles having nothing on us but made it to Khantaak Island as planned. It was dark when we arrived, but since we pulled crab pots around that island several times a week we knew it well. We made camp, had a good dinner of fresh crab, and went to sleep.

We woke on Saturday to a strong wind from the north, so we would be going into a strong headwind as we traveled northeast across Yakutat Bay. With a strong headwind, an overloaded skiff, larger than normal waves, and an undersized twenty-five-horsepower motor, it took most of the morning to cross the bay. We rounded the point to enter Disenchantment Bay and came to a standstill.

Since cold air falls, winds at the bottom of glaciers can be rather swift because they slide down the ice. After falling off of Hubbard Glacier, the cold air got even swifter as it was funneled between the mountains on both sides of the entrance to the bay. The boat motor was wide open, and we even laid down to reduce wind drag, but we were not moving forward. After spending some time laughing at our situation and having a few small icebergs bump into our aluminum skiff, we decided it might be time to be a little more responsible. Besides, where were the life jackets? Had we left them?

We managed to turn around without getting too much water into the skiff, but we weren't ready to go back to town. We adjusted our plans and went to Eleanor Cove on the opposite side of the mountains from Russell Fjord.

On Sunday morning we got up, fought our way through thick Devil's Club, and started moving upward. An hour or so into the trip we got thirsty and learned we both thought that the other had gotten the water. Obviously we didn't do well dividing up the gear, but we didn't want to go back down, so we continued. A few more hours into the journey and we were scooping water from rock depressions and munching on some vegetation for the moisture. We eventually made it to the top and had a spectacular 360-degree view. The Gulf of Alaska was to the west. To the north and south were mountains partly covered by greenery and snow. To the east were snow-covered mountains as far as we could see. Were we able to see into Canada?

We took 360-degree pictures with real cameras—no cell phones then. I still occasionally lay those photos out in sequence and just stare at them to relive the moment. We laughed. We *ooo'd*. We *ahh'd*. We talked about the Tlingit Creation story. We talked about Creation in general. We shouted loudly. We slapped each other on our shoulders and backs. We danced and stomped our feet for joy. We acted like idiots. It felt free and genuine and wonderful. We had worked hard for the experience, and we were going to enjoy it. The challenges of the previous days, the lack of food and water, and our overall level of exhaustion combined with the natural beauty and an absence of distractions led to what I often describe as a spiritual experience.

And there's the main reason I took so much time to tell the story. Jay, who was not religious, also described it as a spiritual experience.

Throughout my time in Yakutat, Jay and I spent a lot of time together pulling crab pots, fishing, hunting, and going on other outings. During those times, Jay often described the above adventure, and others that were just as amazing, as spiritual experiences. Even cleaning the day's catch or kill was a spiritual experience for him. He was grateful that the animal had given its life so he could live. He respected the animals' souls and accepted them into his own. Even though he leaned more toward pantheism, his ability to have spiritual experiences outside of a religious context began to open my eyes to a larger understanding: *spiritual experiences are not limited to theists.*

> *" Spiritual experiences are not limited to theists. "*

Universal Spirituality

Realizing that anyone can have spiritual experiences led me to wonder, *How?* Are there other ways for us to have spiritual experiences? I've had students who were atheists, yet they were highly spiritual. *How?* How can non-believers be spiritual? Was there something common to believers and non-believers? I realized that before I could effectively explore the *how*, I first needed to understand the *what*, in terms that could relate to anyone, not just theists. But since it wasn't a priority for my job, I lazily considered spirituality in general terms over the next few years. I landed on a workable, universal definition of spirituality purely by chance.

I was studying how other teachers with extremely violent students continued to maintain their positive attitudes. Were their methods similar to mine? The teachers had to have had ample time to develop effective stress management methods, so they had to have been in their assignments for more than five consecutive years. The teachers were from several schools around the state. Interview questions did not have any religious overtones; they simply focused on the educational environment.

There was a mixture of religious, agnostic, and atheistic teachers, so I was surprised when, at various times during the interviews, every interviewee brought up the topic of spirituality as a mental health *tool.* All of the teachers used combinations of spiritual activities, such as Bible reading, meditation, prayer (not always Christian in nature), martial arts, fitness, and Pantheism, to obtain physiological, psychological, and sociological benefits. Spirituality (as they defined it) was used to reduce stress because lower stress levels allowed them to continue to build relationships with their students. The ultimate result was that they could consistently have a greater, positive influence on reducing students' violent behaviors. Spirituality was an avenue through stress to better relationships.[25]

During this study, my mind began to combine writings from the medical and educational fields that later led me to create a simple, yet broad, definition of spirituality that could be used in secular education settings: *activities that promote the human longing to be connected.*[26] I realized that the teachers had been sharing their examples of spirituality all along, just in their own words.

At the time I was not familiar with James's work on spirituality. I was familiar with him because he had been used in some of my psychology courses, but I had never read any of his works beyond what had been required. During his early years, James studied biology, physiology, and medicine, and his writings in psychology and philosophy contain clear influences from those fields. He felt that some scientists excluded too much of the human experience, while some philosophers excluded too much science. I agree. The overall result is that James's psychological work promotes a scientific method of inquiry that includes the richness of the human experience—known as the Jamesian approach. This idea culminated in the *Principles of Psychology*, which became the foundation of psychology.[27]

James's work led to him receiving an invitation to give a series of talks for the prestigious Gifford Lectures. He was interested in *all* mental phenomena, and that led him to study areas that some considered *fringe*. One such topic was spiritualism—the belief that certain people could contact the dead—and that led him to study psychics, hypnosis, relaxation techniques, alternative medicine, and seances. He was critical of people who refused to investigate such areas, but he was also critical of those who blindly accepted such practices. Bravo! Since religious and spiritual experiences were of particular interest to James, he decided to address them during the Gifford Lectures, which were later published as *The Varieties of Religious Experience*, one of the most influential psychology writings of all time.[28] So influential, in fact, that it has affected all versions of the *Diagnostic and Statistical Manual* (which you will meet later) and is commonly used as a template for other articles and books.

James's overriding theme for the lecture series was to shift the focus away from the study of specific religious beliefs and doctrines toward the broader area of religious *experiences*. He felt that focusing on experiences might allow him to "succeed in discussing religious experiences in a wider context than has been usual in university courses." One of James's first hurdles was to define religion. Defining a single belief system is much simpler than trying to include all systems in one definition. If you try, you will quickly realize that something seemingly simple is, in fact, quite arduous. After a discussion regarding some of his difficulties, James arrived at a definition that focused on experiences and actions (behaviors) as key components: "Religion, therefore, as I now ask you arbitrarily to take it, shall mean for us the *feelings*, *acts*, and *experiences* of individual men in their solitude, so far as they apprehend themselves to stand in relation to whatever they may consider the divine" *(emphasis mine).*[29]

Notice, in addition to experiences and actions, one of the elements of his definition refers to a relationship ("stand in relation") to anything that an individual considers "divine." Such comments often lead us to think about supernatural things like God, Satan, and spirits, but we rarely consider material objects like humans and pets. But, as you will see later, it is rather common for people to view objects like phones or behaviors like exercise as divine. There is even neurological evidence that the brain reacts in similar ways to both supernatural and physical things if we consider them divine.

James also shared his views of how psychology and biology work together to process experiences. "There is not a single one of our states of mind . . . that has not some organic process as its condition. Scientific theories are organically conditioned just as much as religious emotions are . . . all our raptures and our dryness, our longings and pantings, our questions and beliefs. They are equally organically founded, be they religious or of non-religious content." Because "organic processes" were unobservable, James determined that, ultimately, it is our behavior that allows us and others to judge if we are spiritual. "By their fruits they shall be known, not by their roots. . . . The ROOTS of a man's virtue are inaccessible to us. . . . Our practice [behavior] is the only sure evidence, even to ourselves, that we are genuinely Christian" *(emphasis in original).*

James allowed me to realize the addition of a behavioral component that could be observed would be beneficial. After all, I am largely a behaviorist. When we add James's focus on observable, positive behaviors to my aforementioned definition, we get something like the following: *healthy behaviors that result from activities that help humans to connect.*

Science has progressed since James's time, and we now have a little better insight into the "ROOTS" of our spiritual nature. For example, behavioral geneticist Dean Hamer supported William James's view that spirituality originates internally, suggesting that a person's capacity for spiritual experiences is innate and rooted in their genetic makeup.[30] Biologist Kenneth Miller considers evolution essential for understanding our relationship with God because it provides deeper insights into His living creations.[31] Neuroscientist Andrew Newberg and co-author Mark Waldman wrote that spiritual experiences "can be traced to specific neural processes in the brain, and they

66 Spiritual experiences can be traced to specific neural processes in the brain, and they are available— and ultimately valuable—to anyone who seeks them, including secular individuals. 99

are available—and ultimately valuable—to anyone who seeks them, *including secular individuals" (emphasis mine).*[32]

Spirituality and Medications

Throughout my time as an educator, I noticed that many things affected my students' spiritual natures, but medications and the environment were two big ones for them. Let's focus on medications for now because of their clear influence on biological, physical, and spiritual processes. We'll spend time with some environmental influences later.

Psychotropic medications—methylphenidate, alprazolam, dextroamphetamine, and the like—were prescribed for most of my students. Some took them as prescribed, while others increased or decreased their dosages or mixed them with illegal substances as a way to establish some type of control within their lives. Some simply sold them. There were times when every student in my classroom was taking a prescribed psychotropic in conjunction with illegal medications. The most common were alcohol, marijuana, methamphetamine, spice, and ecstasy. Try to imagine the classroom on those days.

The percentage of those on prescription drugs increased significantly throughout my teaching career in general and special education, though it was more common in special education. This is important because, as prescription drug use increases, so does the number of people affected. Every environment in which I have been involved (secular and religious) has included people who were using some form of drug, legal or illegal or both. The point is, I have had many years to observe how various medications affected students' and adults' spirituality.

You might think that drugs only apply to secular settings. That may be true for some; it's not true for everyone. I've lived in places where several members of a congregation were on various medications, not all of them legal. I've seen more than one young person show up to a youth function with dilated pupils. One even passed out while I was teaching—talk about a blow to my ego. In my current church, it's not uncommon for homeless individuals who are on legal and/or illegal medications to wander into services. Some of our homeless visitors have been admitted to mental health treatment facilities more than once. It's not a stretch of the imagination to realize that as mental health issues increase, so will church attendees who are on medications.

Many years ago I was helping to clean a newly purchased church property. We were cutting trees and brush in the late summer, southern humidity. It was miserable. When not running chainsaws, we made small talk. After lunch, Wayne* began to ask questions about mental health issues and medications. The conversation eventually arrived at the topic he really wanted to discuss—the reality of his spiritual experiences and the affects of his medications on those experiences.

I asked Wayne why these issues mattered to him. I wasn't being mean, I just needed to know the source of his concerns.

"I just want to know, are my experiences real?" he asked.

"Who's to say your spiritual experiences are not more real than mine?"

I could tell that my reply surprised him. He was accustomed to people being hesitant to talk about such things. I was intrigued.

As we talked, I explained why I'd asked that question. Wayne was an intelligent guy who had a broad understanding of the medications he was prescribed and how they affected his experiences. In the end, we talked about how it was possible that, while his mental state caused him some behavioral problems and cognitive issues, it could also cause his spiritual experiences to be more real and deeply felt than mine. The conversation seemed to help. He admitted that he felt more peace knowing that his spiritual experiences might not be the result of his psychosis and was fascinated that his situation might be allowing him to have experiences that were more real than others'.

I was in no position to give spiritual advice or to pass theological judgment. I wasn't his psychiatrist (lucky for him), but I knew enough to just chat about a topic that some would find sensitive or even offensive. Not only was I *willing* to talk to Wayne, he could tell that I *wanted* to talk about the subject. I wanted to explore his experiences as a way to learn more about him. I wasn't trying to change him. I wasn't telling him what to do. I didn't give any definite answers. We just talked, and when he asked for my thoughts, I provided some possible explanations for his situation from an academic (not theological) perspective, even though we were discussing spiritual events.

We continued to attend church together for quite a while until he eventually moved away. We didn't talk much after that workday, but we frequently communicated with knowing smiles, fist bumps, or handshakes, and the occasional hug. We also prayed together at times. One of the few times we did talk he told me again that he appreciated the talk we had and that my lack of judgment regarding his situation was important.

Medications

Among my students, depression was one of the most common mental illnesses, which continues to correspond to current societal rates.[33] Anxiety was also common, but these students were more likely to try and self-medicate with non-prescribed substances like alcohol, marijuana, or barbiturates, while those with depression were more likely to use prescribed medications. My lack of knowledge about those drugs led me to spend some time looking into them. I was surprised to find that some of the more common medications were connected to a class of drugs that may surprise you: *psychedelics*.

I'd guess several of you reacted to the mention of prescription psychedelic drugs—LSD, mescaline, and the like—with something like, *What?!* Even some of the most religious readers may have had to suppress a four-letter word before thinking—*No!* I understand such thoughts. I've had a few myself. They often result from negative stereotypes, illegality, or religious teachings against them. However, many religious traditions commonly use psychotropics—peyote, for instance. Some other traditions don't use drugs, but they do use methods like fasting or sleep deprivation to induce similar alternative states.

But if you look at them medically, psychedelics can make a positive difference. More positive, in fact, than some other currently accepted medications and with fewer negative side effects. If study results continue to be positive, some will need to make moral choices concerning the use of those medications.

Psychedelics are a subset of the *psychoactive* family of drugs, which also includes caffeine and cocaine. Yes, you read that right. Psychoactives impact the central nervous system and influence moods, behaviors, and/or perceptions. Some of the most well-known—LSD, mescaline, DMT, and psilocybin—are called *classic psychedelics*. Users often consider their experiences while using them to be among the most meaningful, spiritually significant, and positively life-changing. They clearly fall within James's definition of general spirituality.

You may ask, *What about the addiction potential?* Well, marijuana (cannabis) and caffeine (stimulant) have similar dependence potentials at *moderate/low*. Moving up the dependence scale, alcohol (depressant) is *moderate*, cocaine (stimulant) is *moderate/high*, nicotine (stimulant) and morphine (narcotic) are *high*, and heroin (narcotic) tops the scale at *very high*.[34] Heroin has been illegal in the US since 1924, but its use has risen since 2007. One explanation ties its rise to the abuse of painkillers such as hydrocodone and oxycodone. All are made from the poppy plant and are chemically related.

On the opposite end of the dependence potential scale are psychedelics such as LSD, psilocybin, and mescaline, which are rated *very low*. In other words, the dependence potential of some medically beneficial psychedelics is lower than caffeine. By the way, I'm on my third cup of caffeinated coffee today, but I've never taken LSD or psilocybin. I am also intrigued by how easy it is to buy things in some stores that are highly addictive. Nicotine gum is a good example.

Dependence potential of some psychoactive drugs						
Very high	Heroin					
High	Morphine		Nicotine			
Moderate/ High		Phenobarbital	Cocaine			
Moderate		Rohypnol	Ephedra			
		Alcohol				
Moderate/ Low			Caffeine	Nitrous oxide		Marijuana
			MDMA			
Low				Ketamine		
					LSD	
Very low					Psilocybin	
					Mescaline	
Legend	Narcotics	Depressants	Stimulants	Anesthetics	Hallucinogens	Cannabis

Figure 1. The general dependence potential of some psychoactive drugs. Elements like dosage, drug quality, gender, biological makeup, psychological state, and others can influence a drug's effect on a user. This table is only a general representation. (Adapted from Gable RS above, 2004.)

Some drugs we think of as bad actually have medicinal uses. While in the Army, I worked in a base hospital while I recovered from surgery. One of the nurses (Jill*) came in with a broken nose, but not from anything heroic. She'd gotten into an argument with her barracks roommate. The roommate shoved Jill out of the room. Jill, who had a temper, pushed herself off of the wall on the other side of the hallway and sprinted back toward the room. Her roommate chose to slam the heavy fire door.

Jill was a tough girl, but the pain from the doctors trying to set her broken nose was too much. They ended up giving her a pain mixture that included cocaine. In topical form, it helps ease surgical pain and is sometimes used for nose, throat, and mouth surgeries. As long as she was stationed there, we often asked Jill to slam a door in our faces. We usually had to dodge a playful punch in response.

The connection between medication and spirituality dates back at least as far as James, who said that some substances may "stimulate the mystical consciousness."[35] In the 1960s, Maslow included LSD and psilocybin in his studies. Maslow developed the famous Hierarchy of Needs, and his work is still used heavily within the field of education in the US. In *Religion, Values, and Peak Experiences*, Maslow described *peak* experiences in ways that are similar to James's spiritual experiences. During peak experiences, individuals perceive the universe as an integrated whole with heightened, objective, and ego-transcending awareness, often feeling a sense of timeless universality, profound emotions like awe and reverence, the resolution of life's conflicts, a loss of anxiety, and an increase in love and acceptance, all while viewing the world as inherently good and desirable.[36]

James and Maslow were certainly not the only ones to support psychedelics in relation to spirituality. The 1960s were dominated by research projects that used psychedelics. One of the most famous is the Good Friday Experiment.

Good Friday Experiment

This experiment took place in Marsh Chapel at Boston University. It was designed by Walter Pahnke, a Harvard University graduate student in theology, and supervised by The Harvard Psilocybin Project. Before the Good Friday service in 1962, twenty graduate student volunteers were divided into two groups. Half received psilocybin while the control group received niacin. Niacin was an active placebo that only affected the physical state of the volunteers. Volunteers listened to the service from the basement. Researchers found that the psilocybin group indicated they had far more meaningful experiences than did the control group (niacin), and the spiritual effects on the psychedelic group lasted far longer.

> **66 While he'd always believed in God, this experiment facilitated his first direct, personal encounter with God. 99**

Huston Smith, later a distinguished religious scholar, received psilocybin during the Good Friday Experiment and in 1997 reported experiences far more mystical than the control group's. The service's peak for him was a soprano's angelic hymn about surrendering to God's will; its verses struck such a profound chord that they became a permanent and deeply ingrained part of him. Smith explained that while he'd always believed in God, this experiment facilitated his first direct, personal encounter with God, akin to those described by Bhakti yogis or Pentecostals.[37]

The use of psychedelics began to fade toward the end of the 1960s because of misuse by recreational users and researchers. They became associated with counterculture, and eventually the government deemed them illegal. However, their medical benefits and low potential addiction levels have caused them to resurface. In 2000, the Johns Hopkins School of Medicine started the process of gaining governmental approval to again use psychedelics in research. The program has now grown into the Center for Psychedelic and Consciousness Research (CPCR). Other labs have also opened in the US and other countries. Also, I recently received an email from Veterans Affairs informing veterans that it (VA) is beginning studies that involve psychedelics for treating some mental health issues in veterans.

Good Friday Experiment (Updated)

In 2006, researchers at the CPCR made some changes to the original Good Friday Experiment. One was to replace the niacin with an active placebo that would also cause psychoactive effects—Ritalin (the previously used niacin only affected physiology). This would allow researchers to look for differences in psychoactive effects. This time, approximately 61 percent of the psilocybin group and approximately 7 percent of the control group had a spiritual experience. And as in the first study, psilocybin was found to have long-term effects. Roughly fourteen months later, 67 percent of the psilocybin participants indicated that the experience remained significant.[38]

Alcoholics Anonymous and Addictions

Another example of someone's life changing for the better through medications is the story of Bill Wilson, founder of Alcoholics Anonymous (AA). Wilson could not hold a job because of his drinking. He tried to stop many times. In 1934, he received a treatment of belladonna by a doctor and later wrote that while lying on the bed, he entered an entirely new realm of consciousness for the first time. A delightful Presence enveloped him, both all around and within, bringing a deep calm that culminated in the reassuring conviction that, despite his problems, all was fundamentally well.[39]

Reportedly, Wilson never drank again. He used LSD later in his life and supported the use of psychedelics for treatment because of their therapeutic benefits. I find it ironic that AA does not currently allow for such interventions despite the success of various medication-assisted treatments (MAT) for addictions. The combination of psychedelics in conjunction with a twelve-step program can increase one's chance of breaking an addiction because both approaches may tap into a shared, neurological pathway. The strength provided by the multiple pathways can help to break the cycle.

Bicycle Day

I'm laughing as I write this section because I went for a bike ride this morning. April 19th, 1943, is quite famously (in some circles) known as *Bicycle Day* and celebrated annually. Albert Hoffman, who synthesized LSD, accidentally ingested some on that day, then rode his bicycle home. He later described the world's first LSD experience. Hoffman's story can be funny at times, but from a more sincere point of view, one reason I share this story is because LSD has helped with the treatment of mental illnesses through some of its modern-day derivatives. One example is that LSD has advanced the scientific study of the neurotransmitter serotonin. Selective serotonin reuptake inhibitors (SSRIs) are structurally similar to LSD and are the most common form of legally prescribed antidepressants. As mental health diagnoses continue to increase, so will the use of SSRIs.

This brief survey of some affects of medications on spirituality is only presented to make you aware of the range of possible spiritual experiences and opinions you may encounter—to have an open mind to the ways others may have experienced the spiritual world. I know theists and non-theists alike who abstain from all drugs, including caffeine. On the other hand, many churches now have coffee shops where members can get a shot of psychoactive caffeine before service. I'm not complaining, believe me! My current church has a coffee shop that also sells things like Bibles and spiritual books. In my twisted mind I often think of it as the *Psycho Shop*. The point is, some church congregations likely include individuals who abstain from drug use while others do, in fact, use drugs. As health problems continue to increase, so will the use of medications. As a result, more spiritual experiences will be affected by chemical substances.

Over There

Many of my students used various combinations of legal and illegal drugs consecutively. The illegal ones were often added because of their living environments. Hunger, abuse, and even death were not uncommon. For some, personal heavy drug use or use by their parents or friends kept death percolating in their minds. Other times the death of a relative or friend because of gang affiliations, suicide, or a drug overdose affected some. These situations, and others like them, sometimes led them to ask about life after death. Lively discussions often ensued, but they usually ended with more questions than at the beginning. They were pure speculation and tended to wander a lot because, at the beginning of my career, I was not aware of scholarly information related to the topic. So I began to study to be able to add more *meat* to the discussions.

There is evidence that our ancestors were interested in life after death since they began burying their dead with their possessions and drew on cave walls. As language became more refined, so did the information they shared.

In the late 1800s, the Society for Psychical Research wanted to use science to prove the soul continued to live after death. For three years they collected data from seventeen thousand people in England, Brazil, Russia, and the United States. One of the questions became known as the *Sidgwick question*: "Have you ever, when believing yourself to be completely awake, had a vivid impression of seeing or being touched by a living being or inanimate object, or of hearing a voice: which impression, so far as you could discover, was not due to any external physical cause?"[40]

About 10 percent (8 percent men, 12 percent women) claimed to have had an experience with an entity not physically present, and about 84 percent of the experiences had a visual element. The researchers suspected their results were underestimates because they noticed that as more time passed, a proportion of the hallucinations tended to be forgotten or ignored. Maybe because they were forgotten or ignored or were mentally justified as having had a logical cause. Subsequent studies have produced similar results, usually around 10–15 percent. Many studies focused on not giving examples of the types of information researchers were seeking, but when examples were included, over 70 percent admitted to experiencing a being who was not physically there.

Many studies like the above explore living people experiencing the non-living, but some others explore areas like experiences by those who died or almost died. Some of those results can be summed up by a statement you may be familiar with: "I saw a light at the end of a tunnel." Several studies produced similar results, but some of my more skeptical students recognized an obvious limitation: there was no ability to triangulate the data; there was no third-party confirmation.

Honestly, even as a theist, the skeptic in me thought (still thinks) the same thing. Sure, similar results from multiple studies, conducted by many people, in multiple countries, spread over hundreds of years are good indicators that the results are valid because they confirm each other. But some skeptics still claim that there is no proof that "Greg" saw, heard, or felt a being if "Terry" couldn't confirm it. Again, I agree. But, while attending a conference, a fellow presenter made me aware of a research area that can allow for further confirmation.

Near-death experiences (NDEs) are more frequent than you might think. They have been reported across time and in all cultures. A little more than 4 percent of the populations within the United States and Germany have reported an NDE. It is estimated that in the past fifty years, more than twenty-five million individuals globally have experienced an NDE. Some populations, like heart attack survivors, report higher levels of 10–23 percent.

While most experiences are positive, some report a negative experience, but even those negative NDEs indicate that something continues to exist after death. Something is *over there*. Something is *unseen*. The 1975 publication of Moody's *Life after Life*, which details patients' NDEs, became an international bestseller and is an influential turning point in this area.[41] In fact, Moody actually coined the term *near-death experience*. Research has continued to grow, become more scientifically acceptable and stringent, and encompassed more areas. Not all studies agree with some conclusions, but most agree that the area is one worth researching because something is going on.

> **66 The argument that the mind is produced only by biological functions weakens the evolutionary argument, while using natural means to study something theists believe is spiritual can make them uncomfortable. 99**

Some atheists and some theists alike are uncomfortable talking about NDEs—the argument that the mind is produced only by biological functions weakens the evolutionary argument, while using natural means to study something theists believe is spiritual can make them uncomfortable. I understand the apprehension of both groups. As a skeptic, I want physical proof; as a theist, I don't need it. NDEs can be either spiritual or non-spiritual, good or bad. In general, there can be five experiences: (1) an out-of-body experience, (2) a holographic life review, (3) an encounter with a deceased relative or friend, (4) a return to the body, or (5) a disappearance of fear of death. Out of these five, we focus our discussion on out-of-body experiences (OBE) because some components can allow for objective verification. As you read the next few sections, recall Descartes' "I think, therefore I am." The stories have greater meaning if we understand that thinking indicates existence.

Pam Reynolds is a semi-well-known example. She had an aneurysm located in her brain stem. If it ruptured, it would kill her, but her doctor did not feel she was likely to survive a surgery that used normal methods. Pam eventually found a surgical technique called hypothermic cardiac arrest. She would be put to sleep and have her eyes taped shut. Small, molded speakers would be put into her ears and secured with gauze and tape. They would eliminate outside noise and emit one-hundred-decibel clicks so her brain stem activity could be measured so medical personnel would be able to verify that she was brain dead. Next, her skull would be cut open and the outermost layer of her brain removed. Pam's blood would be cooled by routing it through a cardiopulmonary machine before being returned to her body to cool it. After Pam's heart stopped, her EEG brain waves were flat, her brain stem did not show a response, and her body was cooled to sixty degrees Fahrenheit by the blood. The operating table would be tilted head up, and her blood would be drained from her body.

At that point, Pam would be clinically dead. The draining of the blood would allow the aneurysm to collapse and be easily removed. Then, the blood bypass machine would be turned on again to rewarm her blood and pump it back into her body, rewarming her body. As Pam's body temperature increased, her brain stem should start to respond to the one-hundred-decibel clicking of the speakers in her ears, letting medical personnel know when she was alive again.

Pam agreed to the process and was taken into the operating room at 7:15 a.m. She was anesthetized, and other pre-operating procedures were completed. At 10:50 a tube was inserted into Pam's left femoral artery. Her heart stopped at 11:05, and her blood was drained and the aneurism removed at 11:25. The bypass machine that rewarmed her blood was turned off at 12:32 after returning it to her body. At 2:10, Pam, in stable condition, was transferred to the recovery room. It was a rather involved process, and Pam was unconscious and clinically dead. But Pam had a story to tell about the time she was "out," and some of her comments were later verified by medical personnel.

Pam said her experience began when the doctor cut through her skull with a saw that sounded like a dental drill. One of her first visions was the way her head had been shaved—she had expected her entire head would be shaved, but it wasn't. All of the surgical tools had been covered before the surgery, so Pam had not been able to see them, yet she said the saw looked like an electric toothbrush. "It had a dent in it," she said, and she hated the sound of it.

She also told about the surgeons having a problem locating the artery in her right groin. She heard a female voice say, "We have a problem. Her arteries are too small."

"Try the other side," a male voice replied.

They were successful with the left femoral artery.

Toward the end of the surgery, as Pam returned to her body she saw "the thing, my body" from above. "I didn't want to get into it. . . . It looked terrible, like a train wreck. It looked like what it was: dead. . . . It scared me. . . . It was communicated to me [by relatives] that it was like jumping into a swimming pool. . . . I didn't want to, but [her uncle] pushed me. . . . It was like diving into a pool of ice water. . . . It hurt!"

She recalled that the assistants were playing "Hotel California" as they finished the operation. She specifically remembered the line, "You can check out anytime you like, but you can never leave." She later told the doctor that that was incredibly insensitive, to which he humorously replied that she "needed to sleep more."[42]

The saw with the dent, the arterial complications, conversations, and music were verified by medical personnel. Pam's description is interesting because she should not have been able to physically process sight or sound. She was dead, her eyes were taped shut and gauze-covered, and molded speakers played loud clicks in her ears. Her NDE ended suddenly with the "plunging into a pool of ice water"—a sensation that correlates with the pulmonary machine slowly warming her cooled blood as it was pumped back into her body. Many other instances of verifiable OBEs have been recorded. Allow me to summarize a few.

« Seventeen-year-old Reinee-Pasarow described watching paramedics try to revive her body in her front yard. She even described some of the behaviors of neighbors across the street. All behaviors that she described were later verified.[43]

« Maria recalled how a medical team tried to resuscitate her. One interesting component of her description not related to the medical team was of a tennis shoe on the third floor on the north side of the building. The shoe had a lace underneath the heel, and the area of the little toe was worn out. Later a social worker went to check on the shoe, and Maria's description was confirmed. It was found where and how she described.[44]

« Al talked about floating above his open chest and watching his surgeon flap his elbows while his hands were under his arms. Like a chicken. When asked about his behavior, the surgeon confirmed Al's description. He had been giving instructions to personnel in the room while pointing with his elbows. He had washed his hands and didn't want to touch anything.[45]

« Tom clearly recalled watching a nurse remove his dentures for intubation. More than a week later, with the dentures still missing, Tom identified the same nurse and directed staff to a specific cart drawer where he said she had placed them. His teeth were found exactly where he indicated. Tom further provided a detailed description of the room and recounted observing personnel as they attempted to resuscitate him and discussed his critical medical condition.[46]

An area of OBEs that some students found particularly interesting is *eyeless sight*—blind from birth but can see during an NDE. Vicki was a married forty-three-year-old female who had been born prematurely at twenty-two weeks. Both optic nerves were destroyed by too much oxygen in the incubator. Apparently that happened to about fifty thousand babies in the US during the 1950s because of improper oxygen regulation. Vicki did not even understand the concept of sight. When she was twenty-two years old, she was thrown from a van involved in a crash. Vicki recalled seeing the crumpled van and, later, floating next to the ceiling while she watched medical personnel work on her. Part of their discussion was about possible damage to her eardrum and their concern that she might become deaf in addition to being blind. Vicki tried to tell them that she was fine. She even recognized herself lying on the table by features such as her wedding ring. Her NDE ended when she felt a nauseating impact and found herself back in her body, feeling pain, and unable to see.[47]

Eight-year-old Brad was a student at the Boston Center for Blind Children. Pneumonia and severe breathing difficulties caused his heart to stop. Brad felt himself floating toward the ceiling and saw his body lying on the bed and his blind roommate leaving the room to get help. He continued through the ceiling until he hovered above the roof. He saw that the sky was cloudy and dark, and snow covered the ground except for the streets. The streets had been plowed, but they were slushy. He described such things as cars and the school playground. Brad was asked if he sensed such things or if he saw them. He replied that he had clear vision. His experience ended when he suddenly found himself gasping for air while two nurses worked on him. The parts of Brad's NDE that were verifiable were verified: his blind roommate leaving the room to get help, the snow, the playground, cars, and so on. Vicki and Brad are only two examples of multiple people who were blind but were able to see during an NDE. One study found that fifteen of its twenty-one blind participants were able to see during their NDE.[48]

> **" For one [materialist], a near-death experience would simply be a sensory distortion or misperception and wouldn't be taken as evidence that his consciousness could exist apart from his brain. "**

How can a human mind continue to function when it is not supported by the brain? How long will it function without the body? How can someone who has never seen be able to see? Scientifically, consciousness should end when the body dies, but some data seems to indicate otherwise, at least sometimes. But, at times, some materialists will not even consider other possibilities. A researcher asked some materialists what it would take to convince them that NDEs are real. For one, a near-death experience would simply be a sensory distortion or misperception and wouldn't be taken as evidence that his consciousness could exist apart from his brain.[49]

Meditation

Meditation is often linked to spirituality and, though far less controversial than the previous topics, was beneficial for some of my students. Those benefits tend to be more well-known than some of the previous topics, so I'll just give a quick summary. Meditation can help to reduce pain during amputation, burn pain, cancer pain, chronic pain, birth pain, pre-operation anxiety, stress, depression, and general anxiety. It can promote the healing of skin diseases, burns, asthma, and bone fractures. Meditation also improves internal functions by helping to lower cortisol levels (a stress indicator), improving immune and endocrine functions (the hormone system), reducing high blood pressure, and reducing arterial wall thickness (coronary disease and a stroke indicator), to name a few. It also helps improve positive behaviors such as exercise, diet, and reduced cigarette smoking.

Addiction and mental health treatment programs have also found benefits in meditation. A relapse rate of 70–80 percent is considered normal for alcoholic veterans who attend traditional treatment programs. When you throw in meditation, the relapse rate lowers to about 10 percent. Post-traumatic stress disorder (PTSD) treatments combined with meditation reduce nightmares, flashbacks, and the use of psychotropic drugs. Groups treated by traditional methods without meditation tend to relapse most of the time, while roughly 80 percent of veterans in meditation groups do not.[50]

Even a few hours of meditation can rewire areas of the brain that are important for learning, attention, memory, empathy, and emotion regulation. In an unusual but interesting study, researchers used London cab drivers to study structural changes caused by meditation. The cabbies who drive the iconic black cabs of London can earn almost twice as much as other cab drivers, but to be able to drive them, they must pass a strenuous test known as *The Knowledge*. This test assesses their knowledge about the streets and neighborhoods in the Charing Cross area in central London—a complex maze of streets, lanes, and squares. It takes the average cabbie fifteen to thirty hours of study (a form of meditation) per week for three years to learn The Knowledge.

Researchers scanned the brains of sixteen London cab drivers and compared them to scans of non-cabbies. The posterior hippocampi of the cab drivers (the part of the brain that combines information from memory and plays a part in spatial navigation) were significantly larger than the non-cabbies'. Researchers also compared posterior hippocampi scans of cab drivers who had been driving for decades to newer cab drivers and found more development in the long-term drivers. These findings suggest that careers with a dependence on navigational skills can literally, physically expand the hippocampus. A broader application of the findings indicates that one's occupation may change the structure of the brain.[51]

These and other studies show that meditation can produce both psychological and physiological changes. Knowing this gives insight into biblical references to meditation. Romans 12:2 tells us to renew our minds. Joshua 1:8 tells us to meditate on the law day and night, while Psalm 4:4 instructs us to "meditate in your heart upon your bed and be still." In general, those references teach us to meditate so that we can keep doing well, change our behaviors, or feel better. We now know that it can accomplish those goals by changing our brains.

Barb* is a good example of how meditation can improve thinking, spirituality, and behaviors, and can modulate dependence on psychotropics. She was extremely intellectually gifted and had been well-behaved before middle school. Several weeks after the beginning of sixth grade, she started getting into a lot of trouble because her behavior grew violent. However, shortly after the Thanksgiving holiday, her behaviors began to improve. So much so that she was better behaved than she had been before she started acting violently. About three years later, while in high school, close to the end of her ninth-grade year she suddenly became violent again. It was like a switch had instantly flipped. She frequently harmed herself by hitting herself in her face or stomach and attacked school staff and other students. Summer break was close so staff chose to see if she would return for her tenth grade year without the violence. No luck. It was at that point that a heavily medicated and violent Barb was sent to me.

Clearly, I wondered what had caused her behavior to turn bad in middle school, then improve, then worsen again in high school. A look at her personal life explained a lot. Barb's biological father was physically abusing her mother, so her mother left. Shortly after, Barb's father began molesting Barb. That was the reason for her initial few months of violent behavior.

Barb surprised me when she told me that the molestation was also the reason for her return to good behavior. *What?!* Barb admitted that she had grown to enjoy her father's molestation, and her level of intelligence allowed her to create ways to justify what became a consensual father/daughter relationship. The reason her violent behavior returned in high school was because someone learned of the incestuous relationship, and her father was arrested. I had known of the arrest from her records, but I had not made the connection that Barb was mad because her father had been taken away from her. I thought she would have been happy, but she saw it from a different perspective. She missed his physical affection.

It took a long time for me to connect with Barb enough for her to share such personal information. For months after arriving, Barb would not talk or engage at all. She simply sat, except when she went to the bathroom or got something to eat or acted violently. I tried all the tricks I knew to get her to talk. I purposely tried to make her mad. That worked with most students, and it usually opened the door to positive interactions. Nothing from Barb. I tried sympathy. I tried indifference. Ignoring. Nothing. I tried humor. Nothing. She was stone-faced and unemotional about it all.

> **66 In the end, the icebreaker was our different belief systems. It was those differences that opened the door to communication. 99**

In the end, the icebreaker was our different belief systems. It was those differences that opened the door to communication (connection).

Barb usually read books about Irish literature or philosophy during her free time, but one day I noticed she brought in a book about Wicca. I knew very little about it, so I asked. This wasn't a communication ploy on my part; I was truly curious. Over a few days she told me the basics. She talked, and I asked questions, listened, and learned. Why was it important to her? How did she apply it to her life? What good did she get from it? What were some of its limitations? She believed in a world beyond our physical one, and within Wicca, her interests leaned toward Pantheism, and she worshipped a monotheistic goddess. I was fascinated.

I never offered any information regarding my views, but after a few weeks Barb began asking questions about my belief system. She wanted to compare. As I shared, I followed a mental outline of topics she had discussed from Wicca to explain my beliefs, approaching my own beliefs from a direction that interested her the most. When I finished, Barb began to draw correlations between our religions. The big commonalities were that we both believed in creation by a higher power, had religion-specific language, and had a monotheistic God, though hers was female. We weren't trying to change or convert each other; we were just curious to learn about different belief systems and see how they compared. We both enjoyed the discussions.

Another of our similarities was in prayer or meditation. Barb mentioned that she enjoyed meditating while she was in nature. We developed a plan that allowed her to meditate at school and a modified plan that allowed her to meditate while at the foster home. There were several components of her plan, but one involved music with positive tones and lyrics (more on this in a later chapter). She learned to use meditation to improve her mood when she felt bad and, since she could be manic, to calm herself when necessary. She also began to reduce her reliance on medications, both legal and illegal. I didn't actually address the inappropriate relationship with her father, but after using meditation for some time, she raised the subject with me because, as her meditation abilities improved, she began to feel more freedom to face her emotions and to eventually address her sexual feelings.

Shortly before she graduated, Barb told me she initially began talking to me because she felt that I was simply curious about her beliefs. That was true. She wanted someone to listen and understand her without trying to change her. This taught me that some of the most deeply wounded and damaged people just want someone to try and understand them. To just listen. To not try to change them. There is a need to experience the feeling of being emotionally connected to an external and trustworthy *someone* before they can begin to connect to their own internal feelings. It was that connection that led to her developing an internal desire to want to improve.

In Summary

Well, this chapter has been something of a wild ride (hippy pun intended). We've covered quite a lot of ground that some may find controversial, such as universal spiritual experiences, evolutionary spirituality, drugs and spiritual experiences, and meditation. Along the way, I argued that our brains can be affected by things like medications and changed by activities like meditation. However, not all of us intentionally do things like that.

Throughout I hinted that the universal nature of spiritual experiences transcends religious boundaries. We began with an anecdote of an Alaskan adventure that I, and the non-religious Jay, called "spiritual" and that led to further exploration of spirituality's broader applicability. Drawing from some of my own research in which I defined spirituality as "activities that promote the human longing to be connected," I later refined that definition to "healthy behaviors that result from activities that help humans to connect" by using William James's focus on behavior. The chapter then examined various influences on spirituality: psychotropic medications and psychedelics (e.g., LSD, psilocybin), as seen in the Good Friday Experiment; near-death experiences (NDEs) with verifiable out-of-body experiences (e.g., Pam Reynolds); and meditation's psychological and neurological benefits.

Science (e.g., neuroscience, genetics) supports spirituality's accessibility to all, including secular individuals. The chapter emphasizes spirituality's role in promoting connections and reducing stress, while acknowledging the controversial nature of topics like psychedelics and NDEs.

Introspective Questions for Chapter 3

? **Defining Spirituality:** How do you define spirituality? Does the chapter's idea of "activities that promote the human longing to be connected" align with or challenge your understanding?

? **Universal Spirituality:** Has the chapter's argument that spirituality is accessible to non-religious individuals, like Jay, shifted your view on who can have spiritual experiences? Explain.

? **Personal Spiritual Experiences:** Recall a moment of awe or connection in your life (e.g., in nature or art). Would you call it a "spiritual experience?" What made it meaningful?

? **William James's Focus:** James valued observable behaviors as evidence of positive spirituality. How do your actions reflect your spirituality? Do you agree that behaviors matter for determining spiritual experiences?

? **Psychedelics and Authenticity:** Could a psychedelic-induced experience, like those in the Good Friday Experiment, be "authentic" in your view? How do your biases shape this perspective?

? **Near-Death Experiences:** How do verifiable NDEs, like Pam Reynolds's, affect your beliefs about consciousness? Are you open to non-physical explanations?

? **Meditation and Brain Change:** Knowing meditation can rewire the brain, as seen in The Knowledge study, would you consider it to enhance your well-being? Does its scientific basis make it more or less "spiritual"?

? **Connection and Healing:** Barb's story shows the power of non-judgmental listening. When have you experienced or offered such understanding? How can you foster it with others?

? **Scientific and Spiritual Integration:** How do you balance scientific explanations of spiritual experiences (e.g., neuroscience) with personal meanings? Where do you see tension or harmony?

? **Personal Growth:** Has the chapter inspired you to explore practices like meditation or connection building for stress management or growth? If so, what steps might you take?

CHAPTER 4

Targeting the Subconscious: Digital Warfare

Muddy Foxhole

My marksmanship training in the military began with agonizingly boring hours learning about the rifle. When we were finally allowed to shoot, one of the first stages was firing at targets from known distances—one hundred yards, then two hundred, then three hundred. We were made to lie in rain-filled depressions created by previous shooters, with temperatures hovering in the twenties and thirties. At least our shivering helped teach us to control our movements. We would shoot three rounds at large, round bullseye targets. There was a berm in front of the targets, and half of our company sat behind it while bullets whizzed above their heads. After three rounds, the behind-the-berm guys would lower the targets using a pulley system, look for fresh bullet holes, insert black or white discs (depending on if the bullet had hit a white or black area) into the new holes, then raise the target so we could see where we hit. We would then adjust the rifle sights or our aim. This process continued until we consistently hit the bullseye. When we were done firing, we switched positions and became the ones behind the berms with bullets whizzing over our heads. This methodical, conscious processing training is still used in the beginning stages of training, but later stages have been changed.

Generally, the intentional thought processes model is how rifle training was conducted up to and through World War II. A simple firing range, known distances, and bullseye targets. However, training methods began to shift *after* WWII because *during* WWII Brigadier General S. L. A. Marshall found that only 15–20 percent of American combat soldiers fired in an attempt to kill the enemy.[52] Some of the warriors who did not shoot to kill were clearly not cowards; they often exposed themselves to enemy fire to rescue injured comrades, run messages, or resupply ammunition for those who were shooting to kill. They just didn't want to kill another human being. This knowledge surprised Marshall, but it was not a new concept.

There is evidence of a hesitancy to kill another human throughout all known history, but let's use some data from America's Civil War. The *Civil War Collector's Encyclopedia* tells us that 27,574 muskets were removed from the battlefield after the Battle of Gettysburg.[53] Approximately 90 percent of them were loaded. Think of that high percentage of unfired weapons. Your first thought might be that a soldier had loaded his weapon and then been killed before firing, but twelve thousand (approximate numbers from here on) of those muskets had been loaded more than once. Of the twelve thousand, six thousand had been loaded three to ten times without being fired. One was correctly loaded twenty-three times. Pause to consider those numbers. Six thousand muskets were loaded three or more times without being fired. Why?

At that time, a large part of military training consisted of repeatedly practicing loading a musket with gunpowder, the wad, and the bullet, and then turning the gun around to be able to insert the firing cap, cocking, then firing. Roughly 95 percent of the firing process was dedicated to loading, leaving 5 percent for firing. So roughly 95 percent of the dead soldiers should have been killed while trying to load their weapons, and many of those muskets should have been partially loaded. Additionally, some of those partially loaded weapons would have been picked up and used by those willing to kill. Most of the weapons should have been found empty or partially loaded.

That's not what was found. Yes, some of the twenty-four thousand would be killed while reloading, but not all. A small percentage of the twelve thousand muskets that had been loaded multiple times can be explained by a soldier forgetting to fire because of combat stress. There are many documented cases of that, even in modern times. However, simply reloading a second time would solve the problem because both bullets would be shot from the barrel. Therefore, combat stress can't explain why twelve thousand muskets were loaded more than once and six thousand were loaded more than twice. The obvious conclusion is that many did not want to kill the enemy.

In those days, a commander wanting to make sure his troops were firing would spend a lot of time watching them reload. But it would be easy for a soldier to go through the motions of reloading, aiming, and simulating the gun being fired. Gunpowder was extremely smoky back then, and that would have made it even more difficult for a commander to verify a weapon had been fired. And this doesn't take into account soldiers who fired their loaded weapons but purposely missed the enemy. Those behaviors are well documented too and would account for some of the empty muskets.

Studies show that, throughout all of human history, many more people should have died in war than did. There has been a consistent aversion to killing other humans. When a World War I combat veteran was asked what surprised him the most about combat, he said that it was the large number of his colleagues who would not fire at the enemy. The point of this short discussion is to show that, if the military wanted to become more proficient at killing, they needed to psychologically condition their soldiers.

Based on Marshall's study, marksmanship training began to change after WWII, and by the time of the Korean War, the willingness of individual warriors to shoot to kill had increased from WWII's 15 to 20 percent to 55 percent. Individual fire rates steadily rose to 90 to 95 percent in Vietnam and remained consistent throughout Iraq and Afghanistan. For the most part, the military achieved its goal of increasing firing rates through training the subconscious, and those methods are now incorporated into modern-day military and law enforcement training. Training still begins with a focus on conscious thought processes, such as shooting at round bullseye targets, but then transitions into using automatic (subconscious) processes. To better understand how this training transition was able to change behaviors that have been evolutionarily engrained for millennia, let's look to the subconscious.

Two-Tiered System

Philosophers and researchers have been trying to distinguish between the conscious and the subconscious at least since the time of the Greeks. More recently, in 1874 William Carpenter wrote, "two distinct trains of mental action are carried on simultaneously, one consciously, the other unconsciously," and the more we examine the mechanisms of the mind the clearer it becomes "that not only an automatic, but an unconscious action enters largely into all its processes."[54] That thought was profound for his time, and modern scientists continue to build on it. We now know that automatic, subconscious processes influence nearly everything we do. In fact, the subconscious is necessary, but the conscious mind can be considered optional. It's sort of like the options we think we need to get when we buy a new car. Surround-sound media and heated leather seats are nice, but in the end, the car will get us where we need to go without those things.

Sigmund Freud was a neurologist who made contributions to the fields of neurology, neuropathology, and anesthesia, though he's probably best known as the *Father of Psychoanalysis*.[55] Some of his more interesting work involved using gold chloride to stain nerve tissue to study the neural connections between the medulla oblongata, the cerebellum, the acoustic nerve, and the posterior columns of the spinal cord.[56] He was ahead of his time. It was decades before others understood the importance of brain connectivity. Freud correctly concluded that much of human behavior was governed by subconscious processing. He did not have the tools to study his conclusions, so he tried getting his patients to talk. The problem, as we now know, is that part of their mental processing happened in their unconscious minds before they spoke. So although Freud tried to understand what was going on within the brain, he apparently did not make the connection that the unconscious processing of information affected what his patients said, and that caused him to make some incorrect conclusions.

> **66 It is the subconscious mind that allows us to survive in a world that requires such a massive amount of informational processing. 99**

Carl Jung believed we could learn a lot about experiences by studying dreams and mythology. They transcend time and culture, and they come from the subconscious. Pretty amazing thoughts since, unlike us, he did not have the luxury of watching as different neurological structures generated different levels of blood flow as thoughts and emotions changed. We perform many automatic, unconscious behaviors because of the interplay between the two-tiered brain, and we like to think that our behaviors are the result of conscious thoughts. In reality, very little of our behavior is the result of conscious thoughts.[57]

The human sensory system sends about eleven million bits of information to the brain every second, but we can only consciously process between sixteen to fifty-nine bits of information. What happens to the remaining millions of bits? They're handled by our subconscious. (Some scientists estimate that only about 5 percent of our cognitive functioning is available to our conscious mind. The remaining 95 percent occurs in the subconscious.) It is the subconscious mind that allows us to survive in a world that requires such a massive amount of informational processing. Our perceptions, memories, decisions, judgments, and activities seem effortless because of the effort expended by the subconscious.

The subconscious uses most of the energy that our brains consume, and a lot of that—about a third of the brain—is consumed by our visual systems. We rarely, if at all, consider all of the factors that go into what we see. Our brains simply process information that identifies color, recognizes motion, sharpens edges, verifies identities, determines depth and distance, fills in blind spots in our vision, and so on without us realizing it. The visual system is so important that it is one of the most studied systems in neuroscience, and understanding its workings is helping to clarify how the two levels of the human mind function together.

We cannot control all of what our subconscious minds process, but we can limit some exposure. While there are many things we cannot keep from seeing, the remainder of this chapter explores some of the effects our vision has on our decisions. Once we become aware of these effects and how easily our brains can be trained, it's easier to stop being controlled by them.

Subconscious and Vision

A fascinating study done on the visual system involved a fifty-two-year-old male called TN. TN was a doctor who suffered a stroke in 2004. The stroke damaged the visual processing area that handled the vision in his left eye, so he could only see with the right eye. Unfortunately, thirty-six days later, TN had another stroke that damaged the other half of the visual region, and he was left completely blind. A doctor verified that TN had lost all vision. The visual areas of his occipital lobe were simply not functioning. He could not detect shapes, movement, or intense light.

Though his processing centers were not working, the rest of his visual system was working fine. His eyes still functioned as normal, and all the other neural pathways were still hooked up. His retinas could gather information and send it to the visual cortex, but the data couldn't be processed when it arrived there. To sum up, TN had a fully functioning optical system except for the part that processed the gathered information. This was an unfortunate situation, but it did make TN highly sought after for some experiments.

In one study, researchers displayed photos of faces in front of TN's eyes. The faces were either happy or angry, and TN was to guess the expression. Facial expressions are one of the main ways we communicate; therefore, the human brain devotes more neural real estate to facial recognition than it does to many other visual processes. If the guesses were purely random, you'd expect the subject to guess correctly roughly 50 percent of the time since there were only two possible choices. TN correctly identified the faces as happy or angry about 66 percent of the time. This indicated that his subconscious and a part of the visual system known as the *fusiform face area* was probably receiving visual information even though his conscious visual processing center had been destroyed, but clearly this left many unanswered questions.[58]

Another group of researchers wanted to raise the stakes a little. They asked TN to participate in a test designed to access the reptilian part of the brain by including actual physical danger. They designed a test that might cause TN to fall if he made a wrong step. The theory was that danger would engage his unconscious mind more effectively than just safely looking at pictures. So researchers asked TN to navigate a hallway that had an obstacle course made of random office objects like a garbage can, stacks of paper, and boxes. TN was not allowed to use his cane. He successfully navigated the obstacle course without stumbling or walking into any objects. TN could not explain how he and done it; he just had.[59]

The term for TN's condition—an intact optical system but no ability to neurologically process visually collected data—is *blindsight*. Blindsight is a strange syndrome that clearly shows how the two tiers of the brain can operate independently of each other. It also illustrates that the unconscious mind has knowledge that is hidden from the conscious mind.

Binocular Rivalry

Binocular rivalry is a way to artificially demonstrate blindsight. To do this, hold two different images (photos, drawings) close enough to each eye so that each eye cannot see the image covering the other eye. Don't move them. When you see the images, they won't be stacked on top of each other the way your brain puts together the images from each eye to create binocular vision. Instead, your brain will automatically alternate between the two images. You will see one, then the other, then back to the first, and so on. Now, let's alter the situation a little. Begin to slightly move one of the images while continuing to hold the other one still. You will notice that you only perceive the moving image. If you play a video for one eye, then only the video will be consciously seen, but the still image will register in your subconscious. How do we know that the brain receives and processes both images?

Researchers placed a constantly changing image in front of each participant's right eye.[60] It was similar to a mosaic. A non-moving image with a small figure on either the left side or the right side of the image was put in front of the left eye. Participants said they only saw the changing mosaic. When asked if the figure on the unmoving image was located on the left or the right side, they were correct about 50 percent of the time. Since there were only two choices, that was the expected outcome if they were guessing, so there was no proof that their subconscious was registering the figures. But what if the unmoving images were more *interesting*? What if they were more appealing to their base desires? Would the percentage of correct choices increase because the subconscious had more motivation to process it?

Researchers decided to use photos from the International Affective Picture System (IAPS)—a collection of 480 photos that produce different levels of arousal. It includes pictures like mutilated bodies, calming photos of wildlife and children, and sexually explicit situations. Afterward, participants were asked again what they had seen. Again, they said they had consciously seen the changing mosaic. But we know that their subconscious minds processed the *highly arousing erotic* images because their ability to correctly identify if the figure was on the left or right side of the image increased significantly. Our unconscious mind sees things that our conscious mind doesn't, especially if we find it emotionally significant. That is often what happens when we get a *bad feeling* about someone or a situation even though we can't quite explain why we feel that way.

> **" Our unconscious mind sees things that our conscious mind doesn't, especially if we find it emotionally significant. "**

Blind Spots

In addition to collecting and processing data of which our conscious mind is not aware, our subconscious also enhances the relatively poor visual data sent to it. A good example is the blind spot we have in our vision. The place on the back of the eyeball where the retina is connected to the nerves that carry visual data to our brain puts a hole in the middle of our visual field. We don't notice the blind spot because our brain automatically fills in the missing data based on the information it receives about the areas around it. It simply extrapolates what should be there.

You can find the blank area in your vision with an easy experiment. Look at Figure 2. Close your right eye, then focus on the number 9 with your left eye. Move the book toward you or away from you until the star disappears while still looking at number 9. The star is now in your blind spot. Now keep your head still, and move your vision from the 9, to the 8, to the 7, and so on. For me, the star reappears around number 6, but your results may vary.

★ 1 2 3 4 5 6 7 8 9

Figure 2. Man-made experiment to find the blind spot in the middle of our vision.

Microsaccades

Additionally, our subconscious compensates for some of the movements of our eyes. Microsaccades are the fastest movements performed by the human body—so fast that they cannot be observed without special instruments. Don't confuse *microsaccades* with *saccades*—the easily observable eye movements that we see when talking to someone. We probably would not be able to stand watching what was going on around us if our minds didn't adjust for those movements. Thankfully the brain compensates for those motions by editing them out while the data is being transmitted to processing centers.

Alcohol slows the microsaccades to the point that you can see them without special instruments. The greater the alcohol level, the slower the saccades. That's why law enforcement officers ask individuals to visually track an item during sobriety tests. An object, usually a pen, is held about four inches in front of the subject's face, and the individual focuses on the tip. The pen is slowly moved from side to side while the pen mover stares at the subject's eyes. Seeing repeated microsaccades can indicate possible drug influence (even a legal prescription).

Peripheral Vision

Our subconscious also improves visual data from our peripheral vision. As an example, look at an object about an arm's length away—maybe a letter on this page. The only part of your vision that has good resolution will be the letter and possibly the area immediately surrounding it. Just outside of your focus area your visual clarity will change drastically, even if you have perfect vision. The data just outside of the middle of your vision will be similar to someone who needs strong eyeglasses but is not using them. We can demonstrate this with Figure 3.

Look at the asterisk in the first line of Figure 3 from a couple of feet away. Stare at the asterisk in the first line. The Bs are about a thumbnail apart. You may want to cover the second and third lines to start while you stare at the asterisk. If you're like me, you may be able to recognize the As and the Bs but none of the other letters. When I stare at the asterisk in the second row, I can recognize the Cs and Ds. Ironically, my vision allows me to recognize the Ds more clearly than the Cs. I am able to read all of the letters in the third row. Your perceptions may be slightly different because of differences in our eyes.

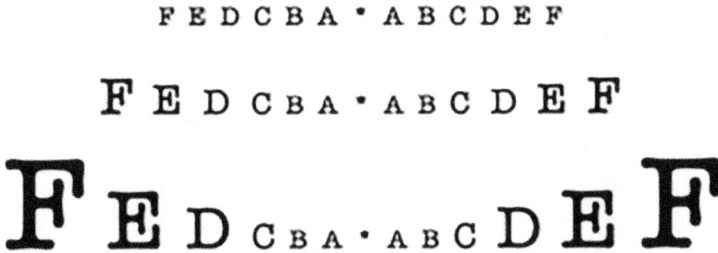

F E D C B A · A B C D E F

F E D C B A · A B C D E F

F E D C B A · A B C D E F

Figure 3. Demonstration of how peripheral vision is affected by size.

Flip It, Process It, Flip It, "See" It

To make things more neurologically difficult, the convex shape of the front part of the eyes bends light and focuses it on the retina at the back of the eye. One of the results of this focusing is that an upside-down image arrives at the retina. Along the processing pathway, meaning is also attached. Is that my child, or is it a lion?

Two visual data streams, inverted images, blind spots, microsaccades, and poor peripheral vision should create severe problems for us. When we look at another person, we should see two images of the same person, standing on his head, curved like one of those carnival mirrors, without depth like a pancake, looking like fuzzy dice, quivering faster than someone going through withdrawals, with a black hole in the middle of his body.

However, the subconscious combines the separate data from both eyes, flattens it, flips it, removes the jiggling, fills in the gaps in the middle of our vision, sharpens the periphery, and gives the image meaning, among many other things. The following images roughly show the difference between what we see with mental processing and what we would see without it. (Note: The manipulated images that follow are not intended to be an exact representation of collected visual data before it's processed by our subconscious; they are only intended to help demonstrate some of the data our minds must process before we can "see" a clear image. Something like those images are what I used to help students better comprehend the complexities of visual processing. If you are interested in seeing more, there are a variety of vision simulators online.) I decided to have a little fun with these images. Remember me telling the story about going to pick up my high school transcripts? Well, stapled to them was my high school identification (Figure 4). Clearly I hadn't attended enough for a teacher to give it to me. Look at that full head of hair.

Figure 4. Author's high school identification used to show what we perceive after our subconscious minds have processed the gathered visual data (e.g., combining dual images, flipping, filling in blind spots, flattening).

Figure 5 demonstrates what the photo might look like before our subconscious corrects for the blind spot in the center of our vision and our poor peripheral vision.

Figure 5. Author's illustration of how the raw visual data may look before subconscious corrections for the blind spot and poor peripheral vision.

Our minds must also process two slightly different visual data streams. Because each eye perceives an object from a slightly different angle, two slightly varied upside-down images are formed. Close one eye and hold a finger up in front of your face. Then, close the open eye and open the closed one without moving your finger. You'll see your finger appear to shift. Rapidly alternating between opening and closing each eye causes your finger to seem to jump side to side in sync with your eyelids. But, we don't see two different fingers with both eyes open because our mind combines them into one. One of the benefits of the two views is that it helps create our depth perception. Figure 6 below demonstrates how my school identification might look if not combined. I say "might look" because there are many reasons why there will be variations in what we see. Let me give you one simple example.

Hold your finger in front of your face like before, but let it barely touch your nose, hold it still, and alternate between opening and closing your eyes, as we did earlier. Now, move your finger away from your face as far as your arm will allow and repeat the procedure. Notice how your finger appears to move side to side more when it's closer to your face? The farther away from your face, the less it moves. To measure how much my finger moves, I just did this procedure with a bookshelf in the background. The shelf is just shy of three feet wide, and with my finger touching my nose, it "moved" beyond the left and right boundaries of the shelves by about forty-two inches each way. So, including the width of the shelf, my finger moved approximately one hundred and twenty inches. However, when I extended my arm as far as possible and repeated the procedure, my finger appeared to move about twelve inches (about the width of nine different sized books). The greater distance from my face made my finger appear to move less.

Of course, the distance of the object you use to measure your finger movement will also affect how much the finger appears to move. For example, the shelf I used as a reference point is about ten feet away. When I go through the same process using my computer monitor, which is about two feet away, my finger moves much less. The overlap in Figure 6 is the approximate distance my finger moves as I hold it about six inches from my face and use my monitor (two feet away) as a backstop. If you would like to see a representation of the two visual streams as they might appear as they arrive at the back of your eyeballs, simply turn the book upside down.

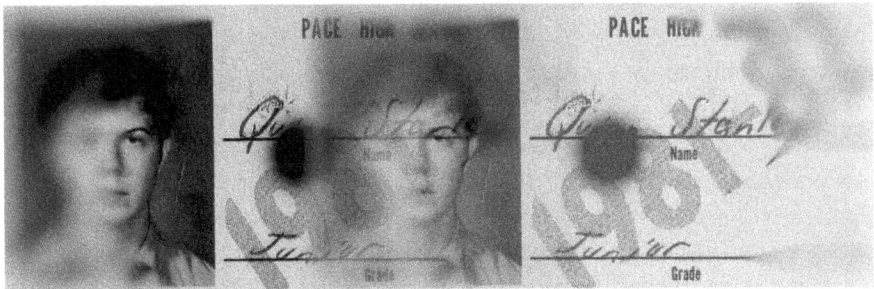

Figure 6. Author's demonstration of the two overlapping, uncombined visual streams, before subconscious processing. (Note: Like the previous image, this image is not intended to be a correct representation of collected visual data before it's processed by our minds. Something like this is what I used to help students better comprehend the complexities of visual processing.)

Subconsciousness and Decisions

The subconscious mind does more than simply adjust our vision; it influences our decisions even when we think it does not. The once-popular Pepsi versus Coke taste test is a good example. In the tests, most people preferred Pepsi to Coke when they didn't know which one they were drinking. When they did know, they said they preferred Coke. (I find myself in that camp.) This has been dubbed the *Pepsi paradox.* One possible explanation is that brand-name familiarity affects choice. The ventromedial prefrontal cortex (VMPFC) is where we find the positive feelings we have when we think about familiar products.

> **Even though we like to think that we make rational choices based on conscious thoughts alone, we don't.**

In 2007 researchers recruited participants for a new Pepsi/Coke study. Some of the participants had damaged VMPFCs, and some did not. Like previous studies, both groups usually chose Pepsi when they didn't know what they were drinking. The difference in this study came when the researchers let the participants know which drink they'd chosen. The group with properly functioning VMPFCs switched their choice to Coke, as in previous studies. However, the group with damaged VMPFCs stayed with Pepsi. The Pepsi paradox only held for the group with properly functioning VMPFCs.[61]

Financial decisions are also affected by our subconscious. Something as simple as sunshine affects how much we tip waiters and waitresses.[62,63] One would think that larger sums of money, such as the amounts stockbrokers *play* with, would be less affected by subconscious thoughts. Not so much. Saunders used both cloudy and sunny days to explore subconscious effects on New York Wall Street trading between 1927 and 1990. He found that stock prices were higher on sunny days and lower on cloudy days in those years.[64]

Others wanted to see if they could verify Saunders's results in other places in the world.[65] They compared stock market indices from twenty-six countries between 1982 and 1998. They confirmed the correlation in Saunders's study, finding similar results in all twenty-six countries. They then went a step further and estimated possible market returns. They concluded that, if the sun had shown in New York for an entire year, the Exchange would have averaged 24.8 percent, while an entire year of cloudy days would have caused the Exchange to average only 8.7 percent. Even though we like to think that we make rational choices based on conscious thoughts alone, we don't. Our unconscious minds affect all of our thoughts and behaviors.

False and Changed Memories

Our eyes can also lead us to false, or changed, memories—good or bad. Researchers gathered participants who had never been in hot-air balloons. Without the participants' knowledge, researchers asked participants' family members to give them photos of the participants when they were between four and eight years old. The photos were to be of the participants at moderately significant events—memorable but not too memorable. The researchers then created fake photos of the participants in hot-air balloons.

The real and fake photos were jumbled together and given to the subjects, and they were then asked to describe everything they could about the events in the pictures. If they could not recall the events, they were asked to close their eyes and mentally envision themselves in the photo. The process was completed three times with three to seven days separating each session. About half of the subjects said they recalled memories of a balloon trip that never happened. Some even recounted details of the non-existent balloon ride that didn't come from the pictures. Even more interesting, some said they could feel the sensations of the ride even after researchers told them that the balloon photos were fake. One even commented that the memories still felt real and some of the scenes persisted.[66]

Another good example of false memories relates to a group of people who had been to Disneyland. They were asked to read and think about an ad they did not know was fake. Participants were then asked to imagine the feeling of their first up-close encounter with Bugs Bunny—an experience encompassing overwhelming excitement at meeting an idolized TV character, parents urging them to shake his hand for photos, hearts pounding and hands sweating so much they'd need to be wiped dry before that momentous handshake.[67]

After reading the advertisement several times, the participants were given a questionnaire that explored their memories of Disneyland. Sixty-two percent recalled shaking Bugs Bunny's hand. Forty-six percent recalled hugging him. One person even recalled that Bugs had been holding a carrot when they met. This study is interesting because Bugs Bunny is a Warner Brothers character so he would not have been at Disneyland. Other false memory studies have led people to believe they had spent time in the hospital, spilled a punch bowl at a wedding, or gotten lost at a mall, to name a few. Misinformation is so easy to implant that gorillas, pigeons, and human infants as young as three months old have had false memories implanted.

Can memories be implanted even more easily than the previous examples? They can. In fact, false memories can be implanted by casually telling a person about an incident that didn't happen. Over time, the person may recall the *event* but forget the source of the memory. The result will be that the false event will be integrated into their memories. Psychologists who try to utilize this procedure for treatment are successful between 15 and 50 percent of the time. This is one reason why, if I am asked if someone should seek counseling, I always recommend that they make sure that the counselor has a good, long-term reputation. Don't allow nefarious people to mess with your head because it's far too easy to do. We've been having a little fun with this topic so far, but in reality, it can be very scary stuff when abused.

Messing with a patient's memories may sound unethical, and sometimes it is. However, it is an accepted treatment method in some cases. You may even do something similar. Have you ever tried to build someone up after they've had a bad day? Rewording a bad situation to make it positive ("Look at the bright side . . .") is the same basic process. Evolutionists even find support for evolution within this process because our survivability increases when others have a more positive outlook. Giving someone else the confidence to handle a hard time will be beneficial to many.

The malleability of memory also provides support for the argument that theists should ensure that the Bible remains unchanged. When you change theological foundations, you allow room for memories and basic tenets to change.

Toward the other end of the spectrum of implanting or changing memories to help someone is the recognition that trying to influence someone to act *appropriately* may in fact influence them to act *inappropriately*. One of the simplest studies to demonstrate this was conducted in the Petrified Forest National Park.[68] Researchers videoed a section of a trail for ten hours. Approximately 3 percent of the petrified wood they'd placed along the trail was taken by hikers. They then placed a sign that condemned visitors for stealing petrified wood and videoed the area for another ten hours. Approximately 8 percent of the wood was stolen. The researchers suggested that condemning a behavior may actually increase it. The unspoken message that the prohibition registers in the subconscious is something like, *Others do it, so why not me?* This is why most teachers quickly learn that *planned ignoring* of some student behaviors is better than addressing them in front of others. Drawing attention to them may entice more students to join.

Educators also quickly learn the benefits of modeling—teaching students appropriate behaviors by acting that way themselves. Kind of like, "Do like you see me do." A benefit, and a possible drawback, to modeling is that students learn from teachers' actions anytime they see a teacher perform an action, or react to a situation, or notice a teacher's facial expression, and so on. So we must be careful to act appropriately at all times. This process is helped by another important component of visual and social learning: mirror neurons. Mirror neurons were discovered somewhat by chance. Researchers were studying the neurons that controlled mouth and hand movements in macaque monkeys. As the monkeys reached for food, they measured the neuronal activity. The researchers unexpectedly discovered that some monkey neurons fired when the monkeys watched the researchers eating lunch. The monkeys didn't need to perform the actions themselves for their neurons to fire.[69,70]

Mirror neurons are of particular interest because virtually all behavior is mimicked. We learn complex movements by seeing them and then modeling them. We may even watch others so that we can improve skills that are declining through age or are suddenly impaired by loss of a motor function, as with a stroke. We may even observe and analyze our own movements so we can improve them—like athletes routinely reviewing training tapes.

When used in a clinical or training setting, modeling is often called *action observant treatment* (AOT). Voluntary movements are typically started by activating motor areas in the frontal lobe, and the cingulate cortex and those movements can be encouraged when we observe the action being performed by others. The process can produce a structural reorganization of the primary motor cortex so the actions can be maintained and improved. The most successful outcomes are produced when an individual observes the action, imagines doing the movement, and then performs it. AOT has shown itself to be beneficial in the rehabilitation, maintenance, and procurement of motor skills.

Motor Learning and Mental Imagery

Motor learning theory has shown that simply thinking about an action causes the related motor neurons to activate and can be used to improve recovery after an injury. When parts of our bodies are immobilized after an injury, the immobility degrades the ability of the brain to cause movement. Other healthy movements also change as a way to compensate for the degradation. Such changes may cause future problems. The longer the immobilization, the greater the possible neurological problems.

One study was trying to find how to best recover the lost abilities of people who had orthopedic surgery for a hip fracture or a hip or knee replacement.[71] Patients were divided into two groups: one group daily viewed clips of motor movements and then imitated them; the other group did not watch the motor movements but still performed the same actions as the other group. At the end of three weeks, all patients in the first group used one crutch (except one), while more than 20 percent of the second group still used two crutches. In all, the evidence for AOT as a help for motor rehabilitation is *strong* for Parkinson's and stroke populations, *moderate* for orthopedic and multiple sclerosis patients, and *small-to-moderate* for children with cerebral palsy.

New Motor Skills

AOT has become quite popular in sports. For athletes who already have a skill, its use helps them to improve motor skills and their abilities to predict an opponent's intention. That ability to predict is often overlooked as a benefit, but it makes sense—if you can learn a movement by observing, you can learn how your opponent will move next by observing. When comparing novice rugby players to skilled rugby players, researchers found that the novices were more likely to fall prey to faking movements than were skilled players.[72] In other words, your skill level can help you spot someone's deceptive behaviors.

Even medical personnel can benefit from observing others. Surgery is one area that has traditionally used observation of surgical procedures within a theater-type setting. However, it's not always possible to be in an operating room, so some students began watching videotapes of expert surgeons. Ultimately their quality and speed were better than students who didn't watch the videos. The training process continues to improve, now incorporating more advanced technologies such as VR-based simulators.

An important, yet often overlooked, component of modeling is that errors made by teachers can help students learn to recognize and correct their own mistakes. Motor skills are improved by this process. Interestingly, students who observe a novice teacher make and correct mistakes learn better than students who watch skilled teachers make and correct mistakes. When all of this information is combined, we see that ideal learning situations are a mixture of novice and expert demonstrations—novice demonstrations to help with the learning of error detection and error correction, and expert demonstrations to show the ideal blueprint that should be followed. Put another way, the traditional approach of master-teaching-learner should also include novice-teaching-learner.

Motor Skills Maintenance

Obviously maintaining and improving skills is important for groups such as athletes and musicians, but they're possibly even more important for first responders, the military, and the elderly. It helps ensure procedures and actions are performed correctly, which assists in injury prevention, reduces hospitalizations, and improves the quality of life, especially for the elderly. Researchers at Otago University have developed the Otago exercise program.

This includes strength training, walking, and balancing tasks for elderly people. The program has improved strength and balance while reducing fall risks for those over seventy years old.[73] When the elderly are allowed to observe someone perform the correct actions, they have an even greater benefit of keeping the frontoparietal networks (attention, complex problem-solving, working memory) from showing age-related degradation.

Conventional wisdom suggests that an observer of any age group should view movements that are slightly better than their own—more advanced, but not so far advanced that they are clearly out of reach. When I played competitive sports, I learned to play against someone slightly better than me because they made me better. A group of people with an average age of 70.5 were asked to perform ball rotation tasks. Separate groups were taught ball rotation movements by (1) a skilled model, (2) a non-skilled model, and (c) verbal directions with no demonstration. Ball rotation speed improved significantly in the group that observed the *non-skilled model* but not in the *skilled* or *no demonstration* groups.[74] In other words, observational training should be kept close to, but slightly better than, the current abilities of the observer.

> *" The 3D nature of VR produces more activation of the frontoparietal networks than 2D videos. "*

Virtual Reality

Virtual reality (VR) is one of the most successful and promising delivery methods for AOT. The 3D nature of VR produces more activation of the frontoparietal networks than 2D videos. VR also produces different levels of activation based on our level of immersion, our viewing devices, and our physical *interaction* with the VR demonstrator. For example, your mirror neurons will have stronger reactions if you can interact with the demonstrator through live stream than they would if you watch a recorded demonstration. The ventral premotor cortex (which prepares for movement based on external cues) is the most activated region within the frontoparietal area of the brain when observing actions using VR. VR is also being used to successfully treat medical conditions like stroke and cerebral palsy.[75,76,77]

Modern VR systems provide the user with visual, auditory, and touch sensations. This creates a more fully immersive experience in which the patient can physically interact with the virtual environment. Some systems even provide optical tracking and visual adjustments to prevent motion sickness. The results are that an expanding number of patients can receive treatment with VR. The treatment becomes even more effective as users grow more excited to participate. This improves transference and use of both simple and complex VR-learned actions into real-life situations.

The visual perspective of the observer—whether it's first person or third person—affects how well the observer's mirror neurons work. First person is your natural viewpoint—how you watch yourself as you do something. Third person views the action from a distance—you watch someone else do something. First-person vision causes more activation of the brain networks related to cognitively demanding tasks. Third-person watching causes visual areas to activate more. Learning upper-body movements seems to work best by combining both first- and third-person perspectives. However, learning lower-body movements seems to work best from the third-person view. This makes sense because a first-person view does not allow the observer to see the entire lower body.

All of this, and other information not discussed in detail here, shows us that the most effective motor learning occurs when the student can switch between first- and third-person viewing, depending on what the observer needs to view (e.g., upper or lower body). From a teaching perspective, the first step should be to provide the patient/student with an overall modeling of the action using the third-person point of view (just watching). Then, depending on the action that needs to be learned (upper or lower body), the first- or third-person perspective can be introduced to help maximize learning. Such an approach combines the advantages of each perspective.

Desensitization, Conditioning, and Denial Defense

Now that we have briefly considered how easily the subconscious mind can be influenced and trained, I would like to return your attention to the US military's need to train personnel to fire at the enemy. Most of us, like those who came before us, have an evolutionarily engrained hesitancy to kill another human, even when legally authorized for duties like the military, law enforcement, or protecting one's family. So I ask, *If we are born with an evolutionarily engrained aversion to harming another human, why are so many of our youth willing, and even eager in some cases, to engage in violence? Why do some view it as a badge of honor?*

To provide a more effective answer, we need to travel down a slightly darker path for a while. You may find the information somewhat unsettling, but it is relevant. Most violence throughout history was for a purpose (though, understandably, our opinions regarding justification may differ). Only in the last few decades have we seen such a large-scale willingness, and sometimes eagerness, to engage in violence that does not have a legal authorization. What has caused such a quick shift in the human psyche?

In the book *On Killing: The Psychological Cost of Learning to Kill in War and Society*, Grossman argues that there is a triad of sociological and psychological manipulations associated with the dramatic shift: *desensitization, conditioning,* and *denial defense.*[78] We focus on desensitization and denial defense because conditioning is included within them. For example, as you are taught that something is good, you can be conditioned to respond with certain behaviors—aspirin is good, so I take some when I have a headache. These concepts were highly influential in urging my severely emotionally/behaviorally disturbed students to engage in harmful behaviors.

Desensitization

In the military, desensitization takes place consistently from the first day of basic training. At least it did in my day. Justified killing was promoted and glorified through even the most basic things like singing cadence during marching. I won't repeat one of our favorite cadences, but it ended with us smashing a yellow bird's head after he landed on our windowsill. If you are a veteran, you probably just smiled a little. Or at least suppressed a smile. I mention singing cadence because, as you will see in the chapters on music, combining movement (especially group movement), music, and words creates a very powerful mental manipulator. Throw in a little twisted, dark humor and its manipulation power grows. Military deification of killing was almost unheard of in WWI, and even in WWII it was rare. It increased significantly by Korea, and by the time Vietnam rolled around it was an institutionalized training method. In simple terms, desensitization can be viewed as a mental smoke screen for the possibility of having to do something our subconscious tells us we should not be doing. We sang and laughed about killing that little yellow bird.

In Vietnam, it took an average of fifty thousand rounds for non-snipers to kill one enemy. I'm sure ammo manufacturers were less happy that Army and Marine snipers averaged only 1.39 rounds per kill. Training can be made more realistic when someone needs more desensitization. Enemy uniforms may be filled with balloons. Milk jugs might be filled with red paint. A well-known sniper who became a trainer for the Israeli Defense Force's antiterrorist sniper course changed all of the targets to anatomically correct full-size targets and dressed them in clothes. He would also pour ketchup into cabbage, put it back together, and put it on the target. He would then tell a shooter to focus on envisioning a head exploding when looking through the long-range optic.[79]

Carlos Hathcock wore a white feather in his bush hat. Yeah, he was confident. Despite the visible calling card, he was so effective that the People's Army of Vietnam put a thirty-thousand-dollar bounty on Hathcock at a time when most bounties ranged from eight to two thousand dollars. After returning to the States, he helped to establish the Marine Corps Scout Sniper School and worked with other branches, special operations groups, and police departments. One of Hathcock's honors was to have a rifle named after him. The M25 Sniper Weapon System was developed for Army and Navy special operations units. The civilian version is known as the Springfield Armory M25 White Feather.

I don't know if Hathcock knew the term *desensitization*, but he used the technique. He made it very clear that the purpose of the training was to kill a bad guy. Hathcock was known for giving very clear instructions like, "Put three rounds inside the inside corner of the right eye of the bad guy." That comment carried some weight. One of his most well-known feats was shooting and killing a Vietnamese sniper (call sign "Cobra") through Cobra's rifle scope, hitting Cobra in the eye. Think of that. Cobra had to have been looking directly at him for the round to make it through the scope and into the eye. How close had Cobra been to squeezing his trigger? Hathcock didn't need fancy props, just the cold, hard fact of a past reality and a future possibility. Simple and effective.

> **" Our denial defense mechanism is a subconscious method we use to deal with traumatic experiences. "**

Denial Defense

Our denial defense mechanism is a subconscious method we use to deal with traumatic experiences. It usually occurs because the soldier rehearsed a process so many times that when the event actually happened he could convince himself he did not *really* kill a human. It was just another target on the range. It was just another training session like those conducted so many times before. Many modern soldiers say they simply think of the enemy as man-shaped targets like the ones in training.

Bill Jordan, an experienced gunfighter, teaches young law enforcement officers to overcome their natural reluctance to shoot another human by mentally dehumanizing their opponent as a mere target, viewing them as someone who disregards societal rules, thus justifying their removal without remorse or emotional attachment.[80]

An important element of the training not discussed to this point is a safeguard that is always incorporated into military and law enforcement training—legitimate authority. Numerous studies demonstrate that this *safety mechanism* is effective. Sure, some veterans commit violent crimes, but statistically they are much less likely to do so when compared to a non-veteran of the same age and sex. In essence, they have been trained to have a greater ability to kill, but they are less likely to do so. The removal of legitimate authority and an understanding of the gruesomeness of killing makes them less likely to engage.

You might expect that the military would be a good place for sociopaths to earn a living. Though there are some, they are less likely to be in the military (or law enforcement) because many have intense aversions to authority. Swank and Marchland studied WWII veterans and noted the existence of about 2 percent of soldiers who were sociopaths who did not have the normal resistance to killing.[81]

Video Games

Violent media often includes *desensitization, conditioning,* and *denial defense.* In Pavlovian classical conditioning, media desensitizes youth by showing detailed, horrible suffering and killing. Games contain peer pressure and rewards that encourage participation in causing suffering and killing. In a Skinnerian, operant conditioning practice, players are presented with simulations that include quick reaction scenarios such as popup targets. Players must quickly (subconsciously) decide if the target is a friend or a foe. They can train elements such as trigger control and shoot-no-shoot decisions at home.

These games are similar to those used by law enforcement and military for training, but unlike law enforcement and military training it is not uncommon for the *enemy* to be a grandma, a child, a businessman, or a cop. Gamers grow accustomed to having a good time shooting non-violent humans/avatars. They learn to engage in socially unacceptable behaviors while enjoying the experience and without the *safety catch* of legal authority. In a social learning process (mirror neurons), games often include graphic and sadistic torture and murder scenes. Youth begin to get the impression that those behaviors are acceptable and even praiseworthy. After all, they get points and praise for them.

The glorification of vigilantes has become popular over the last several decades. Parents, friends, cops, and veterans are portrayed as unstable characters who operate outside of the law to commit murder and torture. The more seamlessly the game can provide a believable connection between realism and the ability to commit violence, the greater its effects. Some games even teach players the most effective and efficient ways to inflict pain and violence and then reward the player for doing so. Given that these conditioning experiences often take place in the presence of friends and food, gamers learn to associate causing suffering and killing with their favorite soft drink or food, with the close relationships often found among their friends or family, with relaxing, with entertainment, with laughing, and so on. They become conditioned to having a good time while committing violence.

Some say that games do not have negative effects on players. I have many possible responses to such comments, and one is to share with them why technologies like VR have been incorporated into realistic shoot-no-shoot training for law enforcement and some special operations personnel. It was first incorporated in the 1970s because LEO deaths were increasing. Many would hesitate to shoot in real-life, life-or-death situations. Sure, the incorporation was out of concern for officers, but the greatest concern was the loss of civilian lives that occurred after the officer died. The results of shoot-no-shoot training show that the saving of both officer and civilian lives has increased. The same general conditioning principles are used in video games, so the effects on civilian players are similar. Officers have seen great improvements in their skills when training only a few hours a year while gamers may play several hours in one day.[82]

Not all video games are bad, and, honestly, some of the effects of violent games are not all bad. Some LEOs and military personnel use games for additional training in concentration and identification of appropriate targets (correct shoot-no-shoot decisions). It helps to nurture and maintain their subconscious training and motor skills because actual force-on-force training is rarely adequate to maintain or improve decision-making skills and motor memory.

Some games are appropriate for anyone at any age. Many promote appropriate learning. Others are designed by neurologists to help people maintain mental fitness. I play word games each day as a way to stimulate neurological pathways to (hopefully) keep them healthy. The more I age, the more I play. Professionally, I sometimes used video games for some special needs students who needed to increase their concentration time and intensity. Motor learning and motor improvement were also a benefit for some. They thought I was cool because I was letting them play a game during class, but in reality, it was a form of treatment. I was often surprised by how much they liked playing the *old school* entertaining games that use a joystick and buttons to aim (Duck Hunt), jump over items (Mario Brothers), eat dots (Pac-Man), or protect one's planet (Asteroid). Those games may seem very basic to you, but for some, they require intense mental concentration and motor coordination. The level of difficulty is relative.

Some other benefits for my students were learning to accept responsibility for their choices and actions, reflect on external and personal struggles, build relationships, explore personal insights, consider future aspirations, and control emotions in stressful situations. These became very useful tools for those who began to understand that many of the processes they learned from playing the games could be used to help them manage real-life situations.

Games and Spirituality

As I ask the following question, recall that we have been relying heavily on the concept that *connection* is a vital component of spirituality: Can games really affect our spirituality? Absolutely. A simple, commonsense response that focuses on negative consequences is that more time spent playing a game means less time on religious or spiritual pursuits. A slightly deeper response is that games affect neural pathways so they can affect one's ideas about spirituality. However, an answer that focuses on positive consequences is that some players claimed that games enhanced their spiritual well-being or helped them feel a deep connection with the universal essence.[83] So, whether games positively or negatively affect a player can depend on the needs of the player and how the gamer uses what was learned. Let's take an even deeper, but still brief, look at some of the methods involved with playing games that can affect our spirituality.

The most popular games are often played in a fantasy world that invites players to take on exploration abilities or increase characteristics that help players perform better in the game than they can in real life. Game themes often center on situations like heroism, apocalyptic doom, outrageous social situations, or quests. Players usually participate in the game while using an avatar.

The term *avatar* derives from the sacred language of Sanskrit and refers to the Hindu idea of a divine being, usually Vishnu, manifesting in a fleshly form. The use of an alternative identity often facilitates an increased willingness to expand one's current identity and try new ones. It then promotes a sense of learning about the new character's self-knowledge. In essence, the player learns to expand boundaries and to try completely new situations that have few or no boundaries.

I have often heard that avatars are virtual, so *living* through them in a game doesn't affect players. However, it has long been recognized that both real and virtual environments affect us. In the 1300s, long before gaming, Catherine of Siena wrote about Communion: "This food strengthens little or much, according to the desire of the recipient, whether he receives sacramentally or virtually."[84] Catherine was saying that when one is actively engaged with a behavior, even if it is a virtual behavior, it can have the same spiritual effect on a person as the actual, physical participation in the behavior. Wise words and a clear understanding of human nature from hundreds of years ago—long before some of the research I have presented indicated something similar.

Most game players recognize that a part of their interest in playing is to escape from reality. They enter a virtual utopia for various reasons (boredom, relationship breakup), and increased game time further increases their need to escape from the pain of the real world. It's a vicious cycle. I have had several students tell me that one of the main reasons they play is because it is easier to pretend to be someone else and to make online friends than it is to make real-life friends. If things don't work out with an online friend, they don't feel as bad, plus they don't have to interact with them in social situations. They just ghost them.

Whatever reasons they have for playing, players' minds tend to wander into a state of semi-unconsciousness. Concentration may increase for some game requirements, like needed reactions, but most players don't sit there and wonder if what they are doing in the game would be appropriate in the real world. As we have seen in multiple examples earlier in this chapter, and will see more later, simply thinking about a behavior can have the same effect as real behavior. Video games naturally stimulate multiple regions of the brain and cause the release of neurochemicals that, in the long run, can have negative effects on spirituality. Gameplay provides a lot of stimulation and causes the release of dopamine (feel good hormone and a neurotransmitter) in large amounts.

Dopamine release can even occur when not playing because players continue to analyze their game performance. Thoughts often pop into a player's mind long after the game is finished. An hour or two of game time throughout a week may not cause long-term negative effects, but a daily hour or two of play will produce significant effects because of the high level of consistent, mental stimulation. The high levels of stimulation combined with the instant gratification of dopamine, lack of virtual moral filtering, and persistent thoughts and analysis after the game ends combine to take away one's motivation to work hard and maintain a consistent train of thought.

That hindrance can also be problematic in spiritual practices. When game players try to pray or meditate and don't get an immediate mental or spiritual reward, they are less likely to continue. Even worse, thoughts of past gameplay may randomly pop into their thoughts and easily distract them, and since they are not getting the mental reward (dopamine) from the spiritual activity, they are less likely to try to increase their concentration for the activity. Gamers find it harder to concentrate on non-game activities and spiritual practices, but they find it easier to engage in behaviors that provide a quick dopamine reward. In essence, games take away focus, motivation, and mindfulness, especially regarding spiritual practices.

TV and Movies

In modern society, the conditioning toward bad behavior often begins with the viewing of cartoons. I grew up without a television, but I would watch the antics of the Road Runner and the Coyote every chance I had. Later in life, I learned that violence is not as funny or painless as in cartoons. TV and movies increasingly present a distorted view of reality. Like the glorified vigilante in the game, media often justifies a vigilante character by beginning a movie with a depiction of an experience that causes the vigilante's actions. In my conversations with students, I often found their typical reactions were to celebrate the vigilante murdering or torturing the initial perpetrator. Horror films seem to have even more freedom to show gore. Even in advertisements it is not uncommon to see things like mutilated bodies, breasts with blood on them, and missing body parts like eyes or arms. Movie creators and actors are rewarded for creating the most violent, graphic, and horrifying films. Mix in some humor, relaxation, food, and family or friends, and viewers learn to associate those positive feelings with violence.

" In psychological terms, there is a step-by-step, systematic, parent-supported desensitization... parents and children learn to feel peace and comfort as they watch others suffer. "

Still believe there is not a connection between media and conditioning? In *War on the Mind*, Peter Watson shares a story told to him about a classical conditioning technique used to help military assassins overcome their resistance to killing.[85] The method began by showing films that included people being killed or injured in violent ways. This process of acclimation was supposed to allow the subjects to distance their natural emotions from such situations (desensitization). The videos grew progressively worse. If a trainee turned his head away or closed his eyes, his head was bolted into a clamp so he could not turn away, and another device kept his eyelids open. He was forced to watch.

I am heartened by the knowledge that at least some of the trainees did not willingly submit to the conditioning. But society as a whole is not as honorable. Large numbers are willingly being desensitized, and parents open their homes through airwaves and cables to the same desensitization and social learning methods. In psychological terms, there is a step-by-step, systematic, parent-supported desensitization. At the same time, parents and children learn to feel peace and comfort as they watch others suffer and die. Such *training* explains how some could support and cheer for the antics that occurred in the Roman Colosseum and will support, and even cheer for, the future suffering of Christians that is depicted in Revelation. Preparation has already begun.

Returning to the question: *If we are born with an evolutionarily engrained aversion to harming another human, why are so many of our youth willing, and even eager in some cases, to engage in violence?* There are multiple answers, but in relation to the information presented in this chapter, it is something like this: During key stages of a child's cognitive development, exposure to violent content in media such as TV, movies, and video games teaches children to kill. This process employs conditioning methods—classical, operant, and social learning—similar to those used in military and law enforcement training. However, unlike the structured environment of those institutions, media exposure lacks the critical components of discipline, ethical guidance, and limitations enforced by legitimate authority.[86,87]

The mass of data related to visual learning shows that it strongly influences conscious and subconscious learning and behavior. The more we learn about the visual system, the more we understand why roughly one-third of the brain is devoted to processing visual information—color, motion, filling in blank spots, clarifying edges, determining distance and depth, learning from others, learning from mistakes, and so on. Like Carl Jung, I now understand that the subconscious processing of normal, daily experiences has a remarkable influence on us. Even though we know it is working out of sight, it still has a lot of information unavailable to our conscious minds. All of this information and more has provided me with a deeper understanding of how my marksmanship training moved from conscious training in the beginning stages to subconscious processing in the later stages.

So, as a seventeen-year-old in basic training, in the final stage of my final marksmanship qualification, I stood in a muddy foxhole, dressed in full combat gear, shooting at human-shaped, steel, pop-up targets from twenty-five to three hundred yards. I had to sight, adjust for distance and wind, squeeze the trigger, and (hopefully) hit the target within a specified amount of time. There were multiple targets at various distances. The twenty-five-yard targets were up for only two seconds. The three-hundred-yard target was up for seven seconds. That sounds like a lot of time, but it's not when you have to survey an entire firing lane, find and identify a semi-camouflaged target that may pop up at any distance in various locations, line up your sights, steady your aim, account for bullet flight time and the effects of wind at longer distances, and fire on targets that appeared progressively smaller to the naked eye (especially at three hundred yards), using only iron sights. The most difficult adjustments were when I had to transition from the twenty-five- to three-hundred-yard target, or three-hundred to twenty-five yards, because that required the greatest mental processing changes of incoming data.

Throughout the decades since, I've improved those initial skills through practice, modeling (AOT), and VR. Like many others who continue to improve and gain new skills, it was to become (hopefully) more effective at protecting innocent lives. Along the way I've acquired new skills, such as room clearing with a pistol, rifle, and shotgun, as an individual and in small groups. I train in active shooter drills and was a recreational competitive shooter for a while. I don't share these things to brag; there's nothing to brag about. I'm nothing special in any one area. Anyone who has been in similar situations, and is honest, will tell you there are always areas for improvement. I only share them to show how a simple, conscious process like learning to consciously fire a rifle at a round target while lying in a rain-filled depression can progress into highly engrained subconscious processes.

In Summary

This chapter explored some ways that can overcome the evolutionarily engrained human aversion to killing that is evidenced throughout history. We focused on low firing rates during the Civil War and WWII to demonstrate the hesitancy and then broadly examined how military training evolved after WWII to overcome this through subconscious conditioning. We then delved into the brain's two-tiered system, where the subconscious processes vast sensory data (11 million bits per second) and automatically corrects visual flaws and influences behavior and memory. The chapter also aligned desensitization and denial defense with media's conditioning. Hopefully the example of my marksmanship training experience combined with neuroscience insights, like mirror neurons and VR's role in learning, has led you to at least briefly consider visual input's impact on our subconscious and to evaluate media consumption and its broader societal implications— especially in relation to children in earlier developmental stages.

I purposely chose to address the topic with some information (violence) that will hopefully cause many of you to stop and think about what you allow into your minds through your eyes. While some sections of this chapter used some potentially unsettling information, the following chapter continues to discuss how our minds and our abilities to connect with others can be affected by what we see, but from a more positive outlook.

Introspective Questions for Chapter 4

? **Human Aversion vs. Violence:** The chapter shows that most soldiers hesitated to kill, yet violence persists in the wider society. How does this shape your view of human nature, and can you recall a situation where you or others showed reluctance or ease with conflict?

? **Ethics of Military Conditioning:** Military training uses desensitization to overcome killing aversion. Is this ethical, considering combat needs and psychological impacts? How would you balance preparing soldiers while preserving humanity?

? **Subconscious Decision-Making:** With the subconscious processing 11 million bits per second versus the conscious mind's 16–59, when have you felt a *gut feeling* guide you differently from conscious reasoning? How does this affect trust in your decisions?

? **Reliability of Perception:** The subconscious corrects visual flaws like blind spots, as seen in *blindsight*. How does this change your trust in what you *see*? Have you questioned a visual experience or eyewitness account?

? **Memory Malleability:** False memories can be implanted, as with the fake balloon ride photos. Have you questioned a memory's accuracy after a conflicting account? How might you evaluate recollections?

? **Media Desensitization:** Violent media pairs violence with positive emotions, potentially desensitizing viewers. Reflect on your media consumption—has violence felt normalized? What responsibilities do creators or consumers have?

? **Societal Violence Trends:** The chapter links media to increased willingness for unjustified violence. Can you identify cultural examples supporting or challenging this? What steps could counteract this trend?

? **Spirituality and Digital Distractions:** Video games' dopamine-driven gratification may hinder spiritual focus. If you practice spirituality, how have digital distractions affected you? How do you balance them?

? **Learning Through Observation:** Mirror neurons enable learning by mimicking, as in AOT (action observant treatment). Reflect on a skill learned by watching others. How did observation shape your process? How does this challenge learning from "experts only"?

? **Mindfulness of Visual Input:** The chapter urges considering what enters your mind through vision. How might you be more intentional about visual content (e.g., social media, games)? What changes align with your values?

CHAPTER 5

Card Catalogs to Cognitive Cargo

Library

A few weeks ago, I was leisurely strolling around a military base while I waited for an appointment. As I walked past a very old, dilapidated building, my peripheral vision caught sight of the word *Library*. I kept walking because the state of the building caused me to subconsciously assume it was not in operation. Someone had simply failed to remove the sign. But after a few steps, I decided to see if the door was unlocked. If it was, I would explore the building. Anyone for some snooping?

To my surprise, the door was unlocked, and when I entered, I found a functioning library that was quite nice. Clearly, the money had been spent on the interior. There were several people of various ages utilizing the services. Some active duty and some retirees. I walked around for a while, reliving the good old days of actual books with the Dewey decimal system on the spines. It brought back some good memories of reshelving library books for one of my college jobs. I even stopped and talked with the librarians at the front desk. The older librarian and I reminisced about the joyful process of using the card catalog, writing down a book's location on a scrap piece of paper, searching for the book, and sometimes getting lost in the stacks of large libraries. The young librarian laughed too, but I think it was more that she was laughing at the two *dinosaurs* chuckling about the "good ole days."

I enjoyed my visit to the library, but it also made me a little sad. It reminded me of a time when there were more physical connections between people and objects (books). Things seemed more real, and people had better relationships with others and with objects—the negativity toward others and physical objects was less. I am one of those who was born before, and began teaching before, the onslaught of technology and media. All of my essays for my first degree were handwritten. Pen and paper. Remember how the pages would begin to curl on the sides as we wrote on the page? If I made a mistake, the entire page needed to be rewritten. Some of you just smiled because you remember the frustrations. I didn't start learning to type properly until I was well into my master's. On the other hand, while in college, and still handwriting my assignments, I learned some computer programming and cybersecurity. Later, I even gave presentations regarding how-tos and a few positives of technology in education. I also taught university students methods for technology integration into their future classrooms. But from the beginning of my technology use, I have always been clear about my concern about the potential for the overuse of technology. Honestly, I miss the simplicity of life before technology. But I tend to be a rather simple man.

> **" Yes, the good can become the bad, and vice versa. It depends on how it is used and how invasive we allow it to become. "**

I straddle the divide of no technology and the use of technology by the masses so I have some perspective on both worlds. My first exposure to serious technology was in the military. There were a few word-processing computers, but there were more advanced technologies like the ability to track eye movements in order to aim weapons. The shooter only had to look at the target, give the weapon a fraction of time to point at the object, then pull the trigger. Similar eye tracking technology is now available for civilian purchase. Video games and VR are common uses of eye tracking technology. I don't deny that technology provides benefits—medical (can help diagnose and heal), safety (know where our loved ones are), and our ability to remain connected (phones, internet) come quickly to mind. But on the other hand, there are downsides—medical (can cause health problems), safety (can track where we are), and disconnection (phones, internet) come quickly to mind. Yes, the good can become the bad, and vice versa. It depends on how it is used and how invasive we allow it to become. That is part of what we explore in this chapter.

The previous chapter laid a very basic foundation for how influential our vision can be on our subconscious and how it can be trained and, thereby, affect our behaviors. In this chapter, we continue to briefly consider those things while shifting our focus to technology. While many subjects relate to this, I limit the topics to areas that negatively affected many former students (secular and religious). I also include an element of how parents can be involved in this process. Don't misinterpret my remarks and think I'm anti-technology. I'm not. Neither am I pro-technology. I label myself as *safe and beneficial technology.*

Does technology help or harm our relationships? It depends on how we use it and how we allow it to affect us. While visiting the library, I noticed all of the users were using computers or iPads to conduct searches and to read—even the retirees. That made me think of two works by Carr. The first is an essay titled "Is Google Making Us Stupid? What the Internet Is Doing to Our Brains,"[88] and the second is a book titled *The Shallows: What the Internet Is Doing to Our Brains.*[89] In these works, Carr writes about how the internet has changed both the way we read and the way we think. In *The Shallows*, Carr shares,

> Over the past few years I've had an uncomfortable sense that someone, or something, has been tinkering with my brain, remapping the neural circuitry, reprogramming my memory. My mind isn't going—so far as I can tell—but it's changing. I'm not thinking the way I used to think, I can feel it most strongly when I'm reading. Immersing myself in a book or lengthy article used to be easy. My mind would get caught up in the narrative or the turns of the argument, and I'd spent hours strolling through long stretches of prose. That's rarely the case anymore. Now my concentration often starts to drift after two or three pages. I get fidgety, loose the thread, begin looking for something else to do. I feel as if I'm always dragging my wayward brain back to the text. The deep reading that used to come naturally has become a struggle.

In 2023, online content consumption increased by about 30 percent from the previous year. For every *minute*, there were,

- « 3.5 billion Snapchats
- « 625 million TikTok videos watched
- « 231 million emails sent
- « 44 million viewing Facebook live streams
- « 16.2 million texts sent

- « 6.3 million Google searches
- « 6 million shopping
- « 3.47 million YouTube videos watched
- « 2.1 million Facebook users
- « 425 thousand hours of content streamed on Netflix
- « 350 thousand tweets sent[90]

The ease of clicking from information source to information source causes us to quickly exceed the brain's *cognitive load capacity*—the limit of our short-term memory. I like Carr's description: it's like zipping "along the surface like a guy on a Jet Ski."[91] Exceeding our cognitive capacity limits our ability to connect new information with already-learned information, and since those mental connections are one of the keys of learning, our constructive memory fragments. The human mind has never encountered such vast stimulation, and there are increasing concerns that relate to the structural changes occurring in the brain and that those changes are happening so fast that we cannot begin to discover and manage negative changes.

Clearly, media affects large numbers of people. Some researchers were interested in digital media's effects on the brains of both *digital immigrants* (researcher defined as people over the age of fifty who were new to technology—that's me) and *digital natives* (born during the digital age). Scans were conducted while immigrants and natives (1) read a book and (2) conducted a Google search. There weren't differences between the groups while they read a book, but internet searching was a different story. The natives' decision-making center of the brain showed twice as much activity as the immigrants'. That made sense because they needed to make decisions while surfing, and they were accustomed to making those decisions.

But why didn't the decision-making centers for the immigrants activate as much as the natives'? The authors felt it was because their brains had not developed the neural pathways needed to make surfing decisions. So they asked the immigrants to participate in further exercises. The immigrants surfed the web for one hour each day for five days, then their brains were rescanned. Scans showed that the same decision-making circuitry as the digital natives was activated. The main point I want you to hang on to is that *it only took a total of five hours for those neurological changes to take shape.*[92]

Multitasking

The previous study is often one of the first that I think about when I see children being babysat by electronic devices. I'm not talking about occasional, short sessions. I'm sure that if I ever have grandkids I will occasionally use electronics for emergency babysitting. What I'm talking about here is using electronics *all* the time. It annoys me because I understand some of the neurological effects. How quickly might those digital babysitters be changing brains? The younger we are, the more easily and quickly our brains can be rewired. Think of that in terms of the effects on the digital immigrants mentioned above. How might those children's long-term memory be affected? A 2004 Kaiser Family Foundation study showed that multitasking allowed eight- to eighteen-year-olds to pack *eight hours* of media content into six-and-a-half hours of clock time. By 2009, the Kaiser Family Foundation found that young people were able to pack *ten hours and forty-five minutes* of media content into seven-and-a-half hours of clock time.[93]

Six years later, Common Sense Media reported that teenagers averaged *nine hours* of media per day while tweens (eight to twelve) averaged *six hours* of media per day. Those figures do not include media used at school or for homework purposes.[94] Such multitasking increases the time effect on the brain beyond the actual clock time—like those algebraic exponents magically increase the value of a number. Digital immigrants and natives alike often believe that multitasking allows them to be more productive and to learn more. Does it? Really?

Before the internet, multitasking referred to one's ability to perform several manual tasks at the same time. Holding a child while picking vegetables is a good example. I was recently in a third-world country and watched as a worker installed a metal roof while his son was in a makeshift child carrier on his back. I was an ironworker for a few years, and I was impressed with his multitasking skills. Such concurrent tasking has been a part of human behavior for all known human existence. These days the term usually refers to performing more than one technology-based task at the same time.

Currently, it is believed that the number of thoughts we can effectively maintain at once (attentional capacity) is four. Even if we maintain four thoughts, it is very difficult to pay *deep* attention to more than one at a time. Four basic mental processes are related to multitasking:

- « *Attentional filtering:* ability to filter relevant from irrelevant information.
- « *Organization of thoughts:* ability to mentally organize the multitasking results and keep them available for later recall.
- « *Task switching:* moving between tasks, returning to a task after a disruption.
- « *Task-switch cost:* the time-lapse between task switching and the related *toll* to cognition, health, productivity, and human happiness.

Two related multitasking studies are shared below. The first explored if multitaskers could focus and not be distracted, and the second explored how efficient the multitaskers were when they shifted between tasks. The researchers thought that the multitaskers would be good in at least one of the four basic mental processes listed previously. They even made good-natured bets, but in the end, everyone lost their bet. People who multitask perform worse across all aspects of it. They have difficulty ignoring distractions, staying mentally organized, and moving efficiently between tasks. Ironically, many multitaskers, particularly those who grew up with digital technology, are convinced they're good at it. The unexpected reality is that they're not.[95]

Some suggest that multitasking hinders learning and information recall because it leads to a neurological *filing error*. Typical processing begins in short-term memory where the information is analyzed and classified as either *declarative* learning (facts) or *procedural* learning (skills, motor learning). Once labelled, the informational packets are sent to the appropriate neurological storage areas. But researchers found that multitasking caused some information to be labelled incorrectly, so it was sent to the wrong neurological storage area. For example, declarative (facts) information might be coded as procedural (skills) and, thus, stored in procedural areas. So when our brain needs to find certain facts, we struggle to locate them because they are not stored in the *facts* area. How many times have you saved a file in the wrong location on your computer and later had a hard time finding it? Same idea.[96]

From a learning perspective, you can't prove you've learned something if you can't recall it. It doesn't mean you didn't learn it; it just means that you can't prove it. If you can't find that file on your computer, there is no proof you saved it. The process of learning and recall relies on correct processing, labeling, and storage. As such, the long-term application of findings like these indicates a bleak future for human learning.

In the early 2000s, on average, *information/knowledge workers* switched tasks every three minutes.[97,98] Interestingly, the workers were just as likely to interrupt themselves as to be interrupted by others. Once interrupted (by others or by themselves), they took an average of twenty-five minutes to return to the original task. In other words, the *task-switch cost* was almost thirty minutes of lost productivity for one task switch. Additionally, normal work notifications (such as emails) and phone calls affect the cost. Even the physical presence of a non-ringing phone affects focus through visual temptations, such as looking at decorative covers, remembering the need to make a call after work, recalling a previous call, and so on. When users pick up their smartphone for whatever reason, they often end up engaging in a string of unrelated activities on the device, prolonging their distraction from the initial task. Additionally, research suggests that interruptions that are more multimedia in nature (for example, combining visuals with words, as opposed to only words) can more significantly impair their capacity to finalize their main objective.[99]

The reality is that information/knowledge worker responsibilities often require multitasking functions. Such high-density work produces large amounts of stress. In 2008, workers who used email switched screen windows approximately thirty-seven times per hour.[100] Some agreed to stop using email for five days. Clearly, the task-switch cost for the emailers was much higher. Heart rate monitors provided more information by showing that the email users remained in consistently high states of alertness while the non-emailers had reduced heart rates and stress. Medically speaking, consistently high stress levels release stress hormones that can have negative effects, such as damaging vital organs and brain cells.[101]

> *" Consistently high stress levels release stress hormones that can have negative effects, such as damaging vital organs and brain cells. "*

Albert Jahn claimed to have developed the first wireless phone in 1908. Eric Tigerstedt filed a patent for a pocket-sized folding telephone in 1917. By 1948, AT&T was providing mobile services to about five thousand customers within a very limited space, but mobile phones did not become widely available until the 1980s. Apple released the first smartphone (mobile phone with computing capabilities) in 2007. By 2009 Richtel had written in *In Study, Texting Lifts Crash Risk by Large Margin* that texting drivers increased crashes by 23 percent.[102]

Studies on phone use remain somewhat limited. When I am asked why there are not more, my response usually involves two areas: speed and funding. The speed with which technology advances is much faster than the time it takes to design a study, get funding, conduct the study, analyze the results, and publish. By the time all of that happens, the studied technology is ancient. Think of it kind of like some people think of the government: it might get the job done, but it takes a very long time to do it and is very expensive.

Besides, funding is hard to achieve because hardware and software companies are not interested in research that would cause their products to look bad. After all, the global revenue from smartphones is around $500 billion (give or take a few billion, depending on who publishes the data). In 2011, 35 percent of Americans owned a smartphone. Ten years later, the percentage was 85 percent.[103] With most Americans now owning a smartphone, the wireless industry has everything to gain by keeping people connected and having their products appear to be all positive.

Research concerning some of the negatives of smartphones is one reason I required that students put their cell phones away during class time. Not on desks where they could see them and be distracted by related thoughts. That was true in K–12, university, and religious settings. More than once I confiscated a phone from a secular or religious student. If under eighteen, their parents could collect it after school. University students were not immune either. Even some graduate students made a scene as they stormed out, while some others simply left. As long as they were not disruptive as they left, they were welcome to try to attend properly during the next class session.

We had a cell phone basket in our church youth classes. It wasn't that the students would be on their phones during class, it was that we knew that even feeling the phone in their pocket could cause their minds to wander. We taught our reasoning to the students (and I taught it to students in secular settings), and most were fine with the practice. But I once observed while teaching the youth group that their reactions to the cell phone basket produced three general behaviors that were good indicators of their current levels of spirituality:

1. Some put their phones in the basket as soon as they entered the room, even if they were early. They were ready to go.

2. Some kept their phones and used them until someone walked around the class with the phone basket. Then they willingly put them in the basket. They would be ready when the time came and were prompted.

3. Some refused to put their phone in the basket, even when I offered money. They clearly weren't ready. (I once offered a student ten dollars if he would put his phone in the basket for thirty minutes—he still refused.)

I later realized that there was a fourth group:

4. Students who reminded others to put their phones in the basket. Many of these were quiet leaders, even if they didn't want to be. They tended to be helpful to others in many situations, even out of religious settings.

Students' behavioral reactions to the phone basket might rotate through different phases, and the relationship to their spiritual fitness at the time may not have always been correct, but most of the time it was a good indicator. The previous paragraphs may seem a bit harsh, but obviously, if someone needed to keep a phone for an important reason (e.g., work, sick relative) it was understandable. We just wanted to lessen their distractions as much as possible. However, we also knew phones could be quite beneficial.

One of our students worked odd hours in a mortuary and cremated bodies. One Sunday, Greg* called and asked if we would stream the lesson. So one of the students put his phone in the front of the classroom. Greg put his earbuds in underneath his silver fire retardant suit and listened to the lesson while he cremated. Classes were usually discussion based, and Greg often participated in the discussions while he worked. Another Sunday I was using the overhead projector during a lesson, and we heard a voice saying, "I can't see." Someone picked up the phone and turned it around so Greg could see the screen. It was an interesting and humorous way to have class. We often chuckled when we saw a silver alien float across the phone screen. It reminded us of an old alien movie with bad special effects. This worked well and became standard practice when Greg worked on Sunday mornings. Some students still occasionally mention those classes, and we laugh.

Internet

It is well known that a lot of internet use can lead to social withdrawal. One of the side effects of that combination is that it can easily lead to technology-based addictions. In the early 1990s, the term *internet addiction disorder* was used to label harmful patterns of internet usage. In the decades that followed, researchers used several other terms but appear to be settling on the term *problematic usage of the internet* (PUI) to represent internet addiction.[104] So for simplicity and clarity, I use PUI to represent all related terms. In general, it can be broadly defined as *online activities that lead to potentially harmful behaviors.* Gambling, cybersex, online purchasing, and uncontrolled use of social media and streaming services are some of the most common. Such behaviors can negatively affect our abilities to make good decisions, concentrate, and stop negative behaviors.

There are some variations between nations, but in general, more internet use leads to more anxiety and depression.[105] When comparing internet addiction in several countries, we find overall addiction rates at about 9 percent, online gaming addiction at about 19 percent, and online social networking addiction at about 33 percent among college students. There is even a relationship between PUI and processing abnormalities within the amygdala (a major processing center for emotions). Neurological functions are affected by structural changes within the amygdala and by connections to other parts of the brain. As PUI increases, so do the negative neurological effects.[106] Social withdrawal is also increased by PUI, and those who socially withdraw tend to display more negative behaviors like deception, escapism, mood changes, and reduction in their abilities to effectively engage in social situations.[107] Indeed, COVID-19 lockdowns led to increases in PUI.[108] Once the cycle starts it can easily continue to push us down a path littered with antisocial behaviors. Especially for people like me who naturally lean toward antisocial behaviors.

Research in this area is increasing quickly. For example, a quick search of the term *internet addiction* on PubMed produced only three results in 1996. By 2015 the same search yielded 1,564 results, and 4,580 in 2022. At the time of this writing (2024), PubMed returns 5,913 results. Such rapid growth is an indication of the recognition of a problem. In general, studies related to PUI indicate that it is widespread and can have negative consequences like poorer health, lower quality of life, reduced social interactions, and diminished vocational and academic outcomes. This very short review of the research in this section hints at some of the coming legal and ethical considerations that will need to be addressed.

Even if we don't have an addiction, most of us are probably aware that the internet can have downsides, like less time spent with the family, less time reading, and less time exercising. But one area often overlooked is *sharenting*. Parents usually have good intentions when posting about their children on social media and are probably not aware that the practice of sharenting can hinder the child's developmental stages. It may also cause family conflicts, and children may feel personal frustration.[109] They may want to remain private, or they might be embarrassed by what is posted, or they know that what is posted is a lie, and so on. I have had many students who were being abused by the very parents who often posted positive things about their children. It seemed as if the child's life was perfect. It only increased the students' anger and bad behaviors. Even other family members, such as siblings or aunts and uncles, can negatively affect emotions and relationships by sharing online.

Overall, studies indicate that internet use affects us, even if we are not addicted. We all need to guard ourselves from becoming addicted because features of social media, such as scrolling and likes, in conjunction with conditioning responses, such as vibrations or earned icons, entice us to continue to use the media. Add predictive algorithms used for marketing or that may manipulate our behaviors, opinions, and choices, and the addiction potential increases.[110,111] Some businesses purposely develop invasive technologies that influence behaviors without us even being aware of the manipulation.[112]

Neuromodulation is one such potentially invasive, manipulative technology. In a medical setting, it is used to treat mental and neurological disorders such as depression and Parkinson's. It provides magnetic or electrical stimulation to modify the neuronal excitability of certain brain regions. The results are that feelings and behaviors are changed.[113] Neuromodulation is becoming more available, and consumers can purchase brain stimulation devices that influence alertness, focus, and productivity, restore sensory data, and more. When connected to apps that allow two-way data transmission, the devices allow businesses and others to collect and analyze the brain data of users.[114] Scary stuff. So, in addition to influencing your brain activity, your specific mental processes and other brain-related data may be shared or even sold.[115]

Some devices known as brain-computer interfaces allow for direct communication between two *beings*. Remote connections to things like robotic prosthetics, games, and mind-controlled electronic devices such as prosthetics and drones can be established.[116] There are even *smart* cell implants that control the release of drugs.[117] The brain-computer connection opens the door to the possibility of the wearable or implantable devices influencing the feelings and behaviors of the wearers in real-time—similar to the previously discussed neuromodulation. Allowing service providers such a high level of access may even impact social behaviors. Some possible influences include contract agreements, elections, medical decisions, etc., through the usurpation of free will. In all, wearable brain-stimulation devices and brain-computer interfaces produce direct interactions that have the potential to trigger addictive behaviors or manipulate our behaviors in real-time by stimulating, or not stimulating, the brain and influencing our decisions.

" Wearable brain-stimulation devices and brain-computer interfaces produce direct interactions that have the potential to trigger addictive behaviors or manipulate our behaviors in real-time by stimulating, or not stimulating, the brain and influencing our decisions. "

Pornography

Technology and the sex industry have had a close relationship throughout history, and many of my students, in both secular and religious settings, were affected by both. The first known pornography occurred in cave wall drawings, but we can now stream it into the privacy of our homes—

which removes many barriers to the creation, sharing, and consumption of pornography. Cave art moved to decorations on pottery, then sculptures. The first publishing of explicit engravings was in the 1500s. (Note: I refrain from mentioning specific publications and some websites in the next few paragraphs.) Photography was invented in 1862, and relatively soon after erotic photos began to appear. The 1920s produced short films, and by the 1970s there were full-length movies. Despite those technological advancements, most of society still viewed pornography as shameful, and it remained expensive and relatively hard to access. This began to change in the 1970s.

Approval grew when creators began to advertise explicit movies and pictures that could be mailed in non-descriptive packaging to homes or to P.O. boxes for greater privacy. I remember seeing magazines loosely wrapped in brown paper being put into some neighbors' mailboxes. Even greater change occurred after the invention of video cassette recorders. People could then purchase or rent videos and watch them in privacy at home. Soon after, cable television arrived and provided soft-porn late at night. In the early 1990s, home internet increased affordability and anonymous access, but, arguably, the most dramatic increase occurred soon after the turn of the century because of webcam technology. Individuals could easily create content that people would pay to watch (subscribers). Production companies were no longer necessary.

Approval and accessibility have continued to increase. A 2023 study demonstrated that the top three pornographic websites had more traffic than some non-pornographic sites like Amazon, Netflix, and Yahoo. Additionally, they had the lowest *bounce rates* (visitors view one page and then leave the site) along with more pages viewed than some non-pornographic sites. Extrapolating to a global level, we can see that some porn sites have similar, and in some cases greater, levels of engagement than some legacy sites.[118] A 2023 meta-analysis presented that over 2.5 million individuals accessed pornographic sites every sixty seconds.[119]

Growing approval is moving porn out of the privacy of the home and into more public environments. Even work is not immune. About 63 percent of men and 36 percent of women watch porn at work. As early as 2000, 70 percent of internet pornographic traffic occurred during work hours.[120] Two obviously negative consequences for viewing porn at work are potential suspension or firing. But one that is easily overlooked is the dehumanization of others, which can lead to unethical behaviors like lying, sexual harassment, aggression, and reduced teamwork.[121] Those dehumanizing effects are not limited to adults.

Specifically regarding the ages of my K–12 students, pornography consumption continues to grow. A 2007 study estimated that 42 percent of youth (aged ten to seventeen) had been exposed to online pornography.[122] In 2011, that early exposure had increased to 48 percent.[123] By 2020, it was estimated that 68 percent of adolescents (aged fourteen to eighteen) in the US had been exposed to online pornography.[124]

One of the negative consequences of youth being exposed to pornography at younger ages is child sexual exploitation. In 2023, the Internet Watch Foundation (IWF) analyzed 392,665 sites for child sexual abuse materials. They removed 275,652 of those sites after confirming abusive content. Ninety-two percent contained *self-generated* images, a 27 percent increase from 2022. Six of the removed sites were from newsgroups.[125] For the IWF, *self-generated* child sexual abuse refers to a child being manipulated, tricked, or coerced into creating and sharing sexual content by someone who is not physically present with them. *Non-self-generated* abuse involves media produced when the abuser is physically present with the victim, or by using media to alter existing images or using AI or other artificial methods to generate such content.[126]

Based on IWF's 2023 data, *self-generated* content for seven- to ten-year-olds was 92 percent, 96 percent for eleven- to thirteen-year-olds, 88 percent for fourteen- to fifteen-year-olds, and 81 percent for sixteen- to seventeen-year-olds. Figure 7 provides some specific numbers.

Age group	Self-generated %	Self-generated	Not self-generated	Total
7–10	92%	104,282	8,458	112,740
11–13	96%	141,920	5,390	147,310
14–15	88%	3,554	502	4,056
16–17	81%	978	224	1,202

Figure 7. Author-created table using IWF's 2023 data regarding specific numbers for each age group related to self-generated and not self-generated child sexual abuse materials.[127]

Looking at those numbers, we see that the second-youngest group (eleven- to thirteen-year-olds) had the greatest total number of sites along with the highest percentage of self-generated content, while the numbers for the two oldest groups dropped drastically.

Moving to the other end of the age spectrum, IWF noted a rising trend of three- to six-year-olds posting self-generated content. Of the 2,401 images, 91 percent were of girls.[128] Another disturbing shift is the use of AI to create child sexual abuse materials (CSAM). In 2024, 90 percent of the 3,512 AI images were realistic enough to fall under the same prosecutorial laws as real CSAMs. Additionally, some images include famous children, and some others show past victims of CSAM.[129]

Despite clearly negative associations, I would be neglectful of the guidelines I established for this book—those of looking at multiple opinions—if I didn't mention that some of my students viewed non-abusive pornography as a healthier example of human interactions than they had experienced. Tom* and Tina's* father locked them in a back room of his business when they were around seven and five, respectively. People could go to the business and pay to spend time with one of the children; a discount was given if the "renter" wanted both at the same time. Law enforcement learned about the situation after a few years. I abstain from describing what I know about the room.

> **Parents often provide access to pornography by paying for their child's access through data plans and then allowing them to take electronic devices to places of privacy.**

Tina was not in my classroom, but Tom once confided in me and his counselor that he struggled to comprehend any sexual boundaries. For him, everything was allowable, with anyone, at any age, at any time, in any place—yes, even school. But he explained that when he had been shown non-violent pornography with consenting adults, he saw a more appropriate form of human interactions than those that had been forced on him. For Tom, it provided some hope for being able to have a different type (consensual versus forced) of relationship in the future. I'm not sure what happened to Tom and Tina, but the last time I heard about Tom he was receiving treatment in a different type of confinement than his father's back room.

Referring back to the broad timeline that began this section, when I was young, pornography was confined, for the most part, to magazines and movies. An underage person usually had to be proactive and put a lot of effort, and sometimes money, into illegally obtaining magazines or movies. My, how times have changed. These days, parents often provide access to pornography by paying for their child's access through data plans and then allowing them to take electronic devices to places of privacy, leading to drastic increases in its use. In general, pornography consumption typically starts while young and increases before it begins to decrease as one moves into the later stages of life. Across developed nations, overall consumption ranges between 46 to 74 percent of men and 16 to 41 percent of women.[130]

In a 2011, slightly less than 90 percent of college-age men viewed pornography, and slightly more than 30 percent of college-age women did so.[131] In my secular teaching environments, male pornographic consumption was similar to the 90 percent and remained relatively steady, but I would estimate females to be a little higher at about 50 percent. (Of course, those estimates are higher than some other educational environments because most of my K–12 career was spent with abused and special needs students.) In religious settings, the rates were much lower—but higher than you might expect—and students often admitted to struggling with pornography because of easy and private online access, even while in the church building.

Clearly, pornography is highly influential. While it's easy to recognize some of the clearly observable behavioral results, it's even easier to fail to look below the surface and miss recognizing that it affects things like our neurology, long-term health, and relationship-building potential.

High neural stimulation makes it easy for addiction to develop. *Pornography addiction* refers to an irresistible desire for visual stimulation through the viewing of pornography. Some common negative consequences are financial, professional, personal, and social problems that may lead to a poorer quality of life, greater depression, and higher levels of anxiety. All addictions (not only sexual) create chemical, anatomical, and pathological changes that can lead to cerebral dysfunctions called *hypofrontal syndromes*. Explained simply, the neurological "braking system" becomes damaged (other events like trauma and brain damage may cause similar results).

Problematic pornography use (PPU), as it is commonly known in the literature, typically ranges between 4 to 9 percent but tends to increase when individuals socially withdraw. A recent example is the increase in pornographic use during the social distancing/confinement created by COVID-19.[132] Most individuals who seek treatment for a compulsive sexual behavior disorder do so because they are not able to control their actions even though they want to. A major hurdle they must overcome is the three components of *Triple A*—accessibility, affordability, and anonymity.[133]

It is easy to see nudity and sexual interactions on social media platforms that may not even be pornographic in nature. Videos can be freely shared, and some services allow users to communicate privately. This increase in access has led to a greater impact on mental health and behavioral changes. Many users are bothered by sexual images and thoughts throughout the day, which causes them to feel increased guilt, shame, confusion, depression, and anxiety. They are also more likely to engage in impulsive behaviors that may or may not be sexual. PPU is difficult to break because it involves physiological, psychological, and biological processes. AI is already being included in pornography, which is only increasing its controlling power.

The industry has little motivation to limit its influence. Estimates for worldwide revenue from pornography are between $6 billion at the low end and more than $97 billion at the high end—more than the combined income of Microsoft, Google, Amazon, eBay, Yahoo, Apple, and Netflix. This leads me to wonder: *Why do some still trivialize the effects of pornography?* One reason is that the sex industry wants to keep making money, so they successfully characterize objections as being only religious or moral. Scientific research is conveniently left out of the discussion. Then, at least in the United States, the industry can label objections as infringements of the First Amendment *right to free speech*. The result is a successful deflection of the reality that pornography causes harm to humans and societies.

Pornography can be a gateway to promiscuous or harmful sexual practices, as can other things like physical or psychological trauma, abuse, or peer pressure. Many don't understand that sexual activity is much more than physical actions; it also involves neurological and psychological actions (as does pornography). Science shows that sex has a broad neurological definition. For example, the seemingly meaningless behavior of touching an arm or staring into another's eyes can release the same neurochemicals, though obviously at reduced levels. Granted, the effects are not as strong, but the knowledge provides insight into how the process of getting to know someone better can begin. The brain is so important to the act that some believe it is the most important sex organ.

It is easy to recognize that pornography can affect us, but we may not realize that sexual conditioning also occurs on television and in movies and video games. In fact, we are led to feel it is OK to engage in promiscuous, dangerous, or coercive sex. Even rape is laughed at, glorified, and rewarded in some media. While most of us understand the possible dangers associated with those behaviors, some parents not only allow such actions—they sometimes promote them. I have had students whose parents encouraged their sexual promiscuousness. One told me that after every sexual encounter, she and her mother would talk about it in detail. When I asked if she was forced to talk about it, she replied, "No." She enjoyed discussing the details with her mother. Some believe such behaviors are healthy for future relationships. Are they? The short answer is, *No*.

During voluntary sex, chemical bonds are created by the release of neurochemicals. The first time they are applied they are sticky, and repeated applications continue to strengthen those bonds. But switching partners leaves some neurological stickiness with the previous partner, and subsequent partners have less stickiness. Too many applications and the stickiness is lost. This clarifies how some people can become promiscuous. They simply go from partner to partner for the dopamine rush or for some other purpose such as manipulation. When the dopamine rush fades, they feel empty, so they seek another conquest. This downward cycle often results in sexual addiction.

Each application also leaves a chemical imprint that can hinder relationships with another partner for many years. Have you ever ended a relationship with "A" and started a new one with "B" only to have memories of A pop up when you are with B? Have you ever heard or said, "I've loved every one I've been with"? Neurochemically speaking, it's true. Chemical remnants of each bond and memory remain, but like the bonds weaken, so do the memories. I don't know how many times I've heard, "You never forget your first." However, I've never heard, "You never forget your fifty-ninth."

When I was young, my friends and I would tease each other a lot (yes, we still do). When we had had enough, we often used the "Sticks and stones may break my bones but words will never hurt me" defense (yes, we still do that too—it's still childishly funny). However, in reality, that defense is false—we now know that words *can* cause us to feel pain. In fact, hurtful words register in the same parts of the brain that register physical pain. So does pain caused by relationship breakups. Pressure to do something you don't want to do can also cause pain. Media glorifying or promoting early or harmful sexual practices when we know better are some

" Hurtful words register in the same parts of the brain that register physical pain. So does pain caused by relationship breakups. "

examples. The message is: *Go ahead, even if your parents don't approve. If you don't do it, you will end up sexually naive or repressed so others won't want to spend time with you.*

However, sexually active teenagers are more likely to be depressed and to attempt suicide when compared to virgins, with percentages higher for girls. Over 90 percent of teenagers, including those who have had sex, think that they should receive a strong abstinence message. Sex before sixteen results in a 58 percent chance that there will be more than five partners before their late twenties. Waiting until after twenty produces a 52 percent chance of having only one partner during the next several years. An unmarried sexual relationship before twenty-one will probably not be permanent. These effects are similar between males and females. The results of media and social pressures are that 75 percent of graduating students had sex in non-committed or short-term relationships.[134]

Even adults receive messages that behaviors like having an affair are acceptable, or that they should allow their children—or even encourage them—to do whatever they want. And, if someone feels shame, it is not because of the sexual behavior; surely those shameful feelings are because of something else in your life. Controlling parent? Unthoughtful spouse? Mean boss? This transference causes us to look in the wrong areas of our lives to heal the stress. We don't find the real source, so it is never addressed, and we and our relationships suffer. Damage is done to one of the most important abilities we are born with: the ability to bond healthily.

Media shows sexual coercion more than ever, and as viewers get more desensitized to it, they are more likely to act on it. Approximately 13 percent of women and 6 percent of men have experienced sexual coercion.[135] Forty percent of girls who had sex before the age of fifteen said that the sex was unwanted or not voluntary. More than 25 percent of women and approximately 11 percent of men experienced some form of unwanted sexual contact, while 32 percent of women and 11 percent of men have experienced an unwanted sexual experience. Approximately 20 percent of women had experienced at least an attempted rape. Date-raped females show lower levels of self-esteem and self-control. Like females, abuse can affect a male's normal development and future interest in sex. Almost 10 percent of abused boys become pedophiles. Brains of abused individuals show reduced activity in the temporal lobes—an indication of reduced abilities to make good choices and consider future consequences of current actions.

Trauma, like coercion and rape, can cause excessive production of chemicals that are beneficial when they are at normal levels. *Brain-derived neurotrophic factor* (BDNF) is one of the most active proteins in the process of neurogenesis (creation of new neurons), and it supports the growth of existing neurons and synapse health. Additionally, it is important for learning, short- and long-term memory, and higher-level thinking skills. At reduced levels, BDNF can result in various developmental problems. At increased levels, it can lead to problems like depression, schizophrenia, Alzheimer's, social withdrawal, a tendency toward addictive behaviors, and an inability to enjoy future intimacy. I sometimes volunteered at group therapy sessions, and during one session, a female shared with the group that her first sexual encounter was a date rape while in high school. We thought of her as *tough*. She was a veteran who had "been there and done that," graduated college on her own, married, and raised children. But the effects still remained—the only way she could be intimate was to leave a light on so she could see her husband. Decades later, she still had to make sure it wasn't the rapist.

In short, when scientific data is analyzed without a manipulative purpose, it supports the idea that sexual relationships should be with one caring partner for life. Never removing the neurochemical tape to reapply it to another person helps protect its stickiness, and the bond is only strengthened with each intimate encounter with the same person. This also benefits children. Studies show that the children of parents with one sexual partner have greater chances of succeeding in life. The neurological impact of sex can affect one's future behaviors and health as well as the future of any children. It does not matter if sex is promiscuous, forced, or in a healthy marriage; its impact will be significant and long-lasting and extend into the next generation.

Video Games

Video games were also a big influence on my students. The first video game was created in 1970, it began showing up in arcades in 1971, and it earned around $1 billion. The Atari 2600 was released in 1977, and games like *Space Invaders* and *Pac-Man* could be played at home. That year total industry revenue was about $22 billion. Income reached a high of $42 billion in 1982, began a three-year decline in 1983, reached a low of $14 billion in 1985, then started to increase again. Nintendo launched the Game Boy in 1989, and the iPhone was released in 2007. Revenue that year was $68 billion and has continued to grow with only a few setbacks over the years.[136]

Between 2000 and 2022, the US video gaming market grew 1,372 percent. Increasing from $6 billion in 2000 to over $85 billion in 2022,[137] though some estimates place the 2022 revenue at over $97 billion.[138] In 2025, US revenue is expected to top $140 billion.[139] Worldwide revenue in 2024 was almost $455 billion,[140] and it is expected to reach $522 billion in 2025[141] and over $690 billion by 2029.[142]

Currently 85 percent of US teens play video games.[143] The Entertainment Software Association's website shows happy people playing games along with messages that games unite over 215 million Americans, provide mental stimulation (91 percent), and improve stress relief (89 percent). Within families, 61 percent say that games helped them stay connected with other family members, and 77 percent of parents now play video games with their children.[144]

Sure, those are some of the benefits. I don't deny there are benefits, but the negatives often get whitewashed. With such a high level of income and influence, it's easy to see why, like the sex industry, the gaming industry is not motivated to fund research that might shed a negative light on some of its uses. Profit margins give companies the ability to influence politicians. However, not all of the fault lies with tech companies and governments. We, the consumers of such devices, are also to blame for the negative results of high task-switch costs, cognitive filing errors, procrastination, and reduced learning. After all, those companies would not exist if we didn't give them our money.

The eleventh edition of the *International Classification of Disease* by the World Health Organization lists gaming disorder with other addictive behaviors such as gambling disorder, online buying-shopping disorder, cyberchondria, cyberbullying, problematic social media usage, and digital hoarding.[145] Compulsive sexual behavior disorder is listed as an impulse control disorder. Gaming and internet addictions can affect similar brain regions as drug addictions. Lack of cognitive controls and the high risk-taking opportunities of gaming can easily lead to increased rates of eating disorders and other addictions through the uncharacteristic functioning of two distinct brain systems: (1) an affective system driven by emotions, rewards, and intrinsic stimuli, and (2) a cognitive system that includes the prefrontal cortex (PFC) and the ventral system (visual, acoustic, spatial).[146]

" Gaming and internet addictions can affect similar brain regions as drug addictions. "

Relationships

Despite the focus on negativity to this point, it is important to point out some positives of scientific knowledge and technology. One is that it can be used to improve relationships. I was asked to give a presentation to parents, foster parents, social workers, counselors, ministers, and others who worked with or housed youth regarding unsafe sexual practices by youth, along with potential treatment methods.

In one section, I discussed that oxytocin (important for bonding and trust) is present in both genders but is most active in females. Oxytocin is values-neutral, and its release is an involuntary process. In *The Female Brain*, Brizendine wrote that a twenty-second embrace triggers the release of oxytocin, strengthening the bond between huggers and activating the brain's trust pathways. Physical and emotional intimacy from activities like touching, eye contact, positive emotional exchanges, kissing, and sexual orgasm also stimulates oxytocin release in the brain. Be cautious about hugging someone unless you're prepared to build trust with them.[147]

I first used the touching/hugging information negatively to help them understand how a boyfriend (or predator) could influence another to want to engage in sex (grooming). I then positively used the information to give an example of how it could be used to build healthy relationships. It was beneficial for the attendees to understand, from a neurological perspective, how they could begin to build positive relationships with the youth they were trying to help—an appropriate look and smile, a good conversation, or a handshake could progress to become a healthy hug that could improve their relationship. The ultimate goal was to try and help the youth develop internal motivation to engage in appropriate behaviors when the adult was not present.

After that secular conference, an attendee asked if I would speak on the topic at his church. I was hesitant because the information is much more candid than I have shared in this book. I told him I would but only if the pastor approved. I needed to share all of the information; watering it down would reduce its effectiveness.

The pastor asked me to present it to his congregation.

William* really hung on to the "twenty-second hug" releasing oxytocin in the previous quote. He approached me after the session and began telling me about the strained relationship with his granddaughter. Her parents were out of the picture, and she was living with William and his wife. They had tried everything they knew to do to improve the granddaughter's behavior and their relationships. Even counseling had not produced long-term improvements. William told me he was going to try simple hugs and touches (appropriate, obviously). I wished him well and never considered I might see him again.

Several years later I was visiting the town again and attended the church. William saw me and began telling me how his granddaughter's behavior had changed and how their relationship had improved. The change had occurred relatively quickly, and they now enjoyed spending time with each other. She had started attending school and was planning to go on to higher education. William mentioned that knowing the value of a touch and having a simple understanding of what happened in the brain was a comforting and motivating bit of information. I still visit that church when I'm in town. When we shake hands and hug, we laugh and say, "We better not hug for twenty seconds!"

Relationship building is not always as easy or as effective as William's situation. Sometimes, nothing is successful. The person may not want to be helped. Positive results may require a long period of time and multiple complex approaches. William was retired and had plenty of time to spend with his granddaughter. Most parents do not have that luxury and simply give up on their children, give in to them, promote inappropriate behaviors, or allow someone (something?) else to babysit them. Two of the most common babysitters these days are media and games.

I am often surprised and feel somewhat vindicated in my teachings when I learn of actors who will not allow their children to watch television or even the films they made. Though acting is how they make a living, they understand the negative side effects. Recently, I have seen several actors say that they are moving from Hollywood because it is negatively influencing their children. Like some others, I applaud their stance. When such statements are made, some Christians wave the *I told you so* flag. Yet many of those same Christians then allow their children to watch the films that the actors will not allow their own children to watch. It is important to recognize the hypocrisy.

Not All Students Are Caving to Societal Conditioning

On another positive note, not all youth are caving to societal pressures. Shortly after the previous presentation, another pastor asked me to spend some time working with his youth group. He wanted me to teach but also gave me leeway to conduct a little informal research if I felt it was necessary to identify some of the causes of their negative behaviors. During one of the sessions, I asked the students to write responses to three open-ended questions:

1. What is your biggest disappointment concerning your family?
2. What is something that makes you sad?
3. What do you wish your parents knew?

After analyzing their responses, I asked to have a parent-only session. They needed to see the effect they had on their children (of course, I maintained students' confidentiality). Using the students' words, the areas of greatest concern were *sin*, *media*, and *relationships*. I categorized behaviors that their church taught against, like smoking, as *sins*. The *media* category included all forms, including games. I subdivided the *relationships* category into "parent-to-child" and "parent-to-parent." *Relationships* were the most referenced category with *media* following. Most responses included elements of more than one category. For example, "We spend more time watching movies than talking" includes *relationships* and *media*.

Proverbs 22:6 tells parents to "Train up a child in the way he should go," while Ephesians 6:2 tells children to "Honor thy father and mother." The problem is that some parents make it difficult for their children to "honor" them because parents "train up a child" using the "Do as I say, not as I do" method. Let's call the behavior what it is: hypocrisy. Below, I provide some of the student responses. It will be easy to recognize that what children see in family relationships affects them. That is one reason why using hypocritical instructional methods can be so damaging to their psyche. I changed the wording to make them more generic and protect identities, but you will get the point. Read them slowly and see which ones apply to you and your relationships. Percentages for each category were rounded to the nearest 5 percent.

> **" Some parents make it difficult for their children to "honor" them because parents "train up a child" using the "Do as I say, not as I do" method. "**

What Is Your Biggest Disappointment Concerning Your Family?

Percentage of relationship (connection)-related responses: 90 percent

- « [Many comments about parents being divorced and/or remarried]
- « They don't have a reason not to trust me.
- « Bringing up my past mistakes and comparing me to my siblings.
- « Favoritism of sibling.
- « Parents fighting.
- « We don't live with them [parents] and don't bond.
- « The arguing, complaints, and negativity.
- « Parent(s) don't communicate with me and I think my parent(s) avoid(s) me.
- « Parent(s) argue and make me not want to get married.
- « I'm afraid that my parents will disown me if I mess up.
- « Parent treats me like a friend.
- « Parents being rude and putting me down. I feel like they hate me.
- « Parents act like they like me in front of other people but not at home.
- « We fight a lot. . . . Instead of talking we text each other.
- « The violence.

What Is Something that Makes You Sad?

Percentage of relationship (connection)-related responses: 100 percent

- « Not seeing my mom.
- « My parents cuss and argue a lot in front of me.

- « I don't get to see my family.
- « My parents fight.
- « I don't get to spend more time with my dad.
- « When my parents argue in front of me.
- « I try to talk to a parent and he/she always has an excuse not to.
- « I try to talk to a parent and he/she cuts me off and gets mad at me.
- « I've never been good enough or pretty enough for my parents.
- « I'm a disappointment to my parents.
- « I get blamed for everything.
- « Parents don't talk about dating each other.
- « Parent changes standards for each sibling.
- « Parents never say they love me.
- « Sibling treats my parents badly and is allowed to run the family.
- « Parents yell at me, even when I didn't do anything wrong.
- « Parents jump to conclusions before finding out what really happened.
- « To hear my siblings say they hate me.

What Do You Wish Your Parents Knew?

Percentage of relationship (connection)-related responses: 95 percent

- « Nothing. I tell them everything. [I included this one so you would know that there were some positive comments.]
- « The real me. I'm scared to let them know. I wish I could do it all over again.
- « Their negative comments toward me. They make me feel unwanted.
- « The impact they have on my life. I hate when they fight.
- « How I feel after I get blamed for something I didn't do. I try to tell the truth, but I am yelled at to be quiet.
- « How bad it hurts when they yell at me and don't forgive my mistakes. And that I really do love them so much.
- « It makes me mad that I was taken from a parent. Now I've been taken from the second parent and he/she is not trying to get me back.
- « Favorites are not cool.
- « How I feel when parents yell at me.

« When you argue we don't forget what you scream.

« I'll never forget you hitting me in anger and calling me bad names.

« You remind me every day of my mistakes and I hide my sadness.

« It hurts when you think my opinion doesn't matter.

« Your fighting leads to nothing good.

« Y'all put me down so much. I wish you would tell me how proud you are of me and that you love me.

« Talk, show affection . . . and handle your problems so I don't have to handle mine and yours too.

« I wish you would love each other.

« It's a relief when a particular parent goes out of town.

« That I forgive them.

These responses are relevant to current times, so you might be surprised to learn that they were collected approximately twenty years before writing this book. At that time, slightly less than 50 percent of the responses identified media as a problem. The media percentage rate is likely much higher now.

You might be wondering why I wrote that this section is positive. It's not obvious unless we look at some of the aftereffects. Occasionally, when I am in town I visit that same church. A few of the students who wrote responses have identified themselves to me over the years. They are parents now, and we sometimes talk about their answers. One of the most frequent comments they make is that they are trying to not raise their children using the methods their parents used. They are focusing on building good relationships with their children and parenting by example (not being hypocritical). Though they experienced pain because of the way they were raised, they are turning the pain into something positive.

A small number of parents talked to me about the student responses. I had shared them in a broad enough manner that they could not determine if their child had written one, but they had related to the general concepts and recognized they needed to try to make some changes.

In Summary

We have spent considerable time in this chapter and the previous one exploring our visual system and how external stimuli can affect our brains and, by extension, our behaviors. Why? The answer is simple: because it affects all of us. It is disheartening that some parents allow, model, and sometimes support the negative conditioning. On the other hand, it is heartwarming that some parents and youth are standing against the negative conditioning

"There are times when we can see the good more clearly by what we refuse to look at rather than what we choose to look at."

and developing good relationships. Isaiah 6:2-3 tells us that the Seraphim covered their faces with two wings while calling, "[T]he whole earth is full of his glory." How could they know that the earth was full of God's glory if their eyes were covered? They couldn't *see* His glory. That leads me to believe that there are times when we can see the good more clearly by what we *refuse* to look at rather than what we *choose* to look at. And, as parents, refusing to look at some things will help teach our children what they should refuse to look at so that they will also see the glory more clearly.

Introspective Questions for Chapter 5

? **Nostalgia for Pre-Digital Life:** What pre-digital activities (e.g., reading physical books) do you miss? How do they compare to your digital habits? How do these experiences shape your view of technology's role in your life?

? **Concentration and Technology:** Have you noticed changes in your attention span or reading habits due to technology use? What strategies could you adopt to regain focus and engage more deeply with tasks?

? **Defining Safe Technology Use:** The author advocates "safe and beneficial" technology. How would you define this in your life? What boundaries might you set to achieve it?

? **Multitasking Efficiency:** Research suggests multitaskers are inefficient, despite believing otherwise. Do you consider yourself good at multitasking with technology? How might you prioritize single-task focus to improve performance?

? **Smartphone Distractions:** How does your smartphone's presence, even when unused, affect your focus during tasks or conversations? What might a phone-free period reveal about your relationship with it?

? **Internet Use and Well-Being:** How do you gauge whether your internet use (e.g., social media, gaming) is healthy or problematic? What warning signs do you monitor? How could you address negative impacts?

? **Sharenting and Privacy:** Sharenting can harm children's development. How do you decide what to share online about yourself or family? What factors influence your balance of connection and privacy?

? **Pornography's Societal Impact:** How has easy access to pornography influenced societal attitudes or behaviors you've observed? What role could education play in addressing its potential harms?

? **Parental Modeling:** Student responses highlight pain from parental hypocrisy. How have your experiences as a child or parent shaped your approach to modeling healthy technology use and relationships?

? **Ethical Concerns with Emerging Technologies:** Technologies like brain-computer interfaces can manipulate thoughts. What ethical guidelines matter most to you for their development? How might you advocate for responsible use?

CHAPTER 6

Sounds and Synapses

I Am Musical—Well, Sort Of . . .

I was the oddball of the family. My mother was a great musician, a music teacher, and a music minister. My sister had a wonderful voice and played the piano. Being the rebellious child that I was, I refused to practice piano. I despised music lessons. During lessons I would sit on the bench and do nothing. I rarely even touched the keys. My mother even hired someone else to teach me. I still refused. Later, I also quit bass guitar lessons after only a few.

In high school I was willing to try percussion. It was an easy class. I could keep time, and I liked hitting things. It was a good fit. We percussionists sat in the back of the band room (yes, if you recall my transcripts, I managed to fail high school band) and usually played a game of our own making. We would start by taking turns hitting each other on the thigh with a drumstick. The first taps were so soft we could barely feel them, but they grew more forceful with each exchange. The first person to succumb to the growing pain levels and quit was the loser. Leaving class with new bruises was not uncommon. They were sources of shame for the loser and pride for the winner. My mother finally accepted that I was not a traditional musician.

I wanted to be a visual artist. I might draw something if it inspired me, and once complete, I would put it in an album. Rarely was a drawing seen again, and all but one is now lost or destroyed due to my travels. I still feel that visual art is important, but I have learned that the most important art forms are not visible—love, faith, purpose, and spirituality, to name a few. Sure, a painting may move us in some way, but the sensation is usually short-lived. It was not until later in life that I realized that music can produce neurological pathways to longer-lasting and deeper emotions. As we shall see, music produces strong neurological connections to experiences. For those of us who believe that there is something beyond what our natural vision can perceive, music can be a way to experience that *something*.

Though I had no interest in making music with an instrument, I was intrigued with sound. I always wanted clear sound and some of the cool, expensive stereo components that go with it. At that time, vinyl and cassettes were what most people played. I managed to get enough odd jobs to buy a turntable that was super cool because it was vertical. I always had to have a dual cassette deck and an equalizer with a spectrum analyzer. There was something about the jumping lines that moved in time with the music that fascinated me. My musical tastes were mostly confined to what I knew at the time, which was a lot of choir music. Mass choirs were big, and I was even able to see Andre Crouch in St. Louis, Missouri. I remember he was wearing a velvet suit coat. He was sweating profusely, but hey, that coat was *bad* (1970s slang), and I wanted one.

While in Bible college, my mother traveled with the college chorale, and my sister and I tagged along on some of the trips. As I grew, and when my mother could not hear what I was listening to, my tastes expanded into secular music. I liked classical, but I also liked blues and rock. Eric Clapton was king, Van Halen was taking the country by storm, Boston had a sound I liked, words could not describe Rush, and the Supremes had a groove that I dug. The more I listened, the more I became interested in older blues and classical. It wasn't until many years later that I realized my interest in those genres was largely because of the vocal harmony and the stringed instruments that often accompany the genres. It was those elements that created positive neurological activations for me.

My mother became a choir director, and the regular sound man could not always be at practices, so I learned as a young teenager to run the soundboard for practices. After a while I found myself operating the board during services when he was absent. I sometimes made some rather unwise decisions. I recall one night I was very tired, so shortly after the preaching began, I started the tape recorder, muted everything except the preacher's mic, and crawled under the soundboard for a nap. It was warm and cozy under there with a slight electrical hum. I awoke to hear the end of the pastor's sermon followed by non-amplified singers straining to be heard. I scurried from under the board and peered over the top to see musicians playing, but no sound was coming from the speakers. I stood up and made exaggerated, frustrated movements like I was having problems with the soundboard. I played with a few cords and then slyly unmuted the mics and instruments and gave them a big smile and a thumbs-up as if I had fixed the problem.

My craziness for music didn't end there. The family car (after the awesome Dodge Charger) was a bright yellow AMC Pacer station wagon. If you're not familiar with those, look them up. You'll be amazed. I decided it needed a better sound system, so I installed some used speakers I had gotten from somewhere. They were too large for the factory-sized hole, so I took a jigsaw to the metal of the door to help them fit. With the panels back in place, it looked normal. I added an amplifier and went for a drive to check out my work. It sounded great, but I wanted more, so I drove to the church to borrow some speakers we used for street services. I had to fold down the rear seats so they would fit in the hatch. I had a great time cruising for a while. Needless to say, Mom was not happy. I don't think she ever learned that I cut the door panels for the speakers. And I am truly sorry for whoever bought that car because I also used it to practice my racing skills.

Despite the craziness, I was pretty good at the soundboard. I learned how elements like special effects, room acoustics, and even some equipment, such as certain microphones and cassette tape brands, could affect the sound. After a few years, I realized that I had unwittingly become a musician. My instrument was not a bass guitar or a piano or my voice. My instrument was a soundboard. I operated an *auditory prism*—I converged all other instruments, including vocal instruments, and then sent the results out for others to hear the *colors*. I realized that my instrument could help or hinder a service. I began to take that role much more seriously.

Music In History

The human fascination with sound is evident throughout history. There is no known culture that has not had music. It can serve many purposes, like providing instruction, developing friendships, cultivating joy, passing on knowledge, exploring emotions such as love, and providing motivation. Interestingly, old musical devices indicate that our ancestors had the mental abilities and physical skills necessary to create instruments long before they made the ones we have today. Some believe that there would have been thousands of years of trial and error before they were able to make instruments that would last. A mammoth tusk discovered in southern Germany dates to about thirty-seven thousand years ago. It was split down the middle and hollowed out, holes were made, and it was put back together to make a flute. That one piece required a tremendous amount of craftsmanship, time, and effort, along with mental images of what the final product should look like, how it should work, how it should sound, and how it should be played. At that time musical instruments were one of the most technologically advanced devices. The drum is the oldest known instrument, and by the nature of their design, vibrating instruments are more fragile, so they probably existed long before the oldest fossils we have found.

Some of those instrument-making skills probably came from other art forms. The oldest known fossils in Europe date to about forty thousand years ago and include carvings, engravings, and cave paintings that record their history on bones and stones. It would have taken a very, very long time for them to learn which materials would stand the test of time. They would also need to learn how to transfer (paint, engrave) onto those materials the information they wanted to leave for future generations. Surely they didn't get it right the first time, so there had to be a lot of trial and error. The resulting hypothesis is that art forms existed for tens of thousands of years before the ancients learned which methods and materials would last.

Music and Relationships

Language and music can both be good methods of communication, but music is far more powerful because it involves more parts of the brain than written or spoken language. When speaking with others, we usually get our point across, but when compared to music, the message is not as memorable. One reason is that there is not as much organizational structure. Normal speech and writing do have some limited structure, but poetry has a little more structure in addition to other elements like rhythm, melody (good poetry has melody when read aloud), and compression of meaning—conveys a message in fewer words than normal communication. Poetry invites us to interpret and participate in the unfolding of the message. So an effect is that we feel a sense of involvement.

" Music can be an even greater effective message transmitter because of the way language and musical structures combine. "

Music can be an even greater effective message transmitter because of the way language and musical structures combine. To create and understand both language and music, we need to have three cognitive abilities. *Perspective-taking* is the ability to think about our own thoughts and to realize that other people may have thoughts that differ from our own. *Representation* is the ability to think about things that are not right in front of us. *Rearrangement* is the ability to combine, recombine, and place items in a hierarchical order. When combined in musical form, these elements lead to neurological and chemical processes that cause one to remember musical messages better than normal spoken or written word.

Social Bonding

Music can promote relationships between performers and audiences. One way is through the release of neurochemicals like oxytocin (social bonding). Another is by the words used. Early performers like Chuck Berry wrote a few songs, but the Beatles were the first group with wide commercial success to write their own songs and to write songs that purposely focused on building connections with audiences. Paul McCartney said that during their early years, he and John Lennon intentionally included a lot of personal pronouns in the lyrics and song titles. They consciously tried to create personal connections with their fans. "She Loves You," "P.S. I Love You," "From Me to You," "Love Me Do," and "I Want to Hold Your Hand" are some of the more famous titles.

Some bands have taken relationship-building with fans even further. The Grateful Dead is one of the most well-known bands to go to an extreme. Hallucinogenics such as peyote, mescaline, and LSD are thought to act on the neurotransmitter serotonin and can create the feeling that time has stopped and sensations of merging with others. The results can be feelings of unity. LSD allowed the Grateful Dead to create powerful relational feelings with audience members. I remember hearing stories during my youth about Dead Heads who would live in vans and travel around the country and attend Grateful Dead concerts. I never understood that level of fascination until I began to study why they felt that way.

A common drug like marijuana can promote a sense of euphoria and connectedness. It stimulates the brain's natural pleasure centers and disrupts short-term memory. The standard subconscious processes continue to function normally, but consciously the user can feel that time is standing still. The result is that users often describe experiencing each note individually. They are *in the moment*. But drugs are not always needed for feelings of connection.

Time and repeated listening to songs also solidifies relational feelings with performers. It imprints voices and messages into our minds. This creates the feeling that we know, and possibly have a close relationship with, the performer. For a time I listened to a lot of Nirvana. Even though I didn't take drugs and I'm not a stalker, I felt a connection with some of Kurt Cobain's lyrics that dealt with issues like internal struggles and homelessness. Because of that connection, I can still remember how sad I felt, where I was, and what I was doing when I heard that he had died. I was working in Houston, Texas. I was on my way to work, driving west away from the rising sun in my burgundy, two-door, 4x4 pickup. Such clear memories were created by multiple musical components like repeated listening and feeling a connection to lyrics.

The application of rhythm, melody, and structure are some other factors that cause the relationship to become more vivid and long-lasting. Rhythm is easily overlooked as a relationship builder, but studies show that humans coordinate movements with other humans better than they coordinate movements with mechanical devices. When asked to tap a finger in time with a metronome and then with another human, they were closer in time to the human. At first this seems strange because a human does not keep beat as precisely as a metronome. But humans accommodate each other, and that leads to a greater drive to coordinate their behaviors. When we successfully coordinate movement with another, there is a release of oxytocin. That is one reason why when people leave concerts, whether rock, classical, or religious, they are giving each other high-fives, laughing, socializing, and generally having a good time. I have been to several genres of concerts, and the general behavior when attendees leave is universal because they have created neurological relationships with each other through the shared musical experience.

Mirror Neurons—Sound/Music

In addition to visual mirror neurons, we also have auditory mirror neurons. Fossil evidence indicates that Brodmann Area 44 (BA44), which is part of the prefrontal cortex and contains mirror neurons that are important for auditory-motor imitation, existed two million years ago. Remember our discussion about our ancestors taking thousands of years to learn to create instruments that would last long enough for us to find them? The FOXP2 gene, which is associated with human language, has been found in Neanderthals, and a variation of the FOXP2 gene has been found in songbirds.

Microcephalin, which is important for brain development, first appeared about thirty-seven thousand years ago. Cro-Magnon, an early form of *Homo sapiens*, are thought to have appeared about the same time. This correlates with the approximate time that historians believe culturally modern humans began to develop. It also coincides with the appearance of artistic artifacts, including musical instruments. A second variation of microcephalin appeared about 5,800 years ago. That timeframe correlates with the first instance of written language, the development of cities, and the spread of agriculture. BA44, FOXP2, and microcephalin are biological indicators of human higher-order thinking abilities that allow us to perform musical and social behaviors, and the biological development of them coincides with historical evidence that they did, in fact, produce related behaviors.[148]

Sensory Domain Transference

Another part of the human evolutionary process related to music is the development of our ability to experience something in one sensory domain and then transfer that sensation into a different sensory domain. We *hear* a song and then we *sing* it. We *hear* a beat and start to *play* the air drums. We *see* words and then we *hum* them. Everything we speak or sing or write is a reproduction of something we experienced in one of the sensory domains. Our ability to transfer information to other sensory domains is thought to have developed when the basal ganglia evolved in such a way that it was able to communicate directly with visual and auditory input structures and motor output structures.

> **"Everything we speak or sing or write is a reproduction of something we experienced in one of the sensory domains."**

Only a few other species can transfer auditory data into a vocal domain. Parrots can reproduce words, and humpback whales, walruses, and sea lions are able to reproduce sounds. Additionally, some animals are able to transfer auditory data into movement. You tell your dog to "Sit," and he does.

Some evolutionists feel that the human ability to compose music arose from a combination of mental components that evolved separately before they combined. Rhythm, timber, and pitch are three examples of musical elements that are processed in different parts of the brain but combine to produce a melody. Clearly, human music has some elements that are unique to us and some that we share with other species. However, one element that is truly unique to us is that we are the only known species to compose songs for particular purposes, like worship or to teach a process.

Motor Mirroring

Though some musical skills are innate to humans, some skills are acquired and developed through musical perception and motor mirroring. Those skills can be maintained by continuously processing the musical stimuli and the motor actions.[149] The importance of the perception-to-production process is often practiced from the very beginning of one's training. Some teachers will have students play a piece and then listen to what they just played and analyze it. Others may be required to first watch the teacher, then mentally imagine performing the movements, and then physically perform the movements. The Suzuki method is a popular teaching theory that has a preliminary learning stage known as the "period of learning by watching."

There is a lot of research that supports the efficacy of such teaching methods. Remember modeling from an earlier chapter?

Audiovisual Mirror Neurons

Simply hearing a sound can produce an unconscious reaction. Experiments with monkeys have shown that some of the same motor neurons that activate when they *see* an action may also activate when they *hear* the action performed by another.[150,151] When they *saw* an action, 75 percent of the monkeys' *auditory* motor neurons were activated. This suggests that both auditory and visual sensations combine, at least somewhat, within the motor system. The combining of those audiovisual mirror neurons are what may allow for the recognition and the motor imitation of others' actions, even if the others' actions are only heard.[152] This convergence of auditory and visual sensations can provide learners with reinforced learning experiences.

Music can also restructure our brains. Advanced musicians have increased activity in brain motor centers related to the hand motions required to produce the sounds of their instruments.[153] Musicians also show overlapping activation in motor and premotor areas when they both listen to music and when they play music.[154,155] Additionally, familiarity with the musical piece increases one's motor movement abilities through the initiation of corticospinal motor movements (movements of the limbs and trunk).[156] Wu and colleagues found that simply listening to a previously practiced musical piece increased the motor actions needed to play the pieces.[157]

In a 2005 study, Haslinger and colleagues found that when a pianist observed someone else playing a piano but could not hear what was played, the auditory regions of the observer were activated.[158] The music was heard mentally by watching. When the researchers combined watching someone playing a piano along with sensory listening, there was an increased activation in several sensorimotor networks. Overall the stimuli from multiple domains have a greater impact on motor networks. The results of such integration means that, as more experience is gained from visual and auditory stimuli, musicians are better able to practice mentally. They will be able to *play* melodies in their minds without external movements. We see this quite frequently in performers of all fields, including sports.

Music creation, performance, and hearing can lead to physical and mental improvements. As we have seen, one of the benefits (and drawbacks) of simply listening to music is it can change brain chemistry. But how does sound, which is a mechanical disturbance, enter our brains and, along the way, get transferred into electrical and then chemical messages that have meaning?

Physics, Vibrational Quality, Ears, and Music

A brief discussion of how foundational sounds are to the human body and psyche will give us a better understanding of why we should try and control the musical vibrations we allow into our minds. After all, sound affects us at the cellular level, and even a slight understanding of that process can clarify why our relationship with music is so important.

Physics tells us that, when broken down into smaller parts, music is simply mechanical disturbances that travel through some sort of medium (e.g., air, water, metal) from one location to another. We usually call those disturbances *vibrations*. To be understood by us, those vibrations must reach our brain. The process begins when the outer ear collects and funnels the disturbances into the ear canal and to the eardrum. As the eardrum vibrates from the external waves, it moves three small bones within the middle ear. Those three bones move in various complex patterns that represent different frequencies. The third bone in the sequence moves the cochlea, which is filled with fluid. Nerve cells that await fluid movement cover the sides of the cochlea. As the fluid moves, electrical signals are created, and neurons transport those messages to auditory portions of the brain. In essence, our ears convert mechanical disturbances into electrical and chemical signals. Amazing.

This oversimplified explanation of how vibrations enter our brains leads to an oversimplified discussion of how our brains process the data and give it meaning. Psychology informs us that the brain extracts information from the signals and then applies meaning after incorporating information from many other systems. Simply put, how does our brain interpret electrical signals and apply meaning? The cochlear nerve transmits the electrical data produced by the inner ear to the brain stem, which houses two cochlear nuclei—one for each ear. The cochlear nuclei organize the signals and distribute them to other brain sections for interpretation. One area is the auditory cortex, which gives meaning to a lot of the data. This is the language center of the brain, and its role is to interpret sounds and make them understandable and identifiable. The prefrontal cortex is also involved. It compiles information from multiple parts of the brain (vision, memory, auditory, situational) in order to provide deeper understandings.

Our auditory system is connected to many body systems, like the nervous system, respiratory system, sense of balance, sense of sight, sense of smell, and sense of taste. It is so well connected that technology can now track heart rate, physical activity, brain electrical activation, blood oxygen levels, vagal tone, body temperature, galvanic skin response, identity security, and emotions (using voice analytics) with only our ears. This ability to gather such a wide range of biometric data is one of the coming revolutions in health, fitness, and behavior modification. Simply put, our ears are one of the most powerful doorways into our mind.[159]

First Line of Defense

What do we do if we don't want to see something? Simple. We close our eyes so those unwanted images don't enter our minds. What do we do if we don't want to hear something? We can't just close our ears or turn them off. We can wear headphones or ear protection, but we can't just throw those on any time we don't want to hear something. But, if we think about it, it is a good thing we can't just turn them off because they are an evolutionary first line of defense. They are part of the warning system that connects to the oldest part of our brain. That bump in the night wakes us. We react when we hear the car horn. The unfamiliar dog growls. Many times throughout the day we hear sounds, and when we hear something and determine it is not a danger, our minds place that sound in a subconscious file marked "safe." This process helps to keep us from getting overwhelmed with too much stimuli.

Some sounds, like a car horn, could be harmful or helpful. At times that sound may be sent to a subconscious file labeled something like "maybe, possibly, or sometimes safe." For example, we may hear a car horn, but if we are on the third floor of an office building, our subconscious tells us we are safe and we won't react. On the other hand, we may react because we are waiting for someone to pick us up, so we grab our stuff and rush out. Our auditory systems also have the ability to focus on sounds we need to, or want to, hear while filtering out sounds we do not need or want. Think of trying to talk in a busy restaurant. The sounds that we do not want to hear still enter our auditory systems, but they are relegated to the subconscious file of "I don't want to hear that."

> **" We hear something and determine it is not a danger— our minds place that sound in a subconscious file marked 'safe.' "**

Tone

Tone, the simplest of vibrational patterns, is the first element the brain works to determine. There is a *primary* and *secondary* auditory cortex located on each side of the brain, and they are almost identical. The primary cortices focus on processing individual sounds before the secondary cortices focus on how multiple sounds relate to each other. The secondary auditory cortex in the left brain focuses on relations between successions of sounds and sequences and has a dominant role in helping us perceive rhythm. From a language standpoint, this makes sense because the left brain is involved in organizing words used in language. The right brain secondary auditory cortex focuses on simultaneous sounds and the hierarchies of harmonic sounds. It is particularly good at analyzing vowel sounds within spoken language. This is understandable because the right brain works at making sense of melodies and detecting relationships between harmonies. The left ear, for the most part, sends its information to the right brain, and the right ear, for the most part, sends its information to the left brain.[160]

Melody

Tones combine to create melodies. Melody processing is much too complex to be processed in a localized brain center, but for simplicity we look at the left and right brain again. The right brain is better at detecting relations between a tone's harmonies, and it excels at making sense of melodies. However, it does not process all of the auditory information alone. There must be a sense of order to the melodies, otherwise they are just noise. This is where the left brain's ability to analyze rhythmic patterns helps with our understanding of the melodies. It provides organization. As musicians improve, their left brain becomes even more active in the perception and organization of melodies. Researchers conclude that those activity changes are necessary for the musician to more successfully integrate melodies into a logical order so that they are more understandable.[161]

Harmony

While melody is concerned with different tones at different times, harmony is concerned with different tones at the same time. Harmony can be thought of as music's depth—tones stacked on top of each other. Brain processing areas are similar to the ones for tones, but harmony causes them to work harder. Melodies are better recognized with the left ear, which funnels the information to the right brain for processing. Maybe a brief history of how harmonies were discovered and how they operate will help to further, but still briefly, explain the complexities with which the brain must contend when analyzing harmony, and why they must work harder than in the past.

Harmonies can be traced to chants sung by medieval Christian monks. At first, they consisted of a single melodic line that wavered up or down slightly. Over time, higher and lower notes were added, but not all singers could reach all the notes, so the chants were broken into separate vocal lines. This process of *organum* continued for hundreds of years. Around the eleventh century, composers began to make the higher vocal parts more complex, while the lower parts continued as before. Around the thirteenth century, composers began to write music in which voices occasionally moved out of sync before returning to harmony. *Polyphony* (two or more melodic parts sounded together) allowed voices to be combined in ways that new sounds could be created. Eventually, the creation of the organ allowed composers to discover even more chords and begin to think in terms of stacking more tones on top of each other in order to achieve even greater depth.[162]

Rhythm

While harmony creates a sense of depth, rhythm allows us to perceive music in relation to time. Rhythm is about grouping sounds and imposing order and timing. While harmony is better recognized by the left ear, rhythm is more accurately recognized by the right ear. It is then sent for processing in the more logical left side of the brain. Rhythm's association with the left brain is understandable since the left brain is more adept with linear processing. However, it is important to note that rhythm interpretation involves more brain areas than harmonic interpretation does.

Though brain sides are similar, there are size differences associated with some parts. Some differences are great enough that psychotic drugs may affect one side more than the other. For example, the front of the right brain is larger than the corresponding left in areas concerned with emotions, while the rear of the left brain is larger in areas affecting language than the corresponding right. These size differences help the right brain score 20 percent higher at identifying melodic patterns and 10 percent better at recognizing non-speech sounds such as laughter, while the left brain scores 90 percent and 70 percent better at recognizing words and meaningless syllables, respectively.[163]

The mechanical waves collected by our ears must be turned into something that can be recognized as music; otherwise it is just noise. Once we recognize music, we are able to listen to it more effectively. However, in our modern industrialized cultures, we rarely listen *actively*, probably because music is so pervasive. In fact, it can be difficult to *not* hear music. Some of us wake to musical alarms. Throughout the day we may use it to concentrate, create energy, reduce stress, reduce pain, help with memory, relax, or go to sleep. Radio commercials often use music to manipulate our emotions. We hear music as we shop because businesses have learned that music affects our buying practices, and some workplaces use music to increase worker productivity. Such musical pervasiveness creates a situation in which we are so accustomed to music that we rarely actively listen to music, though it still enters our brain. The result is that this passive listening can affect us more than active listening because it is not cognitively filtered.

Cognitive Filters

Music is one of the most powerful ways to affect our emotions and feelings and, by extension, our behaviors and relationships. How can unnoticed, mechanical vibrations have a greater effect on human emotions, memories, and behaviors than the vibrations we notice? The simple answer is that the primitive neural circuitry located in the brain stem spends more effort processing it. The primitive circuitry works to *sharpen* the edges of the music (similar to how our peripheral vision is sharpened) and helps to discriminate between frequency, loudness, and locations of sounds. That makes sense because it is part of our evolutionary early warning system. That primitive neural circuitry gives each sound equal weight because the sounds are allowed to bypass cognitive filters in the cerebral cortex and communicate directly with the limbic system (emotions, memory, motivation, behavior).

That makes sense from a survival of the fittest standpoint because quickly processing each sound improves our chances of survival. When that bear surprises us with an attack from behind, we need to automatically know the direction it is coming from, about how fast it is moving, how close it is, and so on. We can then automatically react with protective behaviors. All of that to explain why our survival system is designed the way it is and to explain how unwanted or inappropriate sounds can enter our brains without being filtered. And, just like certain sounds have greater effect on our primal, subconscious minds, music affects our primal brains more effectively when we allow it to enter without actively listening. We allow the musical messages to bypass our cognitive filters so they have greater effect on our subconscious thoughts and actions.

> **" Music affects our primal brains more effectively when we allow it to enter without actively listening. "**

The vagus nerve, which helps to regulate the parasympathetic nervous system, influences feelings of safety, and music influences that nerve. When combined with visual stimulation, the effect of music grows exponentially based on our level of immersion. For example, movies and videos will have less influence when compared to VR or video games. In essence, background music is the auditory version of the previously discussed *blind sight*. I call it *deaf listening*. Even though we may not know it is happening or be able to explain our behaviors (like TN could not describe his), *deaf listening* affects us. This knowledge supports the idea that it may be beneficial to consciously listen to music and its messages because it engages our cognitive filters so the processed information can be put into categories of "appropriate/good" and "inappropriate/bad."

Bodily Movements

Many of us find ourselves moving to music. I often find myself tapping a finger or nodding my head to music in a store, even when I don't know I'm listening. Sometimes I catch myself doing so even if I do not like the song. In such instances, my subconscious processing of the sounds is being produced as visible motor movements. Once I consciously realize what I am doing, my neurological filters engage, and I am then required to make a choice. Should I continue the behavior? Should I change the behavior? Should I stop the behavior?

Moving to the music in any way, whether tapping, head bobbing, or dancing, amplifies the music's effect on us. Think of a cello as an example. Alone, a string produces little sound, but adding the resonator of the large cello amplifies the sound. The much smaller string causes the much larger resonator to move in time with the string. In essence, the larger resonator is played by the smaller string and in the process amplifies the sound. The musician can stop the process and the sound by placing fingers on the strings. The same concept applies to the human body. Small mechanical waves can cause our larger bodies to be *played*. In turn, our bodily movements amplify the musical experience, causing it to have a greater effect on us. Once we realize we are being played by the music, we have choices to make. Do we continue, change, or stop the behavior?

Bodily movements influence our emotions in both good and bad ways. Moving can cause the release of endorphins, which can create a sense of euphoria. This is one reason some people exercise regularly. Runner's high is great. Music is so inclusive that it can cause either great joy or great pain, and, as we know, both can cause neurons to produce endorphins. Endorphins are similar to opiates, and like opiates, they act on pain networks to reduce pain. But if endorphins are released because of our movements, but no pain (or not enough pain) is present to counteract the endorphins, we experience a state of euphoria.

Similar to how pain can counteract endorphins, some manmade medications may have similar counteractive effects. Naloxone is used to treat drug addicts. It works by blocking opiate receptors in the brain so the addict does not feel euphoria. In sum, both naturally occurring *medications*, such as endorphins, and manmade medications influence the intensity of music's effect on us. Combine those feelings with increased or decreased movement, and the effect of the vibrations can be increased or diminished.[164]

Neurological Real Estate

The power of music cannot be fully described by looking at its physical brain structures alone. In terms of total real estate space, the auditory system does not hold any special neurological size advantage. It uses less brain space than the visual system, but let someone drag their fingernails across a chalkboard (if you can find one these days) and watch what happens to those in hearing distance. In fact, just reading those words probably caused some of you older readers to shudder. From where does music get such power to influence? Simply put, music connects to primal and subconscious parts of our brains, and along the processing pathway, it may bypass cognitive filters. It can affect us physiologically and psychologically because it is integrated with other mental processes like vision, memory, situational, and motor.

Phonemic Restoration

In addition to filtering some sounds, our brains can do the opposite. It's similar to how our brain adds information to improve our poor vision; it can add missing auditory data. For example, one study recorded a sentence in which researchers erased the 120-millisecond portions of the first *s* sound in *legislatures* and replaced it with a cough. Participants were told that they would hear a recording that contained a cough. They were given a printed text of the recording and were told to circle the exact position in the text where they heard the cough.

Afterward, they were asked if the cough had masked any of the circled sounds. All twenty said they heard the cough. Nineteen of the twenty said they heard all the sounds. The one participant who reported not hearing a sound because of the cough circled the wrong letter in the text. Even when researchers used a cough to cover the entire syllable *gis* in *legislature,* the participants could not identify the sound that was missing. Their brains automatically inserted the missing or obscured sounds. *Phonemic restoration* is analogous to the filling in of the blind spot in your vision, or other visual improvements, previously discussed.[165]

Phonemic restoration has another interesting effect. What you *think* you hear at the beginning of a sentence can be affected by what you *actually* hear at the end of a sentence. A well-known study demonstrates how later context shapes our perception of earlier ambiguous sounds and illustrates the phenomenon of phonemic restoration. Participants listened to recordings where an ambiguous sound, denoted as **eel,* was embedded in sentences before words that influenced the interpretation of the *. For example, when **eel* preceded *axle*, listeners heard *wheel*. Similarly, when it preceded *shoe, orange*, or *table*, they heard *heel, peel*, or *meal*, respectively.

Each person's brain held onto the missing sound at the beginning of the sentence while it listened for clues later in the sentence. After hearing the words *axle, shoe, orange*, or *table*, their brains went back to the missing or ambiguous data at the beginning of the sentence and filled in the related, missing consonant. Our subconscious automatically overcomes data gaps or hurdles without us consciously being aware of the process. The two previous studies are only a few of the many that indicate that some of the world we hear is artificially created by the subconscious.[166]

Internal Vibrations

This artificially created world can affect us. The average human consists of thirty- to seventy-trillion cells. While the total number of cells may vary widely, researchers agree that music affects all of the cells in an individual's body. In fact, human cell growth and cell death can be affected by playing different acoustic vibrations. Some genres of music have been found to improve cell health, while others have led to cell deterioration. And differences in the *quality* of those musical vibrations can affect our emotions, thoughts, moods, perceptions, and health. Even our mental *products*, like thoughts and moods, produce vibrational frequencies of their own. Indeed, as the musicologist Hazrat Inayat Khan explained, when the energy of sound reaches a person it engages all five senses—sight, hearing, smell, taste, and touch. Though it primarily enters through the hearing process, sound is not perceived solely by the ears; *it resonates through every pore of the body, permeating a person's entire being*. It can either slow or accelerate the rhythm of blood circulation, stimulate or calm the nervous system.[167]

" Some genres of music have been found to improve cell health, while others have led to cell deterioration. "

Music and Health

Our understanding that sound can affect the body is not new. The oldest known use of music as medicine was by the Chinese as early as 2600 BC. These days, an understanding of sound's possible benefits exists in the medical community where sound waves are commonly used for treatment. Ultrasound uses high frequencies to produce internal images to diagnose internal health conditions. It may also be used for treatments like cataract removal, treatment of kidney stones, tendinitis, and surgical tissue cutting. Sound treatments at the frequency of forty hertz (Hz) have been used for pain relief in tendons, ligaments, muscles, nerves, and skin. Forty Hz has also been used to treat Alzheimer's and dementia. So far, treatments have not reversed those diseases, but they have stopped or slowed their progressions. Other frequencies are being used for the treatment of other diseases, and more studies are exploring different frequencies as possible treatments for other ailments. However, vibrational effects are not limited to humans.

Various frequencies have also been found to affect living and harvested plants. Plant acoustic frequency technology (PAFT) uses acoustic waves to improve photosynthesis, nutrient uptake, cell division, and defense mechanisms of living plants. PAFT is also being used to extend the shelf life of harvested plants and to help preserve plant seeds. Though we think of harvested and dead plants and seeds as unmoving, in reality, they are filled with movement.

Weaponized Music

Music can also be used to destroy. A lot of the funding for psychological research between 1945 and the mid-1960s in America came from the US Department of Defense (DOD). One of the no-touch tortures listed in some DOD manuals is music and sound. For more than five decades, Americans have employed music and sound as interrogation tools. This practice isn't exclusive to the current administration or recent conflicts—it has a long history. What's new is that more people are now aware of it, though this increased awareness hasn't led to widespread public outcry.[168]

The DOD operates a Survival, Evasion, Resistance, and Escape (SERE) training program. Personnel are taught various survival techniques based on their risk of capture and exploitation value. Special emphases are placed on air crews, special operations personnel, foreign diplomats, and intelligence personnel. A part of the school's purposes is to teach methods to withstand torture. Unfortunately, some of the techniques that are intended to help personnel survive torture have been reverse engineered and used *for* torture. Music is one of those methods.[169]

The US Military's Psychological Operations Music Program developed specific methods to exploit music's ability to create pathological conditions. Oliver Sacks wrote that music could cross a line and our neurological *off switch* fails at keeping us from mentally *playing* the snippet. It becomes, in a sense, abnormal or unhealthy, replaying constantly, sometimes to a maddening extent for days at a time.[170] Sacks continued that while earworms might seem minor or unimportant, they possess the ability to compel portions of the brain to activate repeatedly and independently in ways that resemble the involuntary actions seen in conditions like tics or seizures. Music can even block our ability to maintain our thoughts. It is even possible to influence us to change our thoughts. Heavy metal, rap, and sexually suggestive music and songs from children's TV shows, like Barney, are often the music of choice in the Music Program.

In addition to the psychological manipulation, music may also be weaponized in a tactile manner. All sound is the movement of air molecules within a medium. The human body can be that medium, and the movement of sound can be used to cause pain, discomfort, injury, and even death. Sound became particularly useful because it meets the no-touch torture requirements found in some US manuals. It also protects vendors of those techniques from prosecution under the Geneva Convention. In 2009, a coalition of musicians whose music was being used for no-touch torture filed a Freedom of Information Act request for the US Government to declassify documents relating to "The Music Program." Groups like REM, Nine Inch Nails, Rage Against the Machine, and Pearl Jam didn't want their music used for such purposes. I find it somewhat interesting that some of the music from bands and shows that are used for torture are, or were, popular within many societies.

Empty Space (and Not Just In My Brain)

As humans, our perspectives are usually limited to what we can easily observe. As I sit at my wood and metal desk, my eyes tell me that the dead, inanimate, solid desk is not moving. However, my scientific mind tells me that the desk is actually filled with a lot of movement. In fact, while it seems solid to me, it is made up of mostly empty space, which allows electron clouds to constantly move around between the atoms. So in reality, my desk is in constant movement and is mostly made up of empty space. This gives more clarity to how sound waves can affect inanimate objects. Think of the singer shattering a glass with her voice.

Music therapy can increase immunoglobulin A (fights mucus system infections), serotonin (sleep regulation, treats some types of depression, supports immune system), and norepinephrine and epinephrine (alertness, brain reward centers). Joyful music tends to have a more positive effect on the chemistry than does negative music. The molecular biologist John Medina suggests that listening to music you like triggers a release of dopamine (feel good) and oxytocin (social bonding) and can reduce cortisol (stress hormone).[171] Overall results are that listening to music you like supports mental and physical health.[172]

Lyrics and Neurochemicals

Lyrical messages can produce different neurochemical responses based on the individual. At times, the results can seem contradictory. Sad songs are a good example. Sad songs can annoy some happy people, while they can help some individuals with clinical depression feel better. That seems odd, until we begin to understand some unseen processes. People with depression tend to feel alone and disconnected. Happy music can cause them irritation and deepen their feelings of depression and aloneness because they can't relate to the positive musical message. Since we often need to feel understood (feel a connection) before recovery can begin, sad music can help us to feel that others understand because they (singers) have gone through sad times as well. The singers have been there, done that, and bought the t-shirt. Once depressed listeners feel that someone can relate to their sadness, healing can begin through the release of the neurochemical prolactin (tranquilizing hormone).[173]

> **" A sad song can cause the release of prolactin even in someone who is happy. "**

Prolactin can be released in tears, but interestingly, only in tears of sorrow. Tears produced for other reasons, such as eye lubrication, because something is stuck in our eye, or for joy, do not contain prolactin. This gives us an even deeper understanding of the power of sad songs. A sad song can cause the release of prolactin even in someone who is happy. Huron suggests that the imagined musical sorrow can trick the brain into producing a comforting emotional response.[174] The results are that our moods are changed for the better. Even a person who is already in a good mood can feel even better. I know that seems counterintuitive, but music affects our electrical circuits and chemicals. That is why music can make us feel happy or sad. Or hearing a song in a store can suddenly ignite long-forgotten memories.

Synesthesia

Synesthesia is an intriguing neurological condition and is a good example of what can happen when our wires get crossed. Causes can be genetic, chemical, or trauma-induced. Simply put, sensory receptors stimulate brain areas that are not normally associated with those receptors. There are many forms of synesthesia, but some examples are sounds that cause one to see colors or touch that causes someone to smell something that is not there. The most common forms of synesthesia relate to colors, and the least common relate to smell or taste. Musicologist Oliver Sacks shared that he once had a musical synesthetic dream that involved Pringles chips. As they crunched in his mouth, they would play a few musical bars of a symphony or concerto.[175] E. S. is a professional musician who experienced either tastes or emotions in response to certain sounds.[176] For example, minor second and major seventh tones produced sour tastes, while major second and minor seventh tones elicited bitter tastes. The minor third triggered a salty taste, and the major third evoked sweetness. The fifth and major sixth tones generated tastes of pure water and low-fat cream, respectively. Octaves produced no taste. Interestingly, the fourth evoked the smell of freshly mown grass, and the tritone triggered feelings of disgust.[177]

The Brain and Energy

Though some individuals can experience neurological anomalies like synesthesia, most brains operate as expected. Our brains take in millions of bits of information while connecting those newly gathered bits of information to other bits of (1) previously gathered information, (2) information gathered at the same time, (3) information that will be gathered in the future, and (4) information that may be regathered. That amount of mental processing requires massive computational power and, as a result, a lot of energy. Only our heart and kidneys require more energy than the brain. Most human brains burn about 22 percent of our total caloric intake, and that burn rate stays relatively consistent if we are relaxing or doing something like studying.[178] Or writing a book that talks about the brain-burning calories.

Our brains are roughly three times larger than other primates and require approximately 10 percent more caloric intake. Evolutionarily speaking, such a relatively large brain does not make sense unless it provides a greater survival advantage. One of those advantages is the ability to think about things that are not right in front of us. Our auditory system is another of those advantages. Our hearing ability is a highly developed defensive system that encompasses both sides of the brain, and even that separation of neurological functions into separate hemispheres provides for *backup systems* should the functions of one side of the brain become damaged. The healthy side of the brain can sometimes evolve to perform some of the functions of the damaged side.

Music Engrained

Auditory collection begins before birth. Babies respond to music while in the womb, and they recognize Mom's voice from the moment of birth. Watch a baby's reaction as Mom coos over him/her shortly after birth. That is somewhat expected because the baby has been hearing Mom's voice for several months. What is less known is that music is much more deeply encoded in our psyche than previously thought. Music is engrained in our genetics. In 2009, Bobby

145

McFerrin gave a presentation at the International World Science Festival entitled, *Notes and Neurons: In Search of the Common Chorus.*[179] As part of his presentation, he sang the first four notes of the pentatonic scale and had the audience complete the scale by singing the missing note or notes. In doing so, McFerrin demonstrated that the pentatonic scale is naturally engrained in humans and is not limited to certain languages or cultures.

> **66 What is less known is that music is much more deeply encoded in our psyche than previously thought. Music is engrained in our genetics. 99**

While in the womb, a baby's rhythms synchronize with Mom's metabolism, heartbeat, singing, and movements. This synching of movements promotes bonding, partly because the same parts of the brain that process emotion also process movement. Remember, emotion causes movement, and movement causes emotion. This helps our understanding of why mothers and babies feel such close connections. It's much more than simply producing offspring (at least it is for most mothers).

When I was young, one of the things that made me feel at ease was my grandmother frequently singing or humming. In my adolescent mind, I just thought she was a happy person, but now I realize that she may have been singing and humming to make herself happy—or happier. The William James quote, "I don't sing because I'm happy; I'm happy because I sing" often comes to mind when I hear people who frequently sing or hum. I may not know exactly why my grandmother was singing, but I understand that there was a cyclical relationship between music and her mood.

In Summary

This chapter intertwined some of my musical journey into a discussion of some of music's history, psychology, neurology, physics, and cultural power. The core of the chapter explored *how* and *why* sound affects us so deeply. It explained the process of hearing—from physical vibrations entering the ear to complex neurological processing that involves multiple brain regions. Some effects include the release of neurochemicals like dopamine (pleasure), oxytocin (bonding), cortisol (stress reduction), and prolactin (consoling effect, especially with sad music), which directly influences our moods and social connections. Along the way, we considered active listening and passive listening and looked at how *deaf listening* can subconsciously bypass cognitive filters. We also looked at some physical effects like cellular reactions, therapeutic uses, and music's potential for weaponization. Ultimately, I argued that music is an innate and powerful force that shapes our experiences, emotions, health, and relationships, even before birth, in ways that operate below conscious awareness.

Introspective Questions for Chapter 6

? **Early Musical Experiences:** How did your early experiences with music lessons or exposure to music shape your current relationship with it? Do you relate to the author's initial resistance to traditional music lessons or his passion for sound?

? **Unconventional Musical Expression:** The author found his "instrument" in the soundboard. Is there an unconventional way you engage with music or sound that feels like your unique form of musical expression or appreciation?

? **Sonic Environment and Well-being:** Considering that sound vibrations affect the body at a cellular level, how do you choose the music or sounds in your daily environment? What impact do you think they have on your well-being?

? **Music, Memory, and Emotion:** What specific songs or musical pieces trigger strong memories or emotions for you? Can you trace why those neurological connections might be so strong in your own life?

? **Passive Listening's Influence:** Considering the concept of passive listening (deaf listening), how aware are you of music playing in your environment (e.g., stores, work, background noise)? Could it be influencing your mood or behavior without your conscious awareness?

? **The Impact of Sad Songs:** How do sad songs affect you personally? Do they bring you down, or do you find comfort or a sense of understanding in them?

? **Artist-Listener Connection:** Have you ever felt a strong connection to an artist through their lyrics, like the author did with Kurt Cobain? How did that connection feel, and how did events in the artist's life impact you?

? **Innate vs. Learned Musicality:** Do you believe musicality or the understanding of basic musical structures (like the pentatonic scale) is purely learned, or does the idea of it being somewhat innate or *engrained* resonate with you?

? **Music's Duality: Therapy and Weapon:** The text mentions music being used therapeutically and as a weapon. How does this duality affect your perception of music's power?

? **Music and Mood Regulation:** Thinking about the William James quote ("I don't sing because I'm happy; I'm happy because I sing"), do you ever use the act of singing, humming, or playing music to actively shift your emotional state?

CHAPTER 7

Cellblock Seasoning and Sonic Harmony

Prison Lunches

When I began working in a prison, I was told staff could get lunch for one dollar. It sounded like a good deal until I was told that prisoners cooked the food. Then, when I asked what they cooked, the reply was, "The same food as the prisoners." I politely declined, but several colleagues insisted that the food was "*really* good." I laughed. My office was close to the cafeteria, and several coworkers walked by my windows each day on their way to eat. I noticed that those who had some flexibility in their schedules would leave for lunch early so they could get a good spot in line.

Eventually I forgot my lunch, and, since I hadn't seen anyone rolling on the ground and foaming at the mouth after eating, I decided to give in. After that day, I stopped taking my lunch and changed my patient appointments so that I could be one of the first ones in line. Still curious about the food, I asked again if they were purchasing different food for the staff. "No, same food as the prisoners." That didn't make sense. The only difference was that the prisoners who cooked our food didn't cook for their fellow prisoners. The flavor was so good that when my family would go out of town, I would buy two lunches. I would eat one at work and take the other home for my dinner. It was hard to beat a good-tasting lunch and dinner for two dollars. And no taxes! The prison was making decent money from staff lunches (of course the labor and food were free), and a lot of us would sit in the cafeteria while we ate and have a good time. Occasionally some of the prisoner trustees would sit with us.

Suddenly, my *gourmet prison lunch world* came crashing down. I went to get lunch one day, and there were different cooks. The taste of the food was as bad as you might imagine prison food to be. I had eaten worse, but that was for survival. We eventually began getting emails telling us that we needed to start buying lunches again because they were losing money. After a few emails, several of us responded that we would when the previous cooks returned. We were finally told that they would not return.

The main cook for the staff lunchroom had been a professionally trained chef at an upscale restaurant. Cool, but how did he make the food taste so good? After all, he used the prisoners' food for us. Well, he had been putting extra spices into our food (nothing illegal or harmful). But where had he gotten the spices? Um . . . some guards had been smuggling them in so the chef could season our food. So he was arrested and sent to jail (if they got arrested for something while in jail, they still called it "going to jail"). The guards who smuggled the spices were fired. I never ate lunch at the prison again. If I forgot my lunch, I would leave the prison, go to the grocery store down the road, and have to go through security again when I returned to work.

I once asked the chef why he was a chef on the outside. He said that it made him happy to make others happy, and he could do that through food. It was very interesting to see that he could still do that in jail and even promote better social interactions with people from different walks of life. It even had positive effects on the trustees who were sometimes allowed to eat with us, though they still had to eat their bland prisoner food. Indeed, the chef had accomplished his goal even in prison. The spices he put into the food made a big difference in its flavor, but even more importantly, they had positive effects on our behaviors and social interactions.

On the other end of the relationship continuum, relationships (connections) were hindered when the chef left. The return of the bad-tasting food caused us to shift from spending time socializing in the cafeteria to eating in our offices alone or in small groups. The group sizes, the frequency, and the quality of the social interactions were greatly reduced. Positive social interactions with prisoners also decreased because, clearly, the trustees were not allowed to go to our offices to eat with us. Even relations with the non-trustee inmates suffered because they no longer saw us sharing a portion of their lunchroom. Some of them felt slighted.

Even though I didn't work with inmates in the general population, the change in the lunch situation affected the ones I did work with in twenty-four-hour lockdown and the mental health dorm. The prison gossip network is a truly impressive machine. People who were not supposed to be having communication with others in "gen pop" heard about the change, and a few of them asked me questions about it. Most understood, but a few held it against me and our ability to communicate suffered a little. Those small, almost imperceptible spices promoted positive relationships, but their removal hindered relationships. Just like those spices, the lyrics (spices) we allow into our brain affect our behaviors and our interactions with others.

Lyrical Diet

I mentioned earlier that I didn't pay much attention to lyrics when I was young. That has changed. The more I learn about the neurological effects of words, the more conscious I am about the music I choose to allow into my mind. I know people who have music playing all the time. It does not matter if they are listening actively or passively; they just like to have background music playing. I do the same thing sometimes. It also helps with my tinnitus (sensation of noise). However, I now make conscious decisions about my lyrical diet, especially when I am not actively listening, because I know that my cognitive filters are not engaged.

Words and Neurochemicals

Like the spices that affect the flavor of food, words can affect us neurochemically. Zatorre and Salimpoor showed that music can activate the same neurological reward centers as food and sex.[180] Cortisol (stress) is released when we hear words with negative associations, while positive words trigger the release of oxytocin (trust). One negative word within an entire conversation can increase activity in the amygdala that will cause the release of neurotransmitters and stress hormones, interrupting brain functions. Unfortunately, our brain tends to respond to negative words almost twice as fast as it does to positive words. Some say that the different response rates prove people are naturally bad, but some others say that the response rate is an evolutionary survival benefit—that *bad feeling* we get can prepare us for danger much quicker.

Even when we think but don't say out loud those painful words, similar effects are produced. In *Words Can Change Your Brain*, Newberg and Waldman wrote, "A *single word* has the power to influence the expression of genes that regulate physical and emotional stress" *(emphasis mine)*. They went on to discuss the benefits of concentrating on positive words: "By holding a positive and optimistic [word] in your mind, you stimulate frontal lobe activity. This area includes specific language centers that connect directly to the motor cortex responsible for moving you into action. And as our research has shown, the longer you concentrate on positive words, the more you begin to affect other areas of the brain."[181]

Simply concentrating on positive words changes our self-perceptions. In the long run, other brain areas are positively affected, and we change the nature of our reality because we see things in a more positive light. At an organizational level, this can have similar effects. I have worked in places that should have been depressing, but the culture made it enjoyable—and vice versa.

Planting Seeds

Seeds produce much larger plants. Some of the most powerful, life-changing conversations may be very short. *Seed* conversations by mentors influenced me to pursue my PhD. I previously shared the abysmal beginning of my high school career and how an English professor offered to ensure I received a graduate assistantship if I applied for the master's program. Though I politely refused, he planted a seed. Over the next few years, the idea that I might have the ability to complete a master's program began to germinate. Toward the end of my master's, another professor offered to write a letter of reference for me if I would apply to his Ivy League alma mater. My response was similar to the one I had given the English professor, but that seed began to grow too. Eventually, like my master's, I decided to give it a try.

> *What you listen to is a strong indicator of the type of person you are.*

The point is, one-sentence statements by individuals I respected influenced my decisions to try the next level of education. Granted, I progressed at my own, slow pace, but the seeds eventually sprouted. Conversations don't need to be big, and change may not happen immediately. In fact, I argue that the message can easily get lost in big conversations and that the most significant changes sometimes need time to grow foundational roots. This same concept applies to lyrics. Lyrics plant seeds that affect us over time. Maybe not right now, but they will. Tiffanie Debartolo explained it well when she wrote that what you listen to is a strong indicator of the type of person you are.[182]

The religious genre possibly contains the most positive messages, but many religious people listen to secular music. In my decades of working with emotionally/behaviorally disturbed students, none of them "acted a fool" while listening to music with positive lyrics or messages. It didn't matter if it was secular or religious. From kindergartners to prison-lifers, the ones who "acted a fool" had consumed a steady diet of negative lyrics. Lyrical content affects our subconscious mind, perceptions, happiness, well-being, behaviors, and states of being. Similar to eating junk food, negative lyrics cause us to feel sluggish and less cognizant and act in unhealthy ways. Since most of the people I have worked with are not believers, I don't usually tell them to listen to Christian artists. However, I have told some believers and non-believers to avoid some Christian artists—some are worse than secular artists. Instead, I tell them to make sure the lyrics are clearly positive—no negative or vague lyrics.

Vague Lyrics

I often get questioning looks when I mention that people should not listen to vague lyrics. As part of my response, I suggest they prioritize their listening choices in this order: positive lyrics, negative lyrics, and, lastly, vague lyrics. Ironically, secular individuals tend to nod in agreement with my preferred rankings more often than believers. Christians often adopt looks of confusion and ask something like, *What's wrong with vague lyrics if it is a Christian song?* In response, I often begin by asking them if they agree that some lyrics are clearly good and some lyrics are clearly bad. Though we may not agree with specific definitions of good and bad, we generally agree that there is a clear difference between the two and that somewhere between the two lies a *line of vagueness.*

I then continue to explain my reasoning. When we subconsciously know lyrics are positive, our cognitive filters don't need to engage. We can let them roam around freely in our minds and do their good work. When we subconsciously know lyrics are negative, our cognitive filters engage and file the received messages as "bad" so that they have less effect on us. But what happens when we don't know the message the lyrics are trying to send?

Remember our discussion of how multitasking can cause labelling and filing errors? Something similar happens here. What are they singing about? Is the message good or bad? Where do I store the information I'm receiving? A negative lyric might be mislabeled as "good" and allowed to roam freely and influence our thoughts and behaviors. On the other hand, a positive lyric may be is mislabeled and stored as "negative," limiting its good influence.[183] Either situation causes us to experience some level of cognitive confusion.

Knowledge Songs and Religious Songs

Occasionally, a fellow conversationalist will comment that one of the beauties of lyrics is that lyrics, like poetry, use *compression of meaning* (though they don't usually use those exact words). I agree. One of the beauties of compression of meaning is that it uses fewer words than normal speech to share its message. One effect is that the listener/reader is invited to participate in the interpretation of the message. But one of the drawbacks is that there is room for individual interpretation. I usually respond by agreeing that compression of meaning is an important art form, and I enjoy it when it is used in the appropriate context.

Some types of songs should not be left open to interpretation. Knowledge songs and religious songs are two examples. Knowledge songs teach a process. Some songs throughout history have taught things like making a medicine or a hunting tool. Some cultures still do this. An unclear step, or incorrect step, in a process may lead to death or a nonfunctioning tool. Think of learning the English alphabet with the ABC song. It was most likely an important tool in learning your ABCs (at least in the US). What if you were told it was OK to sing it in any order you wanted? "However you want to learn it is fine." Now imagine the confusion if each person learned the alphabet in their own way.

A vague meaning in knowledge songs might produce a misinterpretation or a level of confusion that could lead to death if an incorrect medicine or ineffective weapon is produced. Similarly, religious songs are meant to teach a religious process or share a sacred belief or situation. A vague meaning in such songs can easily lead to confusion, perverted beliefs, or even non-belief. Some Christian artists may accidentally combine words in ways that produce unclear or confusing lyrics, but I know some artists who do so intentionally. They may not think it matters much, but Nathaniel Hawthorne was correct when he wrote that words, while in a dictionary, are harmless and weak, but they gain immense power for good or harm when wielded by someone skilled in their use.[184]

> **"Words, while in a dictionary, are harmless and weak, but they gain immense power for good or harm when wielded by someone skilled in their use."**

When discussing the power of vague lyrics, one of the examples I sometimes use is of Jezebel. She was brilliant in the methods she used to pervert the Jewish religion. One way she did this was by placing statues of other gods in places of Jewish worship. The Jews were still allowed to worship their God, but they did so in the presence of the other gods. Over time, the Jews began to associate Jezebel's gods with their God. How could they feel the presence of their God with the others present? Why would their God allow others to be present? They haven't caused us any problems—are they really bad?

Those questions, and others, created confusion for the worshipers. As they continued to worship and question, with no clear answers, they became more accepting of the foreign gods. Slowly, some of their sacred feelings transferred to the other gods, which resulted in a perverted religion that accepted almost all deities and behaviors. They are even known as being one of the most morally corrupt cultures of that time. Vague lyrics in songs by Christian artists can have similar effects. Adding music to words increases their effects, and listening to the songs repeatedly compounds those effects.

One thing to keep in mind is that some lyrics may seem positive but hold negative connotations for some (see previous discussion regarding depression and songs). If that is you, don't play them. Conversely, some secular songs may hold special meaning for you and produce positive feelings. Love songs played at your wedding or a relative's funeral are good examples. I have encouraged some who were stuck in a heavily negative mental or physical state to find positive lyrics (religious or secular) and write them down repeatedly. For them, the positivity was the important part. It was a technique used to intentionally eliminate confusion and negativity and to promote positivity. Adding the concentration and motion of writing the words adds to the effects of hearing them.

Soundtracks

There are neurological reasons why television is one of the most addictive and perception-altering drugs. We visually experience the media at conscious and subconscious levels. Adding audio, such as a soundtrack, enhances the effects by intensifying our emotions and subconscious processing. Being unaware of the degree to which our thoughts and beliefs can be shaped by a soundtrack makes it much easier for us to unknowingly redefine how we think and behave. Such mind games do not happen by accident. In fact, Fitzpatrick wrote that the goal of a film composer is to guide the emotional and mental journey of a large audience, shaping and influencing their interpretation of the story on a subconscious level.[185]

Our media experiences are often at odds with what we know to be right. That dissonance helps explain why some people who watch a lot of media are consistently unhappy. Each time I have counseled someone to stop watching TV, vegging on social media, or constantly playing video games, and they have done so, their mood has improved. I was recently in an undeveloped country. There was no running water or electricity, and there were no solid-walled homes nor roads in a lot of areas. They didn't have material possessions, but not one time did I look at them in pity. They were happy. They talked. They helped each other. In fact, I pitied myself and my country. They had things that were much more important to human mental health and spirituality. They didn't consume media; they didn't have our level of cognitive confusion because their thoughts, words, and actions were aligned.

Music and Consumerism

Our ancestors understood that music was evolutionarily engrained in everyone. No, obviously they didn't think with those words, but they knew that everyone had some type of musicality. Music was a part of everyone. That began to change around the beginning of the Renaissance Period. Music started shifting from being a part of daily life to a commercialized entertainment system. The best music was reserved for the wealthy. This led to a new practice of training those who would play for people who could pay them to play. Concerts were held in palaces or other places where only those with enough money could listen. Many years later, audio recording devices and radio further established music as a commercial commodity. Music became something to be created by a few, sold by a few, and consumed by many. But, ironically, the technology that allowed the few to control access to music eventually allowed consumers to freely share music. Moving into the digital age has caused entertainers to progressively return to paid performances as a way to increase their income.

Music In the Bible

Our ancestors used sounds and music for spiritual purposes long before standardized languages. More recently, the ancient Hebrews used melody as a memory aid to recall the entire Torah. According to the Jewish tradition, Moses knew the complete Torah. He taught it to the elders who then taught it to the million or so people of the Exodus. Though they had written language, Moses instructed them to not write the Torah, and the oral tradition was followed for more than a thousand years. Throughout that time, knowledge, customs, and rituals were shared through oral and musical transmission. Even today, many Orthodox rabbis can sing every word by heart. The music combined with oral alliteration and assonance helps to neurologically encode the information. Even the melody itself contains clues to words and interpretations. Some Jewish spiritualists believe that even if a speaker does not understand the meaning of the words, simply saying the words will still bring divine favor because of the sounds the words make.

Bonding

Music is a biblical practice. We are the only earthly beings known to plan rituals, celebrate rituals, and connect rituals to particular belief systems. For example, "Oh Happy Day" by the Edwin Hawkins Singers celebrates the ritual of Jesus washing "sins away" and connects the washing process to a belief system. Believers often sing such important songs with great fervor, but I have yet to see an animal celebrate its sins being washed away. To do so requires brain structures they either do not have or are not developed enough to use the ways humans do. The human brain has a level of neural activity between the rational and emotional centers along with billions of connections with the enlarged prefrontal cortex not seen in any other living being. It is this ability that allows us to place a sense of importance on rituals.

A choir is a common ritual in many church settings. The songs often include two types of group singing: *strict synchrony* and *alternation*. With strict synchrony, singers vocalize (sing) in time with others. The ability to synchronize requires many abilities, one of which is the ability to predict what will happen. In essence, the singers must combine their cognitive operations of memory (involves the hippocampus) and prediction (involves the frontal lobes). Combining the past and the future helps them create a *motor action plan*—a specific set of neurological instructions sent to the motor cortex so they can sing in time with the others.

❝ The human brain has a level of neural activity between the rational and emotional centers... not seen in any other living being. ❞

Alternation still requires performers to create a motor action plan from their memory and prediction centers, but, in this instance, the motor action plan keeps them from synchronizing with the others. They purposely sing out of time. This makes me think of the "Father Abraham" song from Sunday school, where one group begins the song, then another group begins the song from the beginning and out of time from the other group, then another group, and so on. Such a plan often requires greater concentration than normal, so the prefrontal cortex needs to engage more. Clearly, when I was young I had no idea of the increased level of neurological engagement needed to sing that song.

Simply receiving singing lessons can increase oxytocin (trust, social bonding) levels, but it is also released during communal singing. This is one of the reasons for the comforting effect of group singing. A choir tends to consist of a core group of people along with some others who may or may not change each week. Typically, someone will vocally lead the choir in singing. Along the way she might provide some sort of improvisation and then vocally rejoin the choir. Euphoric interjections may be planned, or they may be spontaneous. The audience usually joins the singing, adding strength to the communal bonding. Musicians tend to have experiences similar to the singers but to a greater degree because of increased concentration, timing, movements, and interpretation necessary to play their instrument. The result is a musical power that may lead the most stoic of people to unconsciously tap a finger or foot. Overall the results are that church songs usually promote social bonding within groups of diverse individuals.

Call-and-response is a technique often used in Pentecostal choirs. A choir director or speaker may sing or say a line followed by the congregation, choir, or both, responding. The responders either repeat the sequence or respond in some other preplanned manner. This is a specialized form of nonsynchronous singing, partially predictable and partially unpredictable. The choir and/or audience may have a rough idea of when the next call will happen and what it might be, but they don't know exactly when the call will happen or exactly what their response should be because their responses will depend on the timing and content of the call. This specialized form of nonsynchronous singing provides a basis of predictability that is balanced with unpredictability. When compared to strict synchrony, this delicate balance usually creates a noticeable excitement and greater neural activity in areas involved with prediction, movement, and timing.

Repetition

Repetition of music increases its familiarity, which causes activity in the limbic and paralimbic regions and the reward centers of the brain to activate.[186] Pentecostal churches sometimes have a stigma that they play certain songs too frequently. At times, they even laugh about it among themselves, and some preachers make jokes about it. But repetition is not always a bad thing. Musical repetition has been found in all human cultures, and it is often quite common in choir performances. While we don't usually think much about the repetition of music, we play songs we like over and over. However, compare such behavioral repetition to normal language. Think of the child (me) who repeatedly asks, "Why?" We know it's normal behavior for a child, but we often wonder, *When. Will. It. Ever. STOP?!* Imagine an adult doing the same thing: "Why?" "Why?" "Why?" That's not something we want to hear all day. So why do we accept, expect, and even enjoy musical repetition? Why do we play some songs over and over?[187]

We even mentally play songs repeatedly when there is no external musical source. When we mentally listen to music, it can lead to auditory imagery so vivid that our primary auditory cortex and other brain areas associated with auditory processing increase their activity to fill in the missing musical parts.[188] This is similar to our vision filling in missing information. Additionally, the more familiar we are with the music, the greater the activation of motor planning and sequencing areas of the brain.[189] In other words, the neurological structures involved with planning and anticipation are more easily activated to a higher degree, even if the music is only in our heads.

Earworms

Sometimes we want to *listen* to our *mental music players*. Sometimes we don't. It's normal. But sometimes an annoying little jingle gets stuck on repeat in our heads, and we can't stop it. This had led to the creation of descriptive words and phrases like *earworms, brainworms, stubborn music, tormenting songs,* and *sticky music*.[190] Some disorders such as obsessive-compulsive disorder (OCD), schizophrenia, some behaviors found in autism, and aphasia may produce repetitive behaviors that have been traced to problems in the cortico-basal ganglia loop.[191] While that loop may work as designed and not be associated with a disorder, the songs continue to play, even when we don't want them to. Earworms can bring to life memories, experiences, and special times in our lives, but they can also reach a level that causes them to hinder our daily lives. There is even some evidence that earworms were a thing before we could record music.

In February 1876, Mark Twain published *A Literary Nightmare* in *The Atlantic*. It's a story of how he read a little jingle in a newspaper. The "jingling rhymes" then "took instant and entire possession of [him]." Twain described how the jingle bothered him so greatly that it affected his thinking, work, walking movements, eating, sleeping, reading, hearing, conversations, and social interactions for several days. It was only after he shared the jingle with a reverend friend that the "torturing jingle departed from [his] brain, and a grateful sense of rest and peace descended upon [him]." However, the reverend then had the same problems as Twain. The *virus* had been passed on. It even affected his sermon at a funeral. Like Twain, the reverend was not able to stop the earworm until he passed it on to a group of students.[192]

This little story is interesting for many reasons, one of which is that something similar has probably happened to most of us at some time in our lives. Two more things to note are that (1) the jingle started playing in his head from reading it, not listening to it, and (2) it happened before the ability to record music was invented. Thomas Edison did not invent the phonograph until 1877. Such stories are evidence that the reading of words can be transferred into another sensory domain (transference), such as music within our minds, and that earworms existed before the invention of recording technologies.

Future Memories

We know that familiar music can transport us to other places and remind us of past events, but we don't often realize it can also prompt us to think of possible future events. Think of a person hearing a song that will be played on his or her wedding day. Even though the day has not yet happened, the music has stimulated thoughts and feelings about a future event along with some related mental imagery. Even mentally processing things that have not yet happened and may never happen creates a lot of neurochemical activity. This *auditory imagery* possesses a significant level of robustness because of the heavy neurological activity that occurs when future memories are created by current music. The strength of those connections is increased the more we hear the music, have those related thoughts, and finally experience the event. In essence, the song's effect is increased because it will be memorable before the ceremony happens, during the event, and more so after.

Rap and Country

How many times have we found ourselves hearing a song we don't even like, yet we bob our heads or tap a finger in time to the music? Even though we don't like it, it causes physical reactions and produces auditory imagery. Personally, I despise any type of rap music. While I appreciate the poetic writing abilities of some writers, I refuse to voluntarily listen to it. One of the main reasons is because I was alive during its birth, and I am familiar with the negativity associated with its mass dissemination. So even when a Christian song that includes a small amount of rap begins to play on the radio, I usually say something like, "Stupid music," or, "What a waste of a good song," or, "OMG!" and change to something else. I do this even if I enjoy the non-rap parts of the song. On the positive side of things, this situation often produces some humor. My family sees and hears my frustration as I make irritated comments and stab the buttons on the radio. In the end, we laugh each time. I even act the same when I'm alone in the truck, and I usually smile and think about how my family would be laughing at me.

Certain styles of music can create negative thoughts even if the music is strictly Christian. I'll use rap and country for this example, but the argument applies to other genres as well. Secular rap is so closely aligned with behaviors like violence, nudity, promiscuous sex, drinking, drugging, anti-cop, and so on, that any representation of it in Christian music can cause negative auditory imagery. I have spoken with many people who like rap and many who don't like rap, and both groups agree that Christian songs that use rap causes them to think about things they find inappropriate. The same can be said of other styles like country and rock. Many of us have probably heard the joke that goes something like this:

> *What do you get when you listen to country music in reverse?*
> *You get your wife, your pickup truck, and your dog back.*

Of course some respond to that joke with, "Well, I'll play my music in reverse until I get my dog and my truck back. Then I'll stop playing it."

Time

Another important component of music is time. Music encourages us to think of the past, the present, and the future all at the same time. We can experience the music in the moment, we relive memories of experiences, we have a sense of expectation because we naturally anticipate what will happen next. When we hear a song for the first time and correctly guess what happens next, we get a neurochemical reward for having guessed correctly. I remember the excitement I had as a young person after buying a new album. My ritual was to purposely sit and focus on the entire album without stopping (except to flip the record). Those events remain neurologically embedded, and I now have a much better understanding of why. But the embedding didn't stop with the first listening. As we experience the music in more environments, in multiple situations, in different times, and with different people, our brains connect new memories to old ones. Our neurochemical responses cause our memories to shift from a *moment* to a more *global* level of memorization. As such, our perceptions of the song deepen and change over time.

Presentational and Participatory Music

Turino presents that Pentecostal music often takes two forms: presentational and participatory.[193] In *presentational music*, there is a clear distinction between the performers and the audience. Think rock concerts and classical symphonies. In *participatory music*, everyone is expected to contribute to the music-making. Think campfire songfests and bluegrass. Turino identifies different levels of repetition as distinguishing between presentational and participatory music.

Participatory music tends to have more repetition for a longer time. While Pentecostals may use presentational music at certain times, participatory music is more often the goal. While the audience may not make *formal* music, most do engage in the musical process. They add to the musical tones through their own singing and movements. But no matter which type of musical presentation is used, the repetition of the music still causes neurological effects like embedding memories, providing neurological rewards, and supporting relationships between singers, musicians, and audience members. This can lead to a deeper sense of connection with the music and others.

" If you want to find the secrets of the universe, think in terms of energy, frequency, and vibration. "

Sound and Creation

Nikola Tesla is widely credited for having said, "If you want to find the secrets of the universe, think in terms of energy, frequency, and vibration." (The quote often appears in discussions of spirituality, science, and metaphysics because of his obsession with energy, electricity, and vibrational phenomena. However, there is no definitive primary source [such as a specific book, letter, or speech] proving he said or wrote those exact words.) Take a few moments and think about those words while thinking about the Big Bang. Can you imagine a silent explosion? Our experiences teach us that explosions are accompanied by energy, frequencies, and vibrations that can be both heard and felt. Surely sound accompanied the explosion that was great enough to create all matter and the universe. Today, that sound can be found and studied with the use of specialized instruments. In fact, one physicist claims to have recreated a possible acoustic rendition of the sound that spread throughout the universe after the Bang.[194] Previously, Plato and Pythagoras saw music as essential to understanding the workings of the universe. That view still exists and is even more supported by modern science.

Energy in all of its forms appears to exist within everything in the universe. As such, some physicists believe that the principles of both math and music can help us explore the mysteries of the universe. One of the reasons for this brief discussion of movement in both living and non-living things is made clearer when we look at some biblical events that include sound. For example, look at the biblical account of Creation. On the first day, God created light by speaking, and each subsequent Creation day begins with "God said." I find it intriguing that God used mechanical sound waves to create things like light, trees, water, oxygen, and beings. Each Creation day began with sound waves, those waves led to the creation of objects, and the descendants, or remnants, of those objects continue to contain sound waves.

Cymatics

I sometimes refer to cymatics when I discuss Creation because it is a way that we can visualize some things that sound can create. Cymatics is the study of sound waves and their visual formations. In short, invisible vibrations are made visible. Common items are flexible enough to allow sound waves to move through it—gases, liquids, flexible solids, or membranes. The vibrations cause the surface, or a different media on the surface, to change into visual representations of the frequencies. This is nothing new. Cymatics can be traced back at least a thousand years to when tribes in Africa would sprinkle grains of sand onto drums and beat them as a way to conjure spirits. When we consider some of our previous discussions, it is easy to understand why, since the drum is one of the oldest musical instruments, it is likely that the practice of cymatics was used for much longer than we know.

Da Vinci noticed that dust on a table created shapes when the table vibrated. Galileo noticed something similar on a brass plate that was being scraped. But Ernst Chladni, sometimes known as the father of acoustics, was the first to conduct a major study into the phenomena. Chladni used a violin bow to cause a brass plate covered with sand to vibrate. He found that moving the bow across the edge of the plate in different locations created different geometric figures.

Later, Michael Faraday studied the effects of vibrations on oil, water, and fine grains. Lord Rayleigh, who won the Nobel Prize for physics in 1904, wrote *Theory of Sound*, which contains a chapter titled "Vibrations of Plates."[195] Margaret Watts-Hughes created *voice-figures* by singing into one end of a tube covered on the opposite end with a rubber membrane and various objects like sand, powder, or seeds, and Mary Waller used solid carbon dioxide chips to vibrate plates as she studied the previously mentioned Chladni figures.[196,197]

Hans Jenny was the first to use the term *cymatics* as a derivative of the Greek word *billow* or *wave*. In *Cymatics: The Study of Wave Phenomena* he concluded that cymatics isn't a state of lawless confusion; it's an ever-changing yet structured design.[198] He used many methods to study cymatics and wrote two volumes in which he described and showed cymatic shapes. Alexander Lauterwasser compared the shapes produced by sounds with shapes that naturally occur in nature. His book *Water Sound Images: The Creative*

Music of the Universe provides many pictures of sound representation.[199] In the *Cymatics Experiment in the Great Pyramid,* a membrane was stretched over a sarcophagus, and the resulting images resembled ancient Egyptian hieroglyphs.[200]

There are many interesting components and applications of cymatics, but within the context of this book, I find myself thinking of the biblical account of Creation. Genesis 1:3 starts a series of verses in which "God said" before something was created. According to the biblical account, the sound waves of His voice created the universe. It is common for me to wonder how much of an effect those sound waves had on the organizational process of the universe. Like some of the shapes created by cymatics, I wonder if the universe, and every particle in it, is a cymatic representation of His vocal frequencies as they move through the universal media of space.

Second Law of Thermodynamics

I also wonder if His voice provided a sense of order following the chaos of the Big Bang, similar to how cymatics creates different shapes. Are the frequencies of His voice somehow the confines of natural laws? The Second Law of Thermodynamics tells us that a system left to itself will decay. Think of a rotting log in the woods. However, the universe is not falling apart. In fact, it is quite the opposite. In order to put this in context, I often think of an explosion. Initially, it causes a lot of havoc, but after a short amount of time, the energy is dispersed, and projectiles slow down and fall to the ground. If this universe truly was created by the Big Bang, it resembles an explosion in the initial steps only. There was a lot of chaos immediately following, but the universe has not lost its energy, and its proton and neutron projectiles have not *fallen to the ground.* Clearly, for some reason, the Second Law of Thermodynamics is not having success destroying the universe. This seems to indicate a controlling force.

$E = MC^2$

The concept of energy creating something is easily expressed in Einstein's simple formula of $E = MC^2$. E represents energy, M represents matter, and C^2 represents the speed of light squared. So physical matter was created by an extremely high level of energy. It is estimated that the cosmic energy level immediately following Creation was $1,000,000^2$ (that's 1,000,000 x 1,000,000—or, as scientists often say, a *million million*) greater than it is now. Particle physics tells us that quark confinement occurred 0.000001 (one millionth) of a second after the Big Bang. In that flash of time, all the protons and neutrons for all the matter in the universe were formed. No new ones could form after that brief moment in time. The fallen tree rots, but the protons and neutrons simply transfer into different energies. If we burn the trees, they change into other forms like smoke and ash before later being used as nutrients for something else. The smoke may get caught in the clouds and come back as rain, and the ash may end up as fertilizer. It doesn't matter if we look at this information with a religious or scientific lens, it works with both and is amazing stuff.[201]

Rushing Mighty Wind

One purpose of this short discussion is to allow you to begin to consider some of the effects of sound. Sound waves are in everything and affect the connections of everything. The sound waves that created the universe still affect us billions of years later. They operate both outside of us and within us, even at the cellular level. And since science tells us that sound waves never stop, I often wonder how the Creation frequencies from billions of years ago affect us now. This is just one more example of how science leads to a deeper understanding of biblical events.

> **" The sound waves that created the universe still affect us billions of years later. They operate both outside of us and within us, even at the cellular level...I often wonder how the Creation frequencies from billions of years ago affect us now. "**

I regularly have other questions that are opportunities for further exploration. For example, I question how the "sound from heaven as of a rushing mighty wind filled all of the house" with "the Holy Spirit" in Acts 2. I wonder *how* it happened and *what* physically happened within the attendees. Like some others, I struggled to put it into a present-day, physical-world context that would allow me to gain a better understanding of the processes. The result was that I was hesitant to share the experience with non-believers. Further adding to my hesitancy was my philosophical belief that I, a material creature, should be able to speak about a supernatural experience in a way that relates to our physical world. Scientific data provides me a way to do that.

In Summary

Using the story of a prison chef whose smuggled spices dramatically improved morale and social interactions, I argued that words and lyrics act like "spices" for the brain. Auditory inputs affect us neurochemically (influencing hormones like cortisol and oxytocin), impact genes, shape subconscious perceptions, and plant long-term "seeds" that influence behavior. Hence, the need to make conscious, positive "lyrical diet" choices. Negative lyrics, and more importantly vague lyrics, can cause cognitive confusion. We also briefly looked at music's role in social bonding, noted interesting annoyances (like earworms), and connected the fundamental nature of sound to physics, cymatics, and Creation. Ultimately, controlling what we hear is vital for personal well-being and healthy relationships.

The last few chapters have used data relevant to me and to my former SEBD students to explore some ways visual and auditory data can affect neurological processes and our abilities to connect to ourselves and to others. I mostly used a *negative* color to shade the data I shared. That was done with a purpose—to present to you why we should try to "See No Evil" and "Hear No Evil." Allowing bad into our minds tends to produce bad behaviors, and those behaviors can create stress within us and in our relationships. However, in the following chapters, I begin to use a more *positive* color to explore the following question: If negative data tends to cause negative effects, will we ever be able to have positive relationships?

To answer that question in a way that combines my unique experiences, I focus on one specific behavior in the following chapters. Any behavior would have been an option for discussing *speaking* because all behaviors communicate something. In the end, I decided to discuss a theistic behavior that (1) is influenced by both sight and sound, (2) is considered by some to be controversial, (3) is a highly spiritual experience, (4) includes some previously discussed neurological data, (5) is often considered to be one of the most significant connections a human can have with another being, and (6) is well-known for producing unusual sights and sounds that, in turn, positively affect the behaviors of others.

Holding myself to my pre-established guidelines for this book, I must ask, *Can science provide support for the teaching and practice of a theistic spiritual experience that still, even now, transcends human attempts to explain it?* The simple answer is, *Yes.* While science cannot provide a complete picture, it can add to the picture by providing a perspective for theists and non-theists alike. This may lead to better understanding. The evidence for my "yes" answer is laid out over the next two chapters. The next chapter focuses on some historical foundations of the practice, a description of the practice, and an exploration of some of its purposes. I spend a significant amount of time discussing medical perceptions and definitions of the behavior. We conclude with a discussion of the practice's *place* in relation to some other well-known practices with which it is often confused. I then provide a conceptual model of the process and some combined auditory and visual data.

Introspective Questions for Chapter 7

? **Language's Neurochemical Impact:** Considering that words can trigger neurochemicals affecting stress or trust, how aware are you of the way daily exposure to positive or negative language—in conversations, music, or media—shapes your own stress levels, mood, and feelings towards others?

? **Lyrical Seeds and Behavioral Influence:** Reflecting on a song whose lyrics significantly affected your emotions or behavior, how aware are you of the "seeds" your typical music choices might be planting subconsciously over time? Does this experience motivate you to consciously adjust your "lyrical diet"?

? **Clarity vs. Ambiguity in Lyrics:** Does the author's warning about vague lyrics causing confusion resonate with you? Can you recall being unsettled or misinterpreting ambiguous lyrics? Explain. How might prioritizing lyrical clarity influence your listening habits?

? **Music, Memory, and Repetition's Effect:** What songs act as powerful triggers for your memories and emotions? How does the repetition of music, whether chosen or via an "earworm," affect your mood or focus? What about the power of repeated exposure?

? **Subconscious Influence of Passive Audio:** How might music or media playing passively in your environment be influencing your thoughts or feelings subconsciously, especially if cognitive filters are less engaged? Does recognizing this potential influence make you want to be more intentional about your auditory environment? Why or why not?

? **Music and Social Bonding:** Have you experienced enhanced social connection or trust through communal music-making (like singing in a group)? What role do you believe shared musical experiences play in building bonds?

? **The Power of Seed Conversations and Cumulative Messages:** Like the "seed conversations" mentioned, can you recall brief interactions or comments that significantly influenced your life path? How might this concept apply to the cumulative effect of lyrics or musical messages heard over time?

? **Media Consumption and Well-being:** Have you observed differences in well-being or social interaction in environments with high media consumption compared to low media consumption? How might consciously reducing your own media use potentially affect your mental clarity or happiness?

? **Alignment of Thoughts, Words, and Actions:** Reflecting on Gandhi's quote about harmony between thoughts, words, and actions, how much alignment versus dissonance do you currently perceive in your own life? What role might your media/auditory consumption play in this?

? **Sound, Science, and Spirituality:** How do you perceive the interplay between science and spirituality regarding sound's fundamental nature, as explored through concepts like cymatics, physics, and Creation stories? How does this resonate with your personal worldview?

CHAPTER 8

Hiccups, Broken Clutches, and Perception Splits

Hiccups

As a young Private First Class in the US Army, I was assigned to be the squad grenadier. The M203 grenade launcher attached to my rifle fired a variety of 40mm rounds. Despite the inconvenience of the extra weight, one of the benefits was that I was able to spend extra days at the firing range. Our range had several types of disabled vehicles like trucks, tanks, and jeeps. Some of our favorite targets were the cabs of trucks and the open hatches of tanks or self-propelled howitzers. During free time we would pick a vehicle and have competitions to see who could lob a high explosive or incendiary round into the top of a truck or open hatch of a tank or howitzer. Truck cabs were cool, but all of that energy being forcefully funneled back up through the open hatch of a tank or howitzer is an impressive sight.

There were also window- and doorframes on the range. Most of the time we fired gas or smoke rounds through those. They were *lame* rounds and didn't create an impressive show like the explosives and incendiaries, so all of those made it through the open windows. But something supernatural happened when we were supposed to fire high-explosive and incendiary rounds through the same windows. An invisible force kept pushing those rounds toward the walls around the open windows or doorways. Strange magic, indeed. The carpenters who built the frames were not happy with us.

We also spent quite a bit of time firing illumination rounds. It can be tricky to fire them effectively during windy conditions because of their small parachutes. One day we had a stiff wind blowing into our faces all day. The range master had put off firing them in hopes that the wind would die down. No luck. Shortly before it was time to leave, he told us to fire all of the illumination rounds directly into the dirt a safe distance in front of us. We were happy to do so because watching them float down wasn't too exciting, but aiming at fire ant beds and watching them burn was another story. In reality, we all knew this was important because it had not rained for a long time, and behind us was a road and on the other side of that was a very dry pine tree forest. Before giving us the command to fire, we all had to raise our hands so that the range master could verify we understood his commands.

Some veterans will begin to smile when I say, *There's always one.* Admittedly I was the *one* more than once, but thankfully on that day it was Private Herbst*. At some point in time between raising his hand to indicate he understood the command to fire into the ground, lowering his hand, hearing "Fire!," and pulling the trigger, he *raised* his M203 and fired his illumination round high into the air. As soon as he did so he began to yell, "No!" as his brain re-engaged and he realized his mistake. As he loudly cussed himself, most of us laughed as we watched the parachute drift over the road and land in the woods. He received legendary *corrective measures* as the rest of us fired the remainder of the illumination rounds into any fire ant beds we could find and waited on the fire department to arrive.

The point to this humorous vignette is that Private Herbst had a mental *hiccup* at the wrong time. He was a good soldier who was known by all of us to be intelligent and levelheaded. He had simply momentarily *checked out* from the situation. Even though we had fun at the range, we understood the dangers. We once made merciless fun of a fellow soldier who had to have shrapnel removed from his back, glutes, and hamstrings because he had mentally *hiccuped* too. The hand grenade exploded as he ran away. He was just a very, very, very slow runner. Besides, he should have used the foxhole to protect himself instead of running away—but that's a whole other story. Private Herbst had heard the verbal commands over the loudspeakers, and he raised his hand high in the air to non-verbally communicate that he had received the message, understood it, and would obey the command. Then, his brain *hiccuped.*

Private Herbst's mental hiccup can be viewed as a normal dissociation. A momentary *checking out.* We all do something similar: *Where did I put my keys? I just had them. Why did I come into this room? What was I telling you?* While those events may increase with age, it is not automatically a sign of a pathology. I don't know why Private Herbst dissociated. Maybe he thought about his girlfriend. Maybe he thought about his coming deployment. Maybe he started playing a song in his mind. Maybe, like the rest of us, he wanted a nap. Whatever the reason, his hiccup was not taken as an indication of mental health problems.

Most of you are probably at least slightly familiar with post-traumatic stress disorder (PTSD), so let's look at it in relation to dissociation (chaos). The US Department of Veterans Affairs (VA) utilizes the DSM-5 in its evaluation of veterans' mental health, and, over time, research led the VA to support a subtype of PTSD that focuses on the two dissociations of *depersonalization* and *derealization* and is now included in the DSM-5-TR.[202] PTSD is included in VAs trauma and stress-related disorders section. Some of its diagnostic criteria includes being exposed to death, threatened with death, actual or threatened serious injury, or actual or threatened sexual violence. Those

> **" Dissociation serves as the primary shield against intense traumatic experiences. "**

events may have happened through direct exposure, witnessing an event, or indirect exposure to details of the trauma. Some dissociative symptoms (flashbacks, amnesia, etc.) are included in the core PTSD symptoms. Concerning veterans, VA notes that dissociation serves as the primary shield against intense traumatic experiences.[203] Dissociation can be a mental protective measure against greater psychological stress.

Mentally reliving a traumatic event is neurobiologically different from depersonalizing and derealizing an event. Those who *depersonalize* or *derealize* show *increased* activation in both the medial prefrontal cortex (mPFC) and the rostral anterior cingulate cortex (rACC), but at the same time, activity in both the amygdala and the right insular context *decreases*. However, mentally *reliving* a traumatic event does the opposite—it *reduces* activation in both the mPFC and the rACC while *increasing* activity in both the amygdala and right insular cortex. Some functions of the mPFC are emotional regulation, motivation, and cognitive processes; some functions of the rACC relate to emotional and cognitive functions and conflict resolution; some functions of the amygdala include memory, decision-making, and emotional responses; and some functions of the insular cortex involve emotions, empathy, motor control, cognition, and compassion.[204,205]

So what do all of those fancy words mean? Too much *dissociation* leads to *overmodulation* (too much control) of emotional responses—the brain's neurological clutch engages too much and over-limits the limbic system, so there is not enough reaction. On the other hand, mentally *reliving* a traumatic event may lead to *undermodulation* (not enough control) of emotional responses—the neurological clutch fails to engage enough to adequately limit the limbic system, so there is too much reaction. Neither action is perfect. The first process does not allow enough emotion, while the second allows too much emotion. Too much of either one leads to failure of healthy emotional regulation. Therefore, emotional conflicts are never *healed* in the veteran or other traumatized individual.

Wyatt's World

While Private Herbst's hiccup was considered normal, Wyatt's* hiccups were not. I share a snippet of his story to demonstrate a clearly malfunctioning neurological clutch and its relation to dissociation and association. Mostly, this story is about too much association (undermodulation of emotions).

Wyatt did not live with his parents. Both were in the Air Force and had placed him in a group home. He was in my classroom because he was severely emotionally/behaviorally disturbed. Some of his other limitations were fetal alcohol syndrome, poor motor skills (especially in his hands), dysphasia (difficulty swallowing, so he drooled most of the time), Broca's aphasia (could understand what I said, but he struggled to speak fluently), damage to his prefrontal cortex, and more. He had a long list. The damage to his prefrontal cortex had happened after birth and was the result of physical abuse. Wyatt claimed he remembered when it happened.

Some of Wyatt's main problems in school resulted from poor impulse control, learning disabilities, cognitive awareness, and spatial awareness. Though Wyatt had some mental processing challenges, he clearly understood that he did not live with his parents, but his siblings did, and that his siblings did not have any of the physical and mental challenges he did; they were *normal*. He also understood that his limitations were because his mother drank alcohol while pregnant and because she abused him after birth. He understood, and commonly voiced, that he would be "normal like my brother and sisters" if not for his mother's behaviors. Wyatt was the oldest, and Mom had *learned* what not to do as she raised him. That was a lot of stress that added up to severe emotional and behavioral issues. Throw in his cognitive issues, and there was never a dull day with him.

My first experience with Wyatt's lack of impulse control (damaged neurological clutch) occurred on his first day in my class. I had read through his file, but there was little information to be gleaned from his treatment records, so I was learning as we went along. His lack of impulse control was the first behavior I recognized. I gave him an easy spelling test as an evaluation tool. He had made a good grade, but it was not 100 percent. As I was placing the graded test on his desk, he looked at it and tried to stab my hand with a pencil. Fortunately I was watching, and I have cat-like reflexes. He then leaped from his desk toward me. My first reaction was to push him away from me.

As Wyatt got up from the floor, I decided to let his behavior play out. I wanted to see what he would do. It didn't take long. He got up and walked quickly toward me with his arms out, grabbed me in a bear hug, and started sobbing. "I'm sorry, I'm sorry, I'm sorry," he said as he drooled and snotted on my shoulder. Wyatt wasn't worried about his new bruises; he was worried that he had hurt me. We talked later and I learned that his trigger had been that he legitimately cared about his grades. When he had seen a grade that was not 100 percent, he became angry at himself, and his neurological clutch could not stop him from performing the first behavior that came to mind, and because of his abusive past, violence was his first thought. However, on the other end of the spectrum, he was a very caring person, and because his clutch was damaged, his attempts to *make it right* were over the top. I had a lot of messy laundry until he graduated.

If a person was close to him, then that person was the focus, so I made sure no students were close by. He might throw a book at me then start crying and run to hug me. He was known to try to hit me with my coffee cup, then start crying and try to hug me. I had to find a place behind my desk for it. He might simply attack me with his fists, and then while I was physically restraining him on the floor, he would start crying and screaming "I'm sorry," asking if he could hug me. Despite his violent behaviors, Wyatt was unlike most of my students because of his gift of emotionally connecting with others. He truly cared about the well-being of others. He was definitely a hugger, and because of his dysphasia his hugs usually came with a wet shoulder that quickly dried to a white crust. He had a huge heart and a laugh that could make everyone else laugh with him. He simply had a difficult time modulating the violence he had learned from the abuse and a difficult time modulating his concern for others. He could immediately switch from one extreme to the other.

If no one else was near, Wyatt's poor impulse control was directed at himself. He might bang his head on the floor or concrete wall hard enough to split the skin. Or drag his fingernails across his forearm until the skin peeled back and blood started to flow. He stabbed himself in the back of his hand many times. One time he stripped to his underwear, removed one of his long, white tube socks, wrapped it around his neck, and pulled it tight. I could see it was a slipknot, so I stood and watched as his face changed color and he stared at me as if to say, *Aren't you going to stop me?*

I interpreted his visual messages and responded verbally: "When you pass out, you won't be able to hold it [the sock] tight anymore, so after you fall down you'll let it go and start breathing."

He paused for a while, then unwrapped the sock, redressed, hugged me, and cried on my shoulder, covering it with snot. We brought the other students back into the room and continued with class. (Yes, he did have some consequences for his bad behavior.)

I understand why you may not agree with some of my methods, and I didn't share that story about Wyatt so you can criticize. I shared it as a way to help you understand how what I was learning about the brain influenced my subconscious. There was not time to consciously think about all of my options in the sock situation. Too much was going on. My aide and I were getting other students safely out of the room while keeping an eye on Wyatt, other staff were running in to help (we had a process to notify all staff when there was a violent situation so anyone that was free would run to help), we were moving any movable objects from around Wyatt (even desks) in case there was a physical restraint, and so on. The point is, my remark about him passing out and then starting to breathe came from my subconscious mind. I was as surprised as Wyatt and the other staff. Where had that come from?

Over the next few weeks, I began to try and understand what had been going on in my subconscious. Do I think it was the correct thing to say in the moment? Absolutely—based on my past experiences, my professional knowledge at the time, what I knew of everyone else in the room, and our environment. It was without question the correct behavior modification tactic for that situation. Other staff had been positioned around Wyatt just in case he passed out. I was confident he wouldn't pass out, but we could lower him to the floor if he did. In general, two broad subconscious understandings were important for my comment: his emotional right brain was overwhelming his logical left brain because his damaged prefrontal cortex was not able to modulate his emotions. Wyatt truly cared about others and himself, he just needed time for his damaged neurological clutch to engage and give the logical side of his brain enough time to counterbalance his emotional side.

My comment that he would begin to breathe after passing out was a seemingly heartless comment that interrupted his uncontrollable thought processes. Like many things that come from our left brains, it seemed cold, but the statement was actually true—he *would* begin to breathe again. My comment simply refocused Wyatt's thinking: *Why isn't he emotional?* or, *Why isn't he trying to stop me?* or, *Does he care?* or, *Will I really start to breathe again?* or *What if I hit my head?* and so on. That interruption directed his attention from his emotions and gave his damaged prefrontal cortex time to engage and begin to balance his behaviors.

This conflict became a relationship builder and a positive behavior management tool. For example, a few days later, Wyatt began to get upset. I said, "What color are your stripes today?" He looked at me curiously, then down his leg as he pulled his pant leg up to his knee and showed me his long, white socks with a red and a blue stripe around the top. He caught on, and when he looked back up, he was smiling and said, "You got me." We chuckled, and he was soon back to work. The joke grew into things like me giving him a package of ankle socks so he wouldn't have to pull his pants up so high. I knew he wouldn't wear them because he loved his white knee socks, but he did keep them in his desk.

> ** *This conflict became a relationship builder and a positive behavior management tool.* **

Sometimes I would ask him something like, "Are you wearing red and blue stripes again?" He'd smile and pull up his pant leg so I could see the stripe colors for that day. If they were yellow and brown, I'd say something like, "Did you wear those just for me?" or, "Yes! My favorite!" just to have some friendly banter. He'd say, "Nope, red and blue."

One time when he started getting upset, I sent him to Mrs. Chloe* to show her his socks. He was laughing as he took the hall pass, and we could hear them laughing next door. Did it always work? No. When it didn't, I would try another tool from my toolbox. There were many events with Wyatt, and they all followed the general pattern of a behavioral disturbance followed by our relationship improving.

Despite Wyatt's cognitive limitations, he was not dumb, and he enjoyed learning a little bit about why he acted the way he did. I taught him that he was good at making friends because the right side of his head worked well. When we talked about it he would point to the right side of his head. He had problems with math because the left side of his head did not work as well, and as we talked he would poke the left side of his head. He had a hard time stopping bad behaviors because the front part of his brain, the part that was right behind his forehead, was *hurt*. Sometimes he would tap his forehead with a book or pencil eraser as we talked. When he calmed down after violent outbursts, he started making comments like, "It ain't work" as he pointed to his forehead. Sometimes he'd tap it with a pen or pencil for quite a while. Wyatt's greatest mental health healing came from the peace of mind he got from understanding *why* he acted out. He had often thought: *I'm crazy.* Learning he was not led to some comfort.

Wyatt and I developed a close relationship. I tend to be a loner, so, honestly, much of our relationship developed because of his desire for close human relationships. I often think of him as a neuron. Individual neurons seek connections with other neurons. The more connections they make, and the more they are used, the greater their chances for survival (evolution). Neurons that do not connect, or are unused, are pruned. They are hauled away to the trash. Taking that to a larger scale, a healthy brain confined to itself will not remain healthy for long. Moving to an even larger scale, the concept applies to humans. Wyatt the individual human desperately wanted to connect to others, and as we worked through his difficult behaviors our relationship grew closer; the behaviors that caused disruption strengthened our relationship.

I shared part of Wyatt's story to hopefully provide you with a clear contrast between Private Herbst's normally functioning brain and Wyatt's legitimately damaged brain. Both produced behaviors that had good and bad effects on others. For example, Herbst's very innocuous hiccup set the woods on fire, and he received significant *negative reinforcement*, but he also provided a lot of laughter and material for endless teasing. And he often laughed at himself.

> **"A healthy brain confined to itself will not remain healthy for long."**

Wyatt's very frequent emotional behaviors often interrupted most of the school, but they also provided a tremendous amount of material we could use to build relationships. For both, their conflicts led to stronger connections.

Another reason I share Wyatt's story is to introduce another topic: *too much association can be a bad thing.* Wyatt's dissociations were within the normal range, but his associations were extreme to the point of physical and mental harm. Sure, like everyone else, he sometimes forgot his pencil, but his reaction is what made him so different from others. He was very concerned about his actions, and he wanted to do well all of the time. He might throw his books and pull some hair out of his head (literally) because he was angry at himself for failing to make sure he had his pencil. Clearly he had endured an extreme amount of abuse when he made mistakes. One of his positive behaviors was his willingness to take responsibility for his actions. Behaviorally, he was far ahead of other students who *never* took responsibility.

We spent a lot of time talking about the idea that some mistakes are completely normal. In other words, I wanted him to learn to dissociate from some emotions. Forgetting a pencil was not the end of the world. At times I would purposely make mistakes so I could model some appropriate ways to handle them. For example, if I was leaving the room for an errand, I might *accidentally* leave behind some papers. After my classroom aide started teaching, I might interrupt his lesson with a grand entrance and pretend to be a little frustrated and, while smiling, make some statements like, "Forgot my papers," "Late again," "Wyatt, it's your fault for not reminding me," or, "Mr. Clinton* [classroom aide], will you give him a detention for me?" Wyatt usually smiled and responded in his ever-present broken speech patterns (Broca's aphasia) with something like, "Nope, that's your fault. You gotta remember your own stuff," or, "Gotcha!" Mr. Clinton, Wyatt, and some of the other students knew the purpose for my disruptions and usually continued to tease me as I rushed out of the room.

When I returned to the room, if he was still there, Wyatt might just look at me and smile. He usually did that if he was concentrating hard on his work. Or he might smile and wag a crooked index finger (broken from abuse) at me if he was mildly concentrating on his work. Or when he absolutely did not want to work, he might chuckle and say something sarcastically humorous like, "Where's your papers?" I might respond by waving them in the air, or I might respond by stopping and acting like I was going to go back to get them. Goodness gracious, I could write an entire book on Wyatt alone. I loved that dude. But don't get the impression he was my only student. Every student in my classroom had their own uniquely traumatic set of circumstances and distinctive personalities and also needed to learn appropriate levels of dissociation and association and correspondingly appropriate relationships.

The point to these two vignettes is to help clarify something we will explore in the coming pages: Too much dissociation (conflict) can be harmful, just like too much association (connection) can be harmful. We need appropriate levels of both to be mentally and behaviorally healthy. Why is this important? Previous chapters have explored how sight and vision can affect our subconscious and conscious mental states and, by extension, what we speak with our behaviors and with our voices. Too much *speaking* of one or the other, or both, will hinder relationships.

We continue with an overview of how medical *bibles* qualify dissociation and association. Then, because neurotheology is a component of our discussion, we apply them to some spiritual practices.

DSM-5-TR

The non-conversational detail presented in the following pages is necessary for our discussion, so please bear with me. One purpose is to show how medical manuals classify and describe dissociation as a pathology. Feel free to skip to the *Dissociation and Media* section if you have narcolepsy.

Dissociative disorders, as described in the DSM-5-TR, involve disruptions in the normal functioning of core experiential elements, including consciousness, memory, personal identity, emotions, perception of the world, body awareness, motor skills, and behavior.[206] Regarding stress, the DSM-5-TR states that dissociative disorders are often the result of a variety of psychological stressors. It also places dissociative disorders next to stress and trauma-related disorders as a way to reflect the close relationships between them. Some risks for dissociative pathologies may include single-event trauma; cumulative trauma; neglect; sexual, physical, and emotional abuse; and trauma or torture associated with captivity (e.g., prisoners of war, human trafficking). Dissociative disorders are broken down into five sections:

1. *Regarding feelings of detachment (Depersonalization/derealization disorder):* This condition involves ongoing or repeating sensations where an individual feels disconnected or as if things are unreal, either in relation to their own self and body (depersonalization) or to their external environment and the world around them (derealization).

2. *Concerning memory loss (Dissociative amnesia):* This is marked by an individual's incapacity to remember significant personal details or life events, a lapse in memory more substantial than everyday forgetfulness. This memory failure might pertain to a particular period, specific elements of an occurrence, or more extensive portions of their personal history and sense of who they are.

3. *Regarding multiple identities (Dissociative identity disorder—DID):* This disorder is recognized by the presence of at least two distinct self-states or identities, or by episodes where an individual feels as though they are possessed. These manifestations are coupled with recurring gaps in memory. In cases resembling possession, the person may act as if an outside force or entity has assumed command; these experiences are distressing, occur against the person's will, and are involuntary, setting them apart from the majority of culturally or religiously accepted possession experiences found globally that do not align with this diagnosis.

4. *For other specific instances of dissociation (Other specified dissociative disorder):* This classification is used when an individual exhibits prominent dissociative symptoms that cause notable personal distress or impair their ability to function, but the overall pattern of these symptoms doesn't precisely fit the full diagnostic requirements for any of the more narrowly defined dissociative conditions.

5. *For unspecified instances of dissociation (Unspecified dissociative disorder):* This category is used in cases where a clinician opts not to detail why a specific dissociative disorder diagnosis is not applicable or when there is too little information to make a precise diagnosis, such as in urgent medical settings.

ICD-11

The *International Statistical Classification of Diseases and Related Health Problems-11* (ICD-11) is published by the World Health Organization and is used by thirty-five countries.[207] The ICD-11 indicates that *dissociative disorders* are characterized by "involuntary disruption or discontinuity in the normal integration of one or more of the following: identity, sensations, perceptions, affects, thoughts, memories, control over bodily movements, or behaviour." This category is broken down into eight categories (as opposed to the DSM's five) and results in "significant impairment in personal, family, social, educational, occupational or other important areas of functioning."

1. *Regarding neurological-like dissociative symptoms (Dissociative neurological symptom disorder):* This condition manifests as physical movement, sensory experiences, or cognitive issues that suggest an involuntary interruption in how these bodily and mental functions normally operate together. These symptoms do not fit the pattern of any recognized nervous system illness, other psychological or behavioral conditions, or another general medical problem.

2. *Concerning memory loss (Dissociative amnesia):* This involves a difficulty in retrieving important personal memories, particularly those related to recent traumatic or highly stressful occurrences, with the memory loss being more significant than ordinary forgetfulness.

3. *Regarding trance states without possession (Trance disorder):* This is characterized by a notable change in an individual's usual

level of awareness or a feeling of losing one's typical sense of personal identity. The person experiences repeated, or a single extended and involuntary, significant alteration in their state of consciousness, taking the form of a trance, but without the sense of being controlled by an external entity.

4. *Regarding trance states with a sense of possession (Possession trance disorder):* This involves a pronounced shift in an individual's awareness, where their normal sense of identity is seemingly taken over by an outside, "possessing" identity. The person's actions or physical movements are felt to be directed by this possessing agent; these episodes are involuntary, unwelcome, and are not recognized as an accepted element of a shared cultural or religious practice.

5. *Regarding multiple distinct identities (Dissociative identity disorder):* This condition is marked by a fractured sense of self, where two or more separate personality states exist. These distinct states repeatedly assume control of the individual's consciousness and how they function, and typically, there are episodes of amnesia where the individual does not recall experiences had by the other personality states.

6. *Regarding partially distinct identities (Partial dissociative identity disorder):* This involves a disruption in identity where multiple distinct personality states are present. However, one primary personality state is usually dominant, though it is subject to unwelcome interferences or influences from one or more of the other, non-dominant personality states, referred to as dissociative intrusions.

7. *Regarding feelings of unreality about self or surroundings (Depersonalization/derealization disorder):* This is defined by ongoing or recurring sensations of depersonalization (feeling that one's self is strange, unreal, or being detached from one's own thoughts, feelings, body, or actions) and/or derealization (perceiving other people, objects, or the external world as strange, unreal, dreamlike, distant, foggy, lifeless, lacking color, visually distorted, or feeling detached from one's environment).

8. *Regarding dissociation due to other medical conditions (Secondary dissociative syndrome):* This is diagnosed when prominent dissociative symptoms (like feeling detached from oneself or reality) are present and are believed to be the direct physiological

outcome of a general medical condition that is not classified as a mental or behavioral disorder. These symptoms are not better explained by delirium, another mental or behavioral disorder, or as a psychologically driven reaction to a severe medical illness.

Dissociation and Media

Frequently, medical literature indicates that dissociation is a complicated mental health problem that involves an interruption or a confusion in how the brain processes information. It can have such a negative effect that it may influence our sense of identity, perception of time, memories, feelings, sense of reality, and thoughts. It may be caused by situations like trauma (e.g., abuse, combat), hypnosis (to deal with trauma, addictive behaviors, etc.), meditation (religious and secular), and certain drugs (e.g., alcohol, prescriptions, LSD). However, it should be noted that hypnosis, meditation, and some drugs also fit into a treatment category. Dissociation is also linked to other mental health conditions, such as schizophrenia, PTSD, acute stress, affective and eating disorders, OCD, and depression.

" Dissociation is a complicated mental health problem that involves an interruption or a confusion in how the brain processes information. "

Media had huge effects on my students' perceptions of dissociation. Ironically, I was surprised to see how some movies could influence some who did not like to talk about their dissociative tendencies to begin to talk about them. Dissociative Identity Disorder (DID), originally known as *multiple personality disorder*, began to grow in popularity after the Academy Award-winning *The Three Faces of Eve*.[208] It is a film about a young girl who developed multiple personality disorders because of abuse. *Sybil* presents a story about a female who developed multiple personalities in response to physical abuse.[209] *Primal Fear* is about Aaron, an altar boy, who had (was he faking?) DID.[210] *Fight Club* won eleven Academy Awards and depicts the narrator (main character) as having multiple personality disorders.[211] During the day he is a mild-mannered middle-class individual who has anxiety and insomnia. His stress eventually leads to the development of Tyler, who is his alternate personality and is free from social and psychological norms such as fear. *Primal Fear* and *Fight Club* were the most influential during my teaching years. *Split* follows Kevin, who has twenty-three distinct identities caused by childhood trauma, and those alters interact with each other as a twenty-fourth alter ("The Beast") develops.[212] These movies, and others, have encouraged the popularity of dissociation and its close connection to mental pathology.

Trance States (Part 1)

A type of dissociation sometimes related to spiritual practices is *possession trance* (PT). PTs can lead to alterations in how a person's mind operates—affecting their consciousness, self-awareness, unique character, or other mental processes—and these may be accompanied by related changes in their physical actions. Three general categories represent different levels of cultural acceptance: (1) it is involuntary and feared (e.g., demonic possession), (2) it is initially involuntary but later gains acceptance through ceremonial acceptance (e.g., zār), and (3) it is voluntary and intentionally summoned (e.g., voodoo).[213]

In addition to movies about DID, students were also interested in horror movies and were heavily influenced by them. The scarier the better. One of their favorite types was demonic possession. If we look back at the DSM-5-TR and the ICD-11 we see references to different types of possessions as disorders. Admittedly, both mention that some possessions are part of religious practices, but those don't get as much attention. For example, the DSM-5-TR lists *possession form identities* under *dissociative identity disorder,* and the ICD-11 lists *possession trance disorder* under *dissociative disorders.* A characteristic of both is that the possession is unwanted and causes behavioral changes. Horror flicks with demonic possession were one of the most popular genres among my students. Ironically, those led to many discussions about religion. *The Exorcist* was one of the most popular.[214]

Interestingly, our discussions about *The Exorcist* led us to discover that many Satanists, whom we initially assumed would believe in demonic possession, don't even believe in the existence of Satan as an entity. Initially, we were surprised and confused. How could they be Satanists if they didn't believe in Satan? Our confusion was cleared when we learned that many of them are atheists, and their concept of Satan is a representation of individualism, liberty, and potential. This helped us understand because if they don't believe in supernatural beings like God, they shouldn't believe in a demonic entity either. Good for them for not being hypocritical and for being philosophically consistent in their idea of the supernatural. Despite our discovery that two of the largest Satanic organizations are atheistic, we also learned about a minority group called Theistic Satanists who do believe in the existence of God, Satan, and other spiritual entities.[215]

Becker indicates that the Catholic church may be partially at fault for the popularity of possessions because of its focus on demonic trances and exorcisms.[216] The church has tests to detect demonic possession, and they are sometimes depicted in media. Unlike some Satanic religions, the Christian or Catholic traditions do not want or tolerate demonic possession. They are often thought of as vindictive relatives, demons, or even Satan himself. Demonic possession is considered an illness that must be removed or cured. The exorcism process reveals the presence of the demon, and the exorcist attempts to expel it. Possession is nothing new. There are written records of possessions going back thousands of years. The Bible documents some accounts as well. Legion (Mark 5) is possibly the most well-known.

According to Goodman, possession-like experiences may be signaled by a wide range of intense physical, behavioral, and psychological disturbances. These can include chronic sleeplessness, elevated body temperature, agitation, and impulsive wandering. Some individuals might engage in bizarre eating behaviors—either consuming repulsive or non-food items compulsively, or refusing to eat entirely, leading to severe weight loss. A strong, unpleasant body odor may be present, along with excessive drooling. Physical symptoms might escalate from uncontrollable shaking to full-body seizures or states of muscle rigidity that resemble catatonia. Additional indicators include extreme abdominal pain, sudden screaming episodes, tooth grinding, emotional breakdowns like continuous crying, abnormal physical strength, and dramatic changes in facial appearance. Aggressive actions may emerge—toward oneself, potentially to the point of self-harm or suicidal ideation, or toward others. In such cases, an alternate voice may speak—deep, raspy, and distinct from the person's normal tone—sometimes laced with vulgar outbursts or proclamations that appear prophetic or supernatural in nature.[217]

Students were also interested in movies that included other types of possessions. Many of them liked movies with voodoo because they often included some type of vigilante justice. Voodoo dolls could be used to torture then kill the rapist or murderer. Students could relate to wanting vigilante justice because of their abusive situations. Though voodoo can be used for good, my students rarely associated it with that aspect. They tended to want revenge. Voodoo is one of the most documented forms of wanted possession, and the Creole population of Haiti is one of the most well-known groups who ask a spirit to possess their bodies.[218] The most common reasons are for healing, divination, protection from spirits and magic, or appeasing of ancestral spirits.

Some shamanic practices also include expected trance states. Vitebsky identified a range of typical physical behaviors that may signify the beginning of a trance state. These signs may include involuntary bodily reactions such as trembling, shuddering, or developing goosebumps; episodes of fainting, falling, or exhibiting extreme tiredness like yawning and lethargy; and more intense responses like convulsions or foaming at the mouth. Other markers are visibly protruding eyes, an insensitivity to temperature or pain, physical tics, loud or heavy breathing, and a vacant, glassy stare.[219] Some of these may also be seen in demonic possession, but the difference is that shamanic trances tend to be controlled and invited and used for good.

> " Trance states may be related to multiple personality disorders, psychological stress, or simply nutritional deficiencies. "

Somewhat different, zār spirit possession is considered to be an illness. It can't be cured, but it may be pacified.[220] The zār spirits belong to a class known as *jinn* ("genie") and are supported by the Quran. Boddy wrote that, even though a zār spirit possession is not wanted by the human, the spirit at least shows concern for its host while it inflicts some level of suffering. Ironic, I know. If a balance can be found, it becomes something of a mutually beneficial relationship that is tolerated and may even be used for some good.

One difference between voodoo, shamanic trances, zār, and demonic possessions is that voodoo and shamanic trances welcome possession, but in zār and demonic possessions it is unwelcome. The first two ceremonies invite a possession, while zār ceremonies try to appease the possessing spirit. A similarity between them is that ceremonies for voodoo, shamanic trances, and zār are structured—unlike demonic possessions. An important consideration for this discussion is the recognition that the continued pathologizing of any spirit possession has led to several anthropological theories suggesting that trance states may be related to multiple personality disorders, psychological stress, or simply nutritional deficiencies.[221,222,223]

If we were to consider these experiences using terms like *least acceptable* and *most acceptable* and place them on a continuum, using the perceptions of the majority of the world's population, it would look something like Figure 8. In terms of behavioral consequences, *demonic* produces the most negative, followed by zār and *voodoo*, respectively. *Shamanic* trances are usually depicted as producing more positive behaviors.

Demonic	Zār	Voodoo	Shamanic
least acceptable			*most acceptable*

Figure 8. Author's conceptual model illustrating the perceived relative acceptability of trance states based on author's interpretation of data presented above.

182

Christian PTs seem to receive more ridicule in secular settings than do others. Make no mistake about my stance on humor—I love it. It can be a wonderful *tool*. I am of the *pre-woke* age when we laughed at everyone. Yes, even ourselves. And I still laugh at myself and others. But, ridicule has never been allowed. I recently heard a comedian who was Muslim, and his college roommate was Jewish. He talked about how well they got along and laughed at their own cultural practices and those of the other. He also spent some time telling jokes about how much he missed his Jewish friend. Honestly, it was heartwarming. They laughed at, and with, each other, but they didn't ridicule.

One Monday some of my students were full of laughter about a movie that had been released over the weekend. Parts of it made fun of some Christian possession trances. Over the next few weeks, their laughter subsided somewhat, and they began to logically wonder about the practices. So when we had some time, we began to discuss different PTs, including the ones from the previous paragraphs. We looked at differences and similarities. One thing that intrigued me about those discussions was the almost universal agreement that students would not laugh at some of the religions that created fear in them. For example, they were less likely to laugh at demonic possessions because, they said, "I don't want them to get me." As we talked about zār and voodoo there was less fear, so more laughter. Shamanic trances came next, and Christian practices opened the door to laughter because they were "not worried about them getting [them]."

The parts of the movie (and some other movies that came up during discussions) they found to be the most humorous was speaking in tongues. It was easy because, as we have seen, PTs are usually considered to be a type of mental pathology. Though the DSM-5-TR and the ICD-11 make allowances for non-pathological trances if they are a part of a religious or cultural practice, they are often overlooked. Add that many do not understand the purpose of tongues, and the likelihood that some will ridicule it grows. I agree that it is easier to discern the purposes for demonic, zār, and voodoo possessions because the reasons are usually clearly stated, and the behaviors and results are usually observable, even by those who don't understand what is happening.

I found it interesting that most students thought speaking in tongues was limited to Christianity, like I did when I was their age. Granted, Christianity is the most common association, but their interests grew as they learned a little more about the history of tongues and, since I was an English teacher, some of the different language intricacies. Documents spanning thousands of years and from around the world contain references to *glossolalia*. In 853 BC, four hundred prophets spoke in a frenzied state at Samaria's gate,[224] and some references connected to Plato deal with whispered words and expressions of profound joy.[225] In Ancient Egypt, magicians received revelations from gods and then shared them using "senseless noises,"[226] and some mystics from regions like India and China were known to speak in unclear or fragmented ways while communing with spiritual entities.[227]

Speaking in tongues is not unique to Christianity. It is observed in various non-Christian religions and indigenous spiritual practices worldwide, including North American Indian groups like the Peyote cult and Haida, shamanistic traditions in African Sudan, West Africa's Shango cult, Haiti's Voodoo cult, South American and Australian aboriginal shamans, subarctic North American and Asian indigenous peoples, Greenland shamans, Borneo's Dyaks, Ethiopia's zār cult, Siberian shamans, South America's Chaco Indians, Andean curanderos, Sudan's Dinka, African Thonga shamans, and Tibetan monks.[228]

Spirit language has also been observed across diverse cultures, including the Chukchee, Asiatic Eskimos, Lapps, Yakuts, Tungus, Samoyeds, and Hudson Bay Eskimos, where shamans, such as those in the Ainu religion, act as conduits for divine messages, speaking without recalling the words. Similarly, Semang pygmy shamans use spirit language to communicate with spiritual entities, the Gusi cult priestess employs a sacred language exclusive to her and the spirits, Micronesian priests channel spirits in a distinct, otherworldly tongue, and some East Greenland Eskimo shamans use a mystical language in rituals.[229]

Additionally, tongues are occasionally encountered among more well-known religions that are not traditionally associated with the practice. Some Islamic mystics,[230] some Catholics,[231] and, according to my previously discussed student Barb, some Pantheists engage in the practice. Joseph Smith listed the "gift of tongues" and "interpretation of tongues" as elements of the foundational beliefs of Mormonism.[232] As students learned some of this history related to tongues, and some of its breadth, they grew more intrigued and were less likely to laugh or ridicule.

However, learning that some evil spirits use spiritual language and that some humans can fall under demonic control created concern in some and, I must admit, happiness in some others.[233] There are some behavioral and linguistic differences between religious and non-religious tongues, but to summarize some of them very broadly, "[d]emonic glossolalia is characteristically harsher or more chaotic than the Holy Ghost counterpart."[234] The "harsher or more chaotic" elements of demonic glossolalia are common to behavior and linguistics alike. Sometimes, a spirit inhabiting a person will use the person's voice to declare its possession or control over the individual.[235]

In contrast, the "Holy Ghost counterpart" does not forcefully control, or communicate with or through, the person—the speaker must seek out the communication. Possibly the most popular example of non-forced glossolalia is found in the book of Acts of the Bible.[236] In that instance, the speakers spent seven-to-ten days seeking before they began to speak in tongues. Most students agreed that if they were to speak in tongues, they would prefer the non-demonic, non-forced type. In short, glossolalia exists around the world in theistic and non-theistic environments.

Such information sometimes led to discussions about the importance of trying to determine the purpose for the practice in each setting. We agreed that possessions and behaviors can be good or bad, healthy or harmful, or have no effect at all.

What Is Speaking In Tongues?

This led to some, *What is speaking in tongues?* discussions. In academic literature, it is often referred to as *glossolalia*. The word comes from the Greek *glōssa*, "tongue," and *lalia*, "talking." Some modern biblical translations use *speak with other tongues, speak in different languages, speak in foreign languages*, or *speak in foreign tongues*. From here on I use *speaking in tongues, tongues,* and *glossolalia* interchangeably to represent non-pathological, sought-after forms of tongues.

For a multitude of Pentecostals, glossolalia serves as a beautiful, God-given, and articulate means of communicating.[237] Two of the brain areas involved with speaking in tongues are the frontal lobes and limbic system. Of particular interest for this exploration are the language and emotion centers located in the frontal lobes, the parts of the parietal lobe that processes where we are within our environment, and the thalamus, which is a part of the limbic system. The thalamus is involved in the transfer of sensory information collected from outside the body to different parts of the brain and body.

Tongues occurs after an overall reduction of frontal lobe activity, except in the language centers, a slight activity increase in the orientation sections of the parietal lobe, and an increase of activity in the limbic areas. Neurologically summarized, glossolalists (1) surrender some mental control (frontal lobes), and that (2) allows the emotional intensity to increase (limbic system and thalamus). However, they often (3) maintain their sense of themselves and their free will (parietal lobe), (4) show no change of activity (more or less) in the language centers, and (5) the produced vocal language remains highly structured and contains articulation. This suggests that glossolalia is not just babbling. It is phonologically structured, and though it may have an occasional intelligible word, but it is not generally a known language.[238,239]

Reduction in frontal lobe activity supports the argument that glossolalists enter a state of dissociation—an altered state of consciousness (ASC). Samarin noted that, from the viewpoint of those who don't believe, glossolalia appears to be meaningless babble, an involuntary effect of a detached mental state, demonic language, or other similar phenomena.[240] The term is used to indicate that there is a change in the speaker's perception of the surrounding environment. In other words, the speaker dissociates from reality to some extent. Goodman undertook a long-term study of tongues in the US and Mexico and described glossolalia as a state of over-stimulation coupled with a sense of dissociation that has features that remain similar across cultures and times.[241]

Those People Are Crazy! Definitely!

The earliest, non-scientific, modern work to explore tongues and pathology was *Speaking with Tongues*.[242] Cutten believed that almost all practitioners were ignorant and illiterate. He also connected their auditory and visual hallucinations to psychopathologies such as schizophrenia and hysteria. Ironically, *Speaking with Tongues* included very little scientific research, but that has not kept it from taking on a seemingly factual stance among critics of the practice.[243] Other writers of the time indicated that the practitioners of the early twentieth century attracted psychotics and connected glossolalia with schizophrenia.[244,245] Such derogatory exercises are easily found in many writings shortly after the beginning of the twentieth century, throughout the remainder of that century, and into the current century.

Such blanket connections come from some writers seeking to place the practice within a strictly pathological context. Jung considered speaking in tongues to be the result of unconscious mental disorders that were intruding into conscious experiences.[246] Others have suggested that tongues are the result of impaired psychological development. For example, those with borderline personality disorder might be more attracted to tongues, and some suggest that tongues might be a sort of self-therapy for those with narcissistic personality disorder.[247,248] Neurodegenerative disorders, some psychiatric disorders, and seizure disorders are pathologies commonly associated with spiritual experiences. In *The God Delusion*, Richard Dawkins presents the idea that all beliefs in God are delusions.[249] Is tongues one such delusion?

In general, there tend to be three broad theories that attempt to explain the origins and causes of tongues: (1) psychopathology, (2) altered states of consciousness, and (3) social learning.[250,251,252,253,254,255,256] *Psychopathology* indicates that there is something unusual or wrong with the speaker. *Altered states of consciousness* are experiences such as hypnosis, hallucinations, trance states, and meditations we may experience while we are awake. In the medical literature, ASCs are often associated with trauma. *Social learning* situations indicate that the behavior is simply learned. Some early research linked pathologies like mood disorders, dissociative disorders, aphasia, and schizophrenia to tongues. Mental instability connections are often made because of the euphoric experiences often observed during the events.[257,258] We have already reviewed ASCs in sections related to DID and possession trances, so let's briefly review psychopathology and social learning.

In the first study of tongues and pathology in a forensic environment, Hempel and colleagues studied 148 prisoners in a maximum security hospital. Eighteen were glossolalists. Inmates were included if they associated their tongues with a supernatural being entering their body or with the Spirit. Researchers found a significant correlation between glossolalia and psychological disorders. The glossolalists in the study tended to be manic, and all were diagnosed with Bipolar 1 and Schizoaffective Disorder, Bipolar type. Their hallucinations *" Some early research linked pathologies like mood disorders, dissociative disorders, aphasia, and schizophrenia to tongues. "* and crimes were of a sexual and hyper-religious nature. The crimes of the glossolalic group showed a majority of sexual and religious themes when compared to the non-glossolalists. Perpetrators tended to be female, and most of the participants heard auditory commands of a familiar voice during hallucinations. The hearing component is important because when the hallucination's voice is familiar to the *hearer*, the likelihood of obeying is increased.[259,260]

Another reason glossolalia receives some negative press is because of its close association with *conversion disorder*. It is easy for some professionals and laypersons alike to automatically make this connection; however, in earlier psychiatric literature, including older versions of the DSM and ICD, conversion disorder represents something very different—unconscious psychological conflicts that are *converted* into physical problems like paralysis, swallowing difficulties, speech problems, attacks or seizures, or sensory problems. Conversion disorder has now been renamed *functional neurological symptom disorder* (FNSD) in an attempt to move away from automatic negative associations and toward more positive spiritual conversions. The DSM-5-TR includes it within *Somatic Symptom and Related Disorders,* and the ICD-11 includes it within *Dissociative Disorders.*[261]

Even though the most recent versions of the DSM and ICD, and much of the most recent research literature, utilize the FNSD label, the process of switching to the new term creates confusion in some newer learners because they may not initially recognize differences between the two labels. As such, the old stigma of automatically relating conversion disorder to spiritual contexts remains in the minds of some and will do so for quite some time. The results are that many readers of both old and new research literature easily make the mistake of assuming that conversion disorder relates to some sort of problem within religious experiences. The implications are that they view a *normal religious conversion* to be the result of a psychological disorder. The stigma continues and is compounded in the general public for many reasons. Apathy and negative media influences are some of the causes.

Not all researchers associate tongues with pathology, yet they continue to look for scientific explanations, so some turn to *social learning theory* (modeling). This can be a compelling argument because most first-time glossolalic experiences tend to happen with others present and involve concentration on what the individual believes should happen.[262,263,264] Spanos is one who posited that tongues is a learned behavior.[265] He had participants listen to recordings of glossolalia and then try to vocally recreate the patterns. Participants were able to reproduce glossolalic-type sounds, so Spanos felt the study supported the social learning hypothesis. More than twenty years before Spanos, Alland hypothesized that religious trance behavior might be caused by psychosis and that others who saw the behavior might imitate it.[266]

Some social psychologists present an interesting idea that a desire for acceptance by the group may pressure one to try and produce glossolalia for the first time.[267] Good argument, but not all first-time experiences are public. About a third of individuals receive the Spirit while they are by themselves, typically during the quieter hours of the late evening, during the night, or in the early morning.[268] One negative to the private initial experience is that there is no verification by others. However, the absence of others may also be a positive—the speaker was not being prompted to speak in tongues, so the experience may be more heartfelt when free from social pressures. Lopes suggests that those individuals are still able to find group validation afterward.[269] While the social learning theory of tongues is compelling, it does not explain how glossolalia has similarities across all cultures around the world despite vast cultural differences.[270]

Let's Focus a Little More

To keep this discussion of pathology and spirituality from going off the rails, let's focus on a theistic group known to welcome speaking in tongues:

Apostolic Pentecostals. Pentecostalism is a form of Protestantism that often involves lively forms of worship and emphasizes a personal connection to the Divine. Glossolalia is a highly sought-after way of achieving that connection, which is often cited as one of the reasons it was the fastest-growing Christian religion in the twentieth century.[271] I use *Apostolic Pentecostals*, *Pentecostals*, and *Apostolics* interchangeably.

The Christian world often views speaking in tongues as visual and auditory indicators that one has received the Spirit (Holy Ghost). This Spirit baptism is different from water baptism. For Pentecostals, water baptism *washes away* sins but Spirit baptism is the Holy Ghost *inhabiting* an individual.

Many trace modern glossolalic teachings back to 1901 in Topeka, Kansas. It then spread to Los Angeles where the Azusa Street Revival began in 1906 and lasted until about 1915. Over the course of about ten years, the movement's teachings spread around the world.[272] However, this timeline is somewhat misleading because Pentecostal theology extends back through the previous two millennia to biblical times.

Possibly the most popular instance of tongues is recorded in Acts 2. Bystanders heard the sounds and began to ask questions. Honestly, being the natural skeptic that I am, I probably would have been a bit of a scorner if I had been there and seen and heard what was happening. Acts 2:5-11 describes people from an array of nations being bewildered because the group was speaking in so many different languages. Verses 9–11 mention some foreigners who were surprised that some individuals, who did not know the foreigners' language, were speaking their respective languages—these days we call it *xenoglossy*. Conversely, glossolalia is understood to be a non-earthly language that requires a spiritual interpretation before it can be understood. Though xenoglossy is an earthly language, it is considered to be a spiritual impartation of the earthly language. Though they are different, xenoglossy and glossolalia are not usually differentiated by speakers.[273] Speakers don't understand either language, and this book does not differentiate because speakers consider both forms to be spiritual languages and both serve special purposes.

> **" Glossolalia is understood to be a non-earthly language that requires a spiritual interpretation before it can be understood. "**

Within two centuries after Acts, the Catholic Tertullian (155–220 AD) wrote that most Christian believers during his time engaged in tongues and could be found easily. Commenting on that, the theologian Warfield suggested that Tertullian's statements implied Tertullian himself felt to be part of a minority because he didn't speak in tongues, but glossolalia was the dominant and virtually official expression of Christian faith in Rome.[274] Around 300 AD, practitioners began to move into more of an underground mode because of an agreement between Constantine and Catholicism that sought to reduce tongues. Still, there is evidence of the practice in all centuries since its first recording in the book of Acts.

Glossolalia can be difficult to trace through some centuries because of destroyed, missing, or nonexistent documents. Some argue that many documents would not have been created because they could be used as evidence against practitioners. The results are that some believe the actual number of practitioners was higher than is estimated. It was likely practiced by many more people than can be verified, but its spread has still been traced through all centuries and to all of the known world, including Asia, Africa, England, and Europe.

More specific to North America, Pentecostal theology can be traced to the early 1700s. The First Great Awakening included Christian revivals that involved Britain and the thirteen colonies. During that time Jonathan Edwards and others promoted the works of the Holy Spirit. The Second Great Awakening also included a series of revivals between about 1795 and 1835. The Pentecostal renewal that took place in America in the twentieth century receives a lot of attention as its beginning, and the Azusa Street Revival is often given credit for launching its rapid, worldwide influence during modern times. But its true beginning can be found in Acts chapter 2 and in the teachings of the biblical apostles— hence the term *apostolic*.

Glossolalic Purposes

There are many purposes for tongues, but three common ones are *communication, unity,* and *confidence.* Communication allows the supernatural to share a message with an individual or a group, or, in reverse direction, the individual or group may communicate with the supernatural. Often this communication is accompanied by strong visible emotions like weeping with joy, but the tongues is understood to be either the Holy Spirit filling the person, the Holy Spirit communicating with the person, the person praying to God in a heavenly language, or some combination of the three at the same time. Observers understand that the communication is between physical and spiritual beings for specific purposes.

Communication through *xenoglossy* is the most infrequent, at least in my experience. Xenoglossy, or xenolalia (*xenos* = "foreigner," *glōssa* = "tongue" or "language"), is a phenomenon that allows a person to speak, write, or understand a language not previously known to him. The physiologist Charles Richet coined the term *xenoglossy* in 1905. Richet was awarded the 1913 Nobel Prize for Physiology or Medicine for his research into anaphylaxis.[275] He was also intrigued by the relationship between mental processes and bodily functions,[276] and over one hundred years later we see that the effect he had on the study of psychic phenomena remains significant.[277] So why was he interested in spiritual experiences? Well, like James, he was interested in studying many phenomena.

One of the more interesting arguments for the phenomenon is that it is caused by reincarnation. Though I don't personally hold those beliefs, I find the discussion intriguing. There have been a handful of times when I witnessed glossolalia and later someone said the tongues had been spoken in the hearer's native language—it had actually been xenoglossy. Sometimes it was a message for a person, or people, who could understand the language. However, not all xenoglossic events contain a message for hearers. Some native hearers have explained that the speaker was simply worshipping God in the hearer's native tongue even though the speaker did not know the language.

The frequency of tongues and interpretations falls somewhere between individual tongues and xenoglossia. The *tongues* portion is usually glossolalia, with xenoglossia being less frequent. The events begin when someone speaks in tongues, usually louder than the others, and the group understands that it is a spiritual message, so they go silent and wait for the speaker to finish. The group then waits for someone to receive the *interpretation*. When, and if, someone receives the interpretation (if it is glossolalia), it is spoken to the group. In some instances, a second cycle of tongues and interpretation may reinforce the message or provide a different, second message. On rare occasions there may be more than two cycles. Occasionally, a group interpretation is not given. When that happens it is understood that the message was for one or more individuals within the group, and they understood the message so an interpretation for the entire group was not necessary.

Another tongues purpose may be to symbolize unity. Glossolalia symbolizes communication and unity with God. It also shows and promotes unity with other glossolalic individuals. Everyone does not need to speak in tongues at the same time to feel the sense of unity, but if they do it usually increases the feelings of unity. Cohesion is also created on a large scale because this process is the same in all cultures and because it provides assurance that the speakers have connected with the Spirit. James 3 talks about the difficulty of controlling one's tongue. It is small, but it can affect the whole body and others. Remember that words matter, and one spoken word or thought can affect behavior. Normally the brain controls speech, but glossolalia requires a reduction of control of some normal cognitive patterns. That process of allowing something else to influence speech patterns requires a connection to the *something else*. When individuals connect with the supernatural, they also feel a connection to humans through the universal connection with the supernatural.

"It is possible that the brain stores the phonological structures ... and some may learn to subconsciously activate those neurological pathways. "

Tongues also increases confidence that the individual has received the Spirit. However, from a social perspective, it is possible that humans can learn to speak in tongues. After all, human physiology is a part of the process. As we have previously discussed, when a new behavior is learned, new neurological pathways are created. In relation to tongues, it is possible that the brain stores the phonological structures. The next time an individual speaks in tongues, those neurological pathways, phonological structures, and remembered spiritual words may be reused, or the Spirit may provide new ones. This explains why some glossolalists may repeat the same structures and phonemes and why others use multiple structures and phonemes. Over time, some may learn to subconsciously activate those neurological pathways and stored phonological structures. This helps to clarify why some can readily speak in tongues.

Trance States (Part 2)

Some authors suggest that trance states can be viewed along a continuum. Goodman, an anthropologist known for her work on religious experiences, proposed a spectrum for understanding possession phenomena. At one end of the spectrum lies learned and ritually controllable possession, which refers to states that are understood, managed, and often integrated into cultural or religious practices (e.g., shamanic spirit journeys, Caribbean voodoo possession trances). She placed both demonic possession and multiple personality disorder (now known as Dissociative Identity Disorder) at the opposite end, categorizing these as uncontrolled and sometimes pathological manifestations.[278]

One problem with such a continuum is that it is presented as a linear model. In reality, it is much more complex and is better understood as a multidimensional model that includes multiple continuum lines that may cross each other at various points.[279] Let's try and simplify the complexity of a multidimensional model but still get a more comprehensible visual representation to help us understand better (see Figure 9). We use the *Demonic, Zār, Voodoo, Shamanic, least acceptable, most acceptable* continuum presented earlier, and for clarity we combine the zār, voodoo, and shamanic trances into one *Possession Trance* category. We then add two areas important for our discussion: *glossolalia* and *PTSD*. PTSD, glossolalia, and possession trance group relatively closely to each other. Acceptability will vary according to cultures, so we use a Western "lens." Of course, placement also depends on specific cultures within the Western tradition. For example, glossolalia is more acceptable in Pentecostal cultures than it is in generalized Western culture. As such, the continuum focuses on a broad Western viewpoint.

Demonic	Glossolalia	Possession Trance	PTSD
least acceptable			*most acceptable*

Figure 9. Author's conceptual model depicting a continuum of perceived relative acceptability for demonic states, glossolalia, possession trance (zār, voodoo, shamanic combined), and PTSD, based on data referenced above and a broad Western cultural lens (ranging from least to most acceptable).

Let's say we add another continuum line and change the labels to *maladaptive* (to local culture) and *adaptive* (to local culture). Demonic possession, glossolalia, possession trance, and PTSD would group closer to the *maladaptive* end but remain in the same order when using a broad Western lens. But again, as mentioned above, positions and distances from *maladaptive* and *adaptive* could change for specific cultures (see Figure 10).

Demonic / Glossolalia / Possession Trance / PTSD	
maladaptive	*adaptive*

Figure 10. Author's conceptual model depicting a continuum of perceived adaptiveness (to local culture) of demonic possession, glossolalia, possession trance, and PTSD, based on data referenced above and a broad Western viewpoint. All phenomena are positioned toward the maladaptive end of the spectrum, with an internal order of demonic (most maladaptive), then glossolalia, possession trance, and finally PTSD (least maladaptive of this set).

If we were to combine Figures 9 and 10 into a Y-axis and X-axis chart we could easily see that the most *maladaptive* possessions are the *least acceptable,* and the most *adaptive* are the *most acceptable,* but in order to keep from adding multiple continuum lines and making things more confusing, let's just put the basic information into a table (see Figure 11). I have added columns with brief explanations for *context* and *functional roles* related to the behaviors. We explore the areas in greater detail later.

Phenomenon	Cultural acceptability	Context	Functional role
PTSD	High (Western settings) Low (universal)	Clinical, trauma-related	Impairs functioning, no communal value
Possession trance	High (cultural settings) Low (Western settings)	Indigenous/shamanic rituals	Fosters communal bonds, spiritual expression
Glossolalia	High (Pentecostal settings) Low (secular settings)	Religious worship, communal rituals	Enhances connection, reduces anxiety
Demonic possession	Moderate (religious settings) Low (secular settings)	Religious, spiritual intervention	Disrupts functioning, negative perception

Figure 11. Author's comparative framework detailing the cultural acceptability, typical context, and perceived functional role of PTSD, possession trance, glossolalia, and demonic possession, emphasizing the variations in acceptability across different societal and cultural settings based on data presented above.

Wier describes trance states as involving a range of altered experiences, including impaired judgment and weakened willpower, which can limit decision-making and free will. He notes a reduced awareness of the body, often shown through a fixed gaze and immobility. Trances may also increase the intensity or frequency of visions and hallucinations. Overall, he depicts trance as a complex state that significantly alters normal awareness, control, perception, and mental processing, with some abilities diminished and others enhanced.[280] Such behaviors are often associated with glossolalia. Since trance states are relatively common in some Pentecostal practices and glossolalia is considered a sub-domain of dissociative trance, it is often associated with possession trances. Because dissociative disorders are by their medical definition pathological, Pentecostal trance states are easily assumed to be pathological as well.

Spiegel noted that dissociation is so closely tied to repression (unconscious, dissociative amnesia) that it's challenging to separate it from these automatic associations.[281] Freud emphasized that *repression* had become the very foundation of our understanding of mental pathologies. Therefore, he focused his attention on mental *conflict*. The results were that for many years, some others also adopted conflict as their focus. The issue with the negative perspective rooted in Freud's work is that it suggests (1) dissociation stems solely from conflicts related to libido (sex drive) or aggression, and (2) material emerging from the unconscious is inherently chaotic. This leads one to assume that the normal mental states of low anxiety levels of the subconscious and the slightly increased anxiety levels necessary for focusing on tasks are conflicts, even though they are normally occurring and beneficial.

The DSM-5-TR differentiates between positive dissociative symptoms (e.g., depersonalization, derealization) and negative dissociative symptoms like amnesia. Our ability to keep experiences out of our conscious mind for a short while can help us while we are in the midst of a stressful situation. It allows us to set the trauma aside until we can process it in a healthy way. As an athlete, I constantly dissociated from the pain or other game stressors so that I could be more effective during the match. Some military personnel and first responders exist within an almost constant state of dissociation for long periods because of physical and mental stressors. As an educator of students identified as being severely emotionally/behaviorally disturbed, I dissociated from the students' physical and mental traumas. If I had not, my effectiveness as an educator would have been reduced because I would have been consumed with pity.

One of the positives of dissociation is stress reduction. Detachment through meditation is a good example of a method that can be found in both secular and religious settings. It helps to reduce stress by mentally partitioning stressors, which helps lead to both psychological and physiological benefits. Religious dissociation can be seen as both beneficial and harmful, but outsiders often portray it as negative. Even when some benefits of segregation are noted by authors, those positives are often rooted in the negative connotations that correlate with dissociation. It's often something like, *Well, at least you were barely able to maintain your sanity by using religious dissociation until you could get here to talk to me—the professional.* It reminds me of the positive colloquialism *make lemonade from lemons* but with a highly negative undercurrent.

Dissociation, Association, and a Continuum

Placing dissociation and association events on a two-directional plane allows for greater recognition of the ever-changing levels of consciousness. Spiegel suggested that mental awareness can be usefully viewed as existing on a dissociation-association continuum, ranging from (1) narrowing, to (2) maintaining, to (3) broadening categories.[282] Going too far in one direction or the other, and staying there for too long, is unhealthy.

Most of us operate within the mentally healthy *maintaining* middle area that involves frequently changing degrees of dissociation and association throughout the day. We may move because of stressful or peaceful situations or because of normal (Private Herbst) or malfunctioning (Wyatt) mental processes. Most of us move fluidly between those different points throughout the day, but we usually return to the healthy sustaining middle. We also need to understand that my sustaining middle may be, and probably is, different from yours.

An interesting component of this process is that we may move toward dissociation and association at the same time. It may be helpful to imagine two separate planes, one conscious and one unconscious, both having the labels of dissociation (contracting), sustaining, and association (expanding) categories. We may consciously choose to dissociate from something so that we can associate more closely with something else. Or, as some behaviors become more engrained, we may complete the necessary process subconsciously.

Or, possibly even more confusing, we might consciously move in one direction on one plane while subconsciously moving the opposite direction on the other. Use the two continua shown in Figures 12 and 13 to try and visual the process. We might register toward the dissociative end on the unconscious plane, while on the conscious plane we register closer to the association end, and vice versa. Where we register on the two planes at any given moment may vary slightly between the two planes, but mentally healthy individuals usually average toward the sustaining middle, even if the two planes register at opposite ends.

Conscious Continuum

Unhealthy	Healthy	Unhealthy
dissociation	*sustaining*	*association*

Figure 12. Author's conceptual model of consciousness as a continuum ranging from unhealthy dissociation through a healthy sustaining phase, to unhealthy association. While moving to one extreme or the other is not necessarily unhealthy, remaining there for a long time is. Most individuals typically operate within the healthy sustaining middle, with fluidity in shifting states throughout the day.

Unconscious Continuum

Unhealthy	Healthy	Unhealthy
dissociation	*sustaining*	*association*

Figure 13. Author's conceptual model of unconsciousness as a continuum ranging from unhealthy dissociation through a healthy sustaining phase, to unhealthy association. While moving to one extreme or the other is not necessarily unhealthy, remaining there for a long time is. Most individuals typically operate within the healthy sustaining middle, with fluidity in shifting states throughout the day.

A parent who needs to control anger, or medical, military, or law enforcement personnel are easily recognizable examples of those needing to dissociate from negative emotions enough to properly handle a situation. Often called *suppression*, this form of dissociation allows them to set aside unwanted emotions so they can focus on more pressing needs. Repression is similar to suppression, but repression involves forgetting (dissociative amnesia) stressful situations and is unhealthy. Even a seemingly routine traffic stop is stressful for the officer, like it is for the driver, because there is no guarantee that it will remain a normal traffic stop. In those situations, an officer needs to maintain a calm (suppressed) yet mentally and physically charged state in order to remain professional and ready to act. Such calm yet excited mental states can be beneficial and are viewed as healthy.

Shortly after getting involved with law enforcement on a part-time basis (I was still teaching full time), I was driving home after church on New Year's Eve. It was late, I was sleepy, and I just wanted to get my family and me home before the serious partiers were on the roads. Thankfully we had driven separately, and they were a few minutes ahead. Then I witnessed a crash as I topped an interstate overpass.

" Repression involves forgetting (dissociative amnesia) stressful situations and is unhealthy. "

A white Hyundai driven by an elderly female had been in the middle lane (three total lanes). An 18-wheeler had just merged onto the interstate and was in the far right lane. An aggressive driver of a Mustang was in the inside lane. He swerved to the right, into the middle lane, in front of the Hyundai. The Hyundai swerved to the right to avoid the Mustang, but the Hyundai began to spin toward the 18-wheeler. When the Hyundai and the truck came to rest, the Hyundai was facing rearward on the highway with the eight driver's side rear trailer wheels of the 18-wheeler sitting up on the driver's side of the Hyundai, partly on the hood and partly on the roof.

I engaged my emergency flashers and parked my truck so that it provided some protection from interstate traffic for the crashed vehicles. By the time I got to the Hyundai, the truck driver had gotten out of the cab and wedged himself as far as he could in between the trailer and the Hyundai so he could check on the driver. The trailer wheels had crushed the hood, dash, A-pillar, and part of the car's roof. The wheels stopped just in front of the elderly female's face. Everything from her chest down was pinned under the crushed portion of the car. As I crawled under the trailer to check on them, I heard them talking. My first thought was, *Oh, Lord God! How is she even alive, much less conscious? Please let her pass out.*

I squeezed up next to them so I could do a quick assessment. They had already developed something of a connection, despite her struggling to breathe from her chest being compressed, so I asked the truck driver to stay with her and try to keep her calm. Struggling would only make her situation worse. As I crawled from under the trailer, I hoped she would lose consciousness so she wouldn't suffer. I wanted her to simply wake up in the hospital on a lot of pain medication. Let's face it—there are times when being heavily medicated is preferable to the alternative. I reported the incident, ensured no one left the scene, and directed traffic until medical, fire, and other state troopers arrived. I passed along the necessary information to the trooper in charge, excused myself, drove toward home, and began to assess my suppressed emotions.

Because I no longer had responsibilities at the crash site, I could allow my suppressed emotions to begin to slide back toward the middle in the direction of *association*—I could begin to process them. At the same time, I could allow the associations to begin to slide back toward the middle in the direction of *dissociation*—I could begin to think about them less because I no longer needed to focus on rational decisions. Was everything hunky-dory by the time I got home? Nope. Not even close. But I started the process as I purposely drove home by a route that was far out of the way. Even now, years later, as I write about the incident, I feel myself beginning to associate with some negative feelings—mostly my anger at the driver and concern for the elderly female. So even as I write, I am consciously choosing to suppress those negative emotions so I can remain closer to the healthy middle until I can relieve some stress by exercising.

As I drove around that night, I consciously forced myself to explore my emotions because (1) some previous life experiences had taught me that the suppressed negative emotions needed to be dealt with or they would cause problems in the future, and (2) my family was at home and I didn't want to take my anger (Mustang driver) or my concern (Hyundai driver) out on them. Experience also taught me that my adrenaline-charged mental energy was a great tool for proactive mental health. I needed to make use of it before the adrenaline wore off because then I would want to sleep (much more than normal), and I would not have any energy or desire to address the stressors. I would bury them, and they would affect my sleep, my mood, and my behaviors. I had walked down that negative path many times, and it is not a good place to be. So I had a choice to make: I could bury them, sleep terribly, wake up in a bad mood, and take it out on the family, or I could begin to deal with them while I had some energy, sleep well, and wake up in a better mood than if I had not dealt with them (obviously, it wouldn't be like the event never happened).

Over the following weeks, I began to think about how I had automatically disassociated from some negative emotions. My anger at the Mustang driver ("Stay in your car!" "Shut up!" "I'll deal with you later!" "Give me your keys!" "NOW!") would have only hindered my ability to attend to more pressing needs. I even had to distance myself from my concern for the Hyundai driver. Being consumed with pity would have led to inefficiency. In other words, I needed to *suppress* negative emotions so I could *associate* with more pressing responsibilities. Some things were suppressed automatically (subconsciously), while some others (like my anger) required conscious suppression, and vice versa for associations.

I also thought about the importance of the elderly female driver's dissociative state (yes, of course was in shock). She clearly had life-threatening injuries, but she was calm enough to talk to us. She was answering questions and describing some of what was going on in her body. Her dissociation allowed her to provide important information for us to pass along to medical personnel when they arrived. But, at the same time, she also had a level of association with the truck driver. I think they automatically had an emotional connection because they both (truck driver and Hyundai driver) experienced the same traumatic event because of the Mustang driver, even though their experiences were from very different perspectives. The truck driver was wonderfully helpful, and that's one reason I asked him to stay with her when I left to check on other things. I didn't want to create more stress for her by needing her to connect with someone else. Later, the truck driver did a good job of passing the association connection to medical personnel when they arrived.

In Summary

This chapter began by hopefully clarifying normal and unhealthy dissociation and association. Private Herbst's normal "mental hiccup" (dissociation) was contrasted with Wyatt's extreme desire for emotional attachment (association) and poor impulse control ("damaged neurological clutch") that stemmed from trauma and brain damage. We then looked at some medical criteria for both and pointed out that dissociation is often linked to trauma (e.g., PTSD) and classified medically as a pathology, but its healthy and normal uses like suppression are often overlooked. Then, in order to stay within our guidelines, we focused on some spiritual experiences related to detachment and attachment. Glossolalia, a practice that is often stigmatized outside of certain cultures (e.g., Pentecostalism), was discussed using DSM-5-TR and ICD-11 frameworks.

We ended with a story that demonstrated how we can create distance from stressors while drawing closer to other, more needed mental faculties. Ultimately, we saw that both excessive dissociation and excessive association are harmful and that being able to mentally dissociate and associate at the same time is important for daily tasks, especially stressful situations. Healthy functioning requires finding a balance between detachment and connection—whether everyday life, trauma recovery, or cultural practice.

Introspective Questions for Chapter 8

? **Mental Hiccups in Everyday Life:** Private Herbst's "mental hiccup" is described as a normal dissociative moment, like forgetting why you entered a room. Can you recall a similar lapse in attention or action? How did it affect you? Does viewing it as normal dissociation change your perspective on such moments?

? **Dissociation as Coping:** The chapter highlights dissociation as a protective response to overwhelming stress, especially for veterans. Have you ever detached from a stressful situation to cope? How did this help or hinder your ability to process the experience later?

? **Neurological Clutch and Emotional Balance:** The "neurological clutch" metaphor illustrates emotional modulation, with overmodulation causing numbness and undermodulation leading to overwhelm. Can you think of a time when your emotions felt too controlled or out of control? How did this impact your decisions or relationships?

? **Wyatt's Self-Understanding:** Wyatt found comfort in learning his behaviors didn't mean he was "crazy." Have you gained insight into your own behaviors that reduced self-criticism? How did this knowledge change your approach to yourself or others?

? Creative Interventions for Behavior: The author used unconventional methods, like commenting on Wyatt's socks, to de-escalate his distress. Have you used or experienced a creative approach to calm a tense situation? How might such strategies apply to your interactions with challenging behaviors?

? Pathological vs. Cultural Dissociation: The DSM-5-TR and ICD-11 distinguish pathological dissociation from culturally accepted practices like possession trances. Do you see a tension in labeling spiritual experiences as disorders? How should such experiences be understood in your view?

? Glossolalia's Universal Presence: The historical and cross-cultural prevalence of glossolalia surprised some students. Did this broader context change your view of speaking in tongues or similar practices? Can you think of other universal practices that connect diverse cultures?

? Media and Spiritual Perceptions: Films like *The Exorcist* shaped students' views on possession trances. Have you been influenced by media to form opinions about a spiritual or cultural practice? How did further exploration alter your perspective?

? Fear, Familiarity, and Ridicule: Students avoided mocking feared practices (e.g., demonic possession) but ridiculed peaceful ones (e.g., Christian trances). How does fear or familiarity influence your respect or judgment of unfamiliar beliefs? How can you foster greater respect for diversity?

? Processing Emotions Proactively: The narrator processed suppressed emotions after a car accident to avoid long-term issues. How do you approach processing difficult emotions or experiences? What strategies could you adopt from the narrator's proactive approach to maintain mental health?

CHAPTER 9

Runway to Revelation

Skydiving Before Sunday School

I awoke early one Sunday morning in a Chicago hotel room and felt like going skydiving. So I put my suit in the truck, drove to a country airport that was surrounded by corn fields, jumped, put on my suit in the airport parking lot, then drove back into town for church. I vividly remember that morning's taxi down the runway. I was the last one in, so I was next to the door. The jump master hadn't closed it, so I sat on the floor and held the bar above the open door with my right arm and let my upper body hang out of the plane. My cheeks fluttered from the propeller blast, but the heat felt good, and I loved watching the runway zip by as we gained speed and slowly lifted off.

The jump master looked back and yelled at me to get in and pull the door down. I had to yell back to ask, "Why did you leave it open if you didn't want me to hang out?" He responded with a sarcastic comment that he didn't want me to fall out. I responded, "Why? I'm wearing a chute." The other jumpers laughed, but he looked like he wanted to unbuckle my chute and push.

The weather that morning was special: very little wind, not a cloud in the sky, and mid-seventies. There was lots of laughter and a greater than usual sense of peace. Everything was right with the world. I opened my chute early so I could float for as long as possible. The plane had dropped us on the east side of the airport because the winds were from the west/northwest. As I steered into it, the sun was to my back, and the reflection from the dew on the ground and crops made the visual experience more vibrant than expected. The colors *popped*. It was also quiet except for the occasional, lazy flapping of the chute. It is a surreal experience to float over civilization (roads, businesses, homes) and not hear the noises associated with them. Everything was just right, and it was one of those spiritual experiences we remember for the rest of our lives. It was made even more memorable by the events that followed.

I was over an hour late for service, and a missionary by the name of Nona Freeman was already speaking. She noticed me when I walked in because everyone else was sitting quietly, and we had spent a few moments greeting each other at Friday evening dinner with the pastor. I sat on the back row against the wall, but the sanctuary was small enough that I could see her give a *Hey, you finally made it. Where you been? Better late than never. Glad you could make time for God* look. You know what I mean.

The pastor invited me to eat lunch with them, and I was a little awestruck with Sister Freeman sitting across from me. I didn't say much. I just ate my food and smiled politely at the conversations going on around me. Eventually Sister Freeman began to ask some general questions about why I was in town, about my past life, future plans, why I was single at my age, and so on. The look on her face and the tone of her voice told me she was going somewhere with her questioning. She was not simply conversing; she had a purpose. She was directing the conversation down a certain path. I couldn't figure out where she was going, so I just went along for the ride. I was interested to see where it went.

One of her questions was how long I planned to continue with my traveling construction job. At the time I was a journeyman carpenter who built kitchen and bath displays in new home improvement stores around the US. A new hotel every couple of months and restaurant meals were the norm. Honestly, I enjoyed the solitude and freedom. One year a hotel chain sent me a Christmas card. I told Sister Freeman that I would finish the job in Chicago and then head to one in Houston. That would take me about three months, and I would then begin working as a teacher at the Tupelo Children's Mansion (a residential treatment facility for abused children) in Tupelo, Mississippi.

With a half smile, she commented: "I noticed you got to church late this morning. After I had started my message."

I tried to be coy. I didn't want to lie, but neither did I want to tell the truth about my tardiness.

I said, "Well, I'm in town for work, and I got tied up with something this morning, and it took me longer than usual to get to church. Traffic was terrible because of construction." As I spoke, I made some mental justifications that kept me from outright lying. I *was* in Chicago *for work*. I *had* been *tied up* in my parachute (*something*), and I *had* gone *up* in an airplane. It *had* taken me *longer than usual to get to church* because I *had* driven from the city into the country, jumped, and then driven back into the city. And the city traffic really *was terrible because of construction.* I was proud of my word games.

Sister Freeman responded with a comment about my suit looking nice, but my "hair was all messed up" when I had walked into church. I knew there was more to her side of the conversation, and she knew there was more to my side. I was a big boy and could take her correction, so I ultimately confessed. We both laughed as I began to explain that morning's events to her. She found my mental justification of my *non-lie* humorous. I thought she was going to fuss at me, but after a few moments she smiled and said, "The Mansion needs someone like you." Yes, I realize she meant my sense of adventure and not my word games. Although, I'm sure that some who worked at Tupelo can confirm that my word games continued.

I shared that vignette because it is a decent example of two strangers who were able to connect and communicate on multiple levels at the same time. Our subconscious minds were working overtime to process the visual and auditory behaviors of the other. At the same time, we both had a mental idea of where we were trying to direct (mental planning) the conversation without bluntly asking the other what we wanted to know. We quickly and easily developed a communication system that began with cautious distance (dissociation) but eventually drew us closer together. The stronger the connection became, the more the distance reduced. Amazingly, all of this processing, and much more, was going on between the two of us without the others realizing the communication was happening. Sure, they could hear our words and see our actions, but they were missing all of the subtle, unspoken messages.

> **" The key criterion for reality is not necessarily objective, independent existence, but rather the demonstrable impact of concepts—whether gods or ideologies— within human practices and experiences. "**

The concept of observers missing subtle messages that pass between others who are communicating is important for this chapter. Like those who were with us at the table, people not involved in the communication *circle* can miss or misinterpret messages. This is sometimes the case with tongues. Let's begin by considering the reality of glossolalia.

Is glossolalia real? Or is it just made up? In 1912, James wrote about *radical empiricism*, which focuses on the reality of the experience, not our experience of reality.[283] Eighty years later, Chakrabarty proposed that the reality of gods should be considered equivalent to the reality of researchers' own ideological notions. If researchers recognize their ideologies as having genuine existence and tangible influence in the world, intellectual consistency demands researchers grant similar reality to the divine beings revered by the communities they study. The key criterion for reality is not necessarily objective, independent existence, but rather the demonstrable impact of concepts—whether gods or ideologies—within human practices and experiences. Thus, a researcher who views an ideology as a real, shaping force in society should logically acknowledge the gods of the studied communities as equally real and influential.[284] That's great, but if you are like me, you want some evidence you can see. Not just words. I'm a behaviorist, so what are some behaviors that are shaped by beliefs?

Are Those People Sane?

Greeley noted that people reporting spiritual experiences scored highest on a standardized test measuring healthy personality traits, surpassing other groups. They also exhibited significantly higher levels of psychological well-being compared to the national average.[285] Considering the significant positive relationship between healthy minds and spiritual experiences, it's puzzling that these experiences are often associated with mental pathologies. Why is this the case? Two common reasons are *knowledge* and *understanding*.

Over the years I have learned that the common ground may be made more apparent by clarifying differences. For example, I didn't view the outbursts of my severely emotionally/behaviorally disturbed students with a completely negative perspective. Sure, their behaviors were socially unacceptable and often unsafe, but those outbursts also contained some golden nuggets. We just had to recognize and define them before we could use them to understand and improve the behavior.

Maybe a sports analogy will help with my explanation. When I was a kid, my friends and I liked to play "kill the man with the ball." It was one of our favorites. The rules were very general and something like, *no permanent damage.* Bruises and accidental blood were normal (and badges of honor), but kicking someone in the face would lead to all of us beating the tar out of the offender. At its core, the game is simple: tackle the guy with the ball. But it could also be confusing and difficult to follow for those unfamiliar. The game might flow from yard to yard, from the front of a house to the back, onto a roof if a ladder was there, or into the street. Yes, tackling was allowed in the street if the guy with the ball was brave enough to go there. We once tackled a guy out of a tree. The chaos is part of what made it fun, but my point is that the lack of clear boundaries and clearly defined and standardized rules made it appear confusing.

In organized sports things are clearer because the teams agree to follow established rules (though some still cheat) within a specified area (this concept even applies to sports like shooting and racing). It is the agreed upon rules that promote a uniform and easily recognized contest. It is clear to both the players and the audience members, at least those who understand the rules. Rugby is a good example of a more organized version of "kill the man with the ball." Almost every person I talked to after they had watched their first match made a comment like, "It's so confusing." My responses can be summarized with something like this: "It's actually a very organized sport. Once you understand the rules and strategy, you can then understand its fluid organization and simplicity." What usually followed was watching videos with them, pausing when necessary, and explaining what was happening. Over time, as they learned the rules, common elements like fitness and teamwork became clearer. It is with this spirit of clarifying commonalities by explaining differences that I provide a few examples.

Saver and Rabin tackled some distinctions between pathologies and spiritual experiences.[286] Both spiritual and psychotic experiences may include common elements like delusions, hallucinations, social withdrawal, and unusual social behaviors. However, one difference between them relates to the descriptions of the events. Psychotics use more negative descriptors like *confused* and *terrified* and often include an angry god; spiritualists often describe the events with more positive words like *clarity, joy, unity, serenity, wholeness,* and *love* and often include a loving god.

Psychotics do not welcome the altered states of consciousness, and their descriptions of the events often become confused and difficult for them to explain and for the hearer to understand what happened. They also tend to lead to greater social stressors, withdrawal, and negative relationships. Religious grandiosity, an inflated ego, and an agitated state of mind are not uncommon. Psychotic events can have negative effects for years. Conversely, spiritualists usually welcome the altered states of consciousness and are later able to coherently describe the event. They also return to normal social functioning, and, in some cases, their social skills improve. A loss of unhealthy pride and ego along with a healthy quieting of the mind are also common.

In order to increase clarity, Saver and Rabin explored some relationships between spiritual and epileptic events. Like some spiritual experiences, some types of temporal lobe epilepsy produce experiences that include ecstasy, out-of-body experiences, religious awe, religious conversion, unity, and the presence of God. However, the authors parse some differences. Seizures tend to happen frequently and with some regularity. Any associated hallucinations are usually similar and contain the same voices and messages. On the other hand, spiritualists' experiences don't contain similar messages or voices, and they don't happen frequently or with regularity. In fact, some may have only one experience during a lifetime.

There are also some differences related to sensory input. Pathological events usually involve only one sensory system. Individuals feel, see, or hear something but do not usually experience a combination of them. On the other hand, spiritual events usually involve multiple sensory systems, and the sensory complexity is similar to our normal state of mind. This is one reason spiritual events feel real even after normal mental functioning returns. The reality does not fade. *Spiritual* events have the same clarity as *real* events, while delusions, dreams, and hallucinations do not. They are often murky and confusing. The clarity and realness of spiritual experiences indicate that they are not the result of neurological malfunctions; they are products of healthy brains that provide a stable platform from which to search for greater meaning.

The authors of the study used a behavioral approach to compare temporal lobe seizures to the experiences of some well-known religious figures. Saint Paul (Christian), Muhammad (Muslim founder), Joan of Arc (Catholic), Emanuel Swedenborg (New Jerusalem Church founder), Ann Lee (Shaker founder), and Joseph Smith (Mormon founder) were included. Paul's experience of seeing a bright light, falling down, and then having a conversation with a voice from an unseen entity was interpreted as being consistent with his post-seizure blindness.

Even as a theist, I find such mental exercises intriguing. There is no way to know for sure if they were truly epileptic events or if God used epileptic-type events to get the individuals' attention. Possibly God had been trying to communicate with them for a while, but they had ignored Him or refused to engage. Interrupting their normal cognitive processes could have been a way to get them to communicate. Or, possibly, they weren't epileptic, but the events were purely spiritual. Or, maybe, they were epileptic events that lead to spiritual experiences. Without medical documentation we can't know for sure.

So, within the preset guidelines of this book, and in my own behaviorist mind, we return to James's criteria of observing behaviors to gauge the event. Afterward, how did they behave? What did they teach? Did they live what they taught, or were they hypocritical? In the end, epileptic or not, the analyzed events clearly fall within James's definition of spiritual experiences.[287]

Saint Paul is a good example. Even if it was an epileptic event, it caused him to change from one of the greatest persecutors of Christians into one of the greatest Christian defenders. (Theologically I don't think his experience was epileptic because Matthew mentions that others saw a light.) Paul's behavior changed drastically for the better, and a large portion of his subsequent writings are about how people should behave. Who knew Paul was a behaviorist? He is credited with writing slightly more than 5 percent of the Bible. That puts him in fifth place behind Moses at a little more than 20 percent, Ezra at about 7 percent, Luke at a shade over 6 percent, and Jeremiah at a tick under 6 percent. So even if his experience was truly epileptic, can it be classified as *only* pathological if it produced such positive behaviors and results? Can't it be spiritual too?

Tongues and Health

Some of Paul's teachings refer to speaking in tongues. There was a surge of academic literature regarding tongues and health around the 1920s and 1930s—relatively soon after the Azusa Street Revival ended around 1915. There was renewed focus around the 1960s and 1970s and the late twentieth- and early twenty-first centuries have seen renewed interest. The 2002 publication of *The Link Between Religion and Health: Psychoneuroimmunology and the Faith Factor* established a connection between religion and health, and the *Handbook of Religion and Health* outlines rational arguments for the connection between religion, spirituality, and health.[288,289,290] But let's focus on tongues.

Jumping back to the start of the twentieth century, Cutten's 1927 *Speaking with Tongues* connected glossolalia to psychopathology, but it lacked scientific data.[291] That means that Boisen's 1939 *Economic Distress and Religious Experience: A Study of the Holy Rollers* holds the distinction of the first relatively modern work to include scientific exploration.[292] Boisen analyzed psychiatric patients who had behaviors similar to Holy Rollers and then compared the actions of the two groups. While he found some behavioral similarities, he did not find any evidence of Holy Roller mental illness.

Interest in tongues seemed to renew in the 1960s. At the start of the decade, Alland wrote in *Possession in a Revivalistic Negro Church* that glossolalists were well-adjusted and, aside from their lively church behaviors, they were well-behaved.[293] Later, Kiev compared West Indian schizophrenics to Pentecostal immigrants and found that the Pentecostals could clearly identify behavioral differences between psychotics and non-psychotics.[294] In a different study, Kiev mentioned that speaking in tongues seemed to give people a sense of security and relief from anxiety,[295] which is what other researchers found in 1967.[296] By 1969, glossolalia was fairly common around the world, and when it happened during religious experiences, it was not a sign of mental illness.[297] That same year, Hine argued that theories that tried to paint glossolalia as a mental illness were flimsy.[298] In fact, she wrote that the idea of tongues as an indicator of a pathology should be discarded.

The positive findings continued into the 70s, and in 1972, Samarin suggested that individuals might participate in the practice because the experience itself seems to provide them with a sense of fulfillment.[299] That same year, Kildahl reported that those who spoke in tongues had less depression,[300] and Goodman did not find evidence of psychosis in tongues speakers.[301] Who doesn't need a little more joy and less psychosis? At the end of the decade, Spanos and Hewitt's study didn't find a link between glossolalia and psychosis. In fact, those who spoke in tongues were less likely to be depressed.[302]

Jumping to the 1990s, we recognize another swell of interest similar to the 60s. Grady and Loewenthal wrote that some people claim to feel better when they practice glossolalia because it's relaxing and they can do it often.[303] The *feel better* effect increased with more frequent practice. Daily indulgence provided the greatest positive effect. After surveyed research, the researchers determined that glossolalia wasn't a mental illness. Others found that Pentecostal ministry candidates were more mentally stable than non-candidates.[304] And, after a literature review, they concluded that people who were naturally outgoing and confident were more likely to have the charismatic experience.[305]

> **66 Tongues was not associated with neurotic tendencies. Instead, it showed a more significant correlation with individuals who are both emotionally stable and extraverted. 99**

Moving into the new century, Johnson, like many before and since, proposed that there is little evidence that glossolalia is an unusual event.[306] Francis and Robbins found that glossolalics were less likely to have mental disturbances and were more psychologically stable. Tongues was not associated with neurotic tendencies. Instead, it showed a more significant correlation with individuals who are both emotionally stable and extraverted, and it bore no relationship to a psychological disorder.[307] Indeed, in 2016, First and colleagues gave structured clinical interviews to glossolalists and determined that they did not meet the disorders criteria of the DSM-5.[308]

Later, in 2020, Kéri and team explored the cognitive functioning of tongues speakers compared to those with psychotic disorders. The glossolalists were better able to understand complex mental states of others by looking at facial expressions, and they were better at predicting the future actions of others than were the schizophrenics. Notably, the levels of anxiety, depression, or schizotypy (unusual fears and beliefs, relationship issues) exhibited by glossolalists were similar to non-schizophrenic participants who did not engage in glossolalia.[309] In a separate cognitively related study, Kéri and colleagues found that tongues speakers had enhanced verbal learning abilities, and the time spent speaking in tongues increased learning abilities.[310]

Despite such evidence, many still connect tongues and pathologies. It is easy to understand why observers could misinterpret and mislabel such an odd behavior. I often think of it like the ancient Greeks who had many gods to help explain some natural events. Zeus controlled the weather. Poseidon was the god of the sea. Aphrodite was the goddess of love and beauty. Demeter was the goddess of agriculture and affected the seasons. Apollo was the god of music, art, light, and medicine. Hermes was the messenger of the gods and also guided the dead to the underworld. Hades was the god of the underworld and ruled over the dead. I understand how the Greeks could make such assumptions, and I probably would have been right in line with them if I had lived then.

In the Greek setting, random gods might decide to do something to, or for, humans. It may have simply been for entertainment (like a human video game?), or it may have been for a particular purpose. It was hard to know what to expect. This is one reason some scholars argue that Monotheism is one of the most significant historical, sociological developments. It provided order. It provided logic. It allowed people to see that events could be the result of natural laws. Humans no longer needed to sacrifice their children to a random god to appease it. However, there were some who continued, and still continue, the practice of child sacrifice even though we now know that things occur through natural processes, and Zeus does not control the weather.

It is for reasons similar to the multiple gods theory of ancient times that I understand how some pathologies might be associated with the present-day practice of tongues—people search for ways to explain things they don't understand. The easily made association between glossolalia and aphasia is a good example because both relate to language functions. Aphasia, schizophrenia, some autistic behaviors, and OCD may include repetitive behaviors because of problems in the cortico-basal ganglia loop. Wernicke's aphasia causes difficulty understanding and producing speech. They may speak in long sentences that have no meaning, or they may add or make up words and be unaware of their mistakes. Those with Broca's aphasia can understand the speech they hear and know what they want to say, they just struggle to say it. It often takes a lot of effort to produce short phrases, and they sometimes omit small words like *and*, *is*, and *the*.

Both types of aphasia seem to have characteristics similar to glossolalia. However, again, a deeper understanding shows fundamental differences.[311] One of the clearest and most consistent is that aphasiacs have consistent speech problems while glossolalists easily switch between tongues and their native speech. They do not have repetitive behaviors associated with the cortico-basal ganglia loop. Granted, there have been some documented cases of glossolalists being so connected with the Spirit that they spoke in tongues for hours or days, but normal speech eventually returned. Glossolalists know that their tongues' language is not understandable, but some aphasiacs do not. When we gain deeper understandings of human behavior, distinguishing between pathologies and tongues becomes easier.

Biocultural Glossolalia

I ran across Lynn's study as I was updating some research data in preparation for a conference presentation. A previous study of mine had explored the relationship between stress and occupational efficacy, but Lynn's dealt with the relationship between stress and glossolalia.[312] I found it interesting that we both explored stress, but the glossolalist (me) did not study tongues, while the non-glossolalist (Lynn) did. One of the intriguing components of his study was his biological exploration of tongues. It allows a look past observable behaviors into a rarely seen world. As far as I can determine, it is the first biocultural study of glossolalia. Lynn's work is a wonderfully conducted study, and I find his exploration of the topic to be quite respectful.

> [F]rom a cultural neurophenomenological perspective, the best way to fully understand the questionnaire [that Lynn had given to participants] and biochemical data I have collected would have been through Apostolic practice, experiencing the Holy Ghost, and discerning the distinctions myself, through my own embodied insight, as to what constitutes HGG [Holy Ghost Glossolalia], backslider [aware demonic glossolalia], iatrogenic [unaware demonic glossolalia], and factitious [fake] glossolalia. This, at any rate, was the continual suggestion of the brethren. . . .
>
> So, for a true phenomenological exegesis [interpretation], I need to go through it and come out the other side. *Does this*

. . . then, truly convey the embodiment of glossolalia? Perhaps, perhaps not. . . . I can simply say that *only those who have experienced the Holy Ghost can make that assessment.* As I stated in the beginning . . . it is not that I did not want to experience tarrying at the altar in supplication, but I did not want to be false as I was working to develop an honest relationship. I often consider going to a charismatic church where they don't know me and I am not conducting research to have this experience, and perhaps, . . . I will. But there are two sides to that as well: practice insinuates acceptance of the moral code, so, *if I have not accepted but merely want to embody the practice, will the phenomenon I apprehend be the same phenomenon the brethren do?* Hmm. On the other hand, I daresay the brethren would tell me to give Jesus a chance, to supplicate myself at the altar and let Him surprise me. . . . The brethren have said to me, "you will not know if you do not try."[313] *(brackets [ ] and emphases are mine)*

Let's consider the statements I italicized above. Lynn is to be applauded for recognizing and sharing these concerns. Some authors simply gloss over such questions. Some don't want to address them, while others want to act as if they have all of the answers because their findings are *gospel*.

> **" Apostolic glossolalia reduces both cortisol and α-Amylase. The results are less stress and an enhanced mood. "**

Lynn measured stress responses to glossolalia by using cortisol and α-Amylase. Cortisol is a hormone that helps manage blood sugar, reduce inflammation, manage bold pressure, control metabolism, form memories, and manage stress. It is often referred to as the *stress hormone* because higher levels indicate greater stress levels. Alpha-amylase's primary function relates to digestion, but it is also involved with energy production and blood sugar management, and it is a possible cancer treatment. Like cortisol, too much α-Amylase is an indicator of high stress levels.

In sum, Lynn found that Apostolic glossolalia reduces both cortisol and α-Amylase. The results are less stress and an enhanced mood. Longer-term and frequent glossolalists saw greater stress reduction and better mood enhancement benefits. Both physical and mental health are also improved because stress and mood influence both. At a biological level, these results do not indicate theistic tongues should be automatically labelled pathological. Quite the opposite.

Brain Scans and Neurological Functioning

Newberg and Waldman were the first to use brain scan technology to explore the neurological functioning of Pentecostals as they sang gospel music and spoke in tongues.[314] The authors tested four hypotheses: (1) glossolalia would be "associated with decreased activity in the frontal lobes" (involved in willful control of behaviors), (2) there would not be a decrease in the superior parietal lobe (would indicate an altered sense of self), (3) there would be increased blood flow in the thalamus (processes and transmits sensory and motor signals), and (4) there would be increased activity in the limbic areas (i.e., amygdala) because glossolalia tends to be an emotional state.

Participants had practiced tongues for more than five years. Before being included in the study, structured clinical interviews confirmed there were no psychiatric conditions. Neither did they have any neurological or medical conditions or take prescriptions that might affect mental functioning. In the first (singing) session, each subject sang for five minutes before the researchers injected a medical radioisotope (radioactive isotope tracer) through an IV that had been inserted before they began singing. The participants continued singing for fifteen more minutes and were then taken to a SPECT (single-photon emission computerized tomography) scanner for a forty-minute scan.

After the first scan (singing), participants returned to the room where they had completed the singing portion of the study. The second session began by singing until they entered into a glossolalic state (usually around five minutes), at which time they were injected with a different radioactive isotope tracer. The subjects continued to speak in tongues for fifteen more minutes before being taken for a second thirty-minute SPECT scan using the same parameters that had been used on the first scan. The researchers observed the participants in all settings to ensure similarity.

Hypothesis #1 was supported (glossolalia would be "associated with decreased activity in the frontal lobes" [involved in willful control of behaviors]). There were "significant decreases in the prefrontal cortices, left caudate and left temporal pole." Reduced blood flow in the frontal lobes while speaking in tongues is consistent with glossolalists' descriptions of a lack of control over the glossolalia.

Hypothesis #2 was supported (there would not be a decrease in the superior parietal lobe [would indicate an altered sense of self]). There were no significant decreases in blood flow to the superior parietal lobes, so, also consistent with glossolalists descriptions, they rarely experience a loss of their sense of self.

213

Hypothesis #3 was not supported (there would be increased blood flow in the thalamus [processes and transmits sensory and motor signals]). There was not an increase in the activity in the thalamus. At least not in the overall measure of blood flow. But the authors also looked at the left and right sides of the thalamus and compared the activity differences between them (laterality index). They found "a significant negative correlation between the singing and glossolalia thalamic [laterality index], indicating that the more the thalamic activity was asymmetric [lopsided] to begin with, the more the asymmetry reversed [became more balanced] during glossolalia." The knowledge that the greatest lopsidedness between the sides produced the greatest balancing (corrective) measures is intriguing. The authors wondered if the corrective process might be "important for altering the sense of control in which practitioners no longer feel as if they are willfully making vocalizations."

Hypothesis #4 was partially supported (there would be increased activity in the limbic areas [i.e., amygdala] because glossolalia tends to be an emotional state). The right amygdala showed a small activity increase but not enough to clarify the relationship between tongues and the limbic system. On the other hand, the left caudate showed a significant decrease in activity, and the authors wondered if it related to the change in emotional activity during glossolalia.

Newberg and Waldman mention some of the limitations of this study, including that they measured the cerebral blood flow relatively early in the process and at single points of time during the glossolalia. There was also a small number of participants. Another limitation that stands out from the others, at least for me, is the admission that it is difficult to find glossolalists willing to perform it in a laboratory setting. And for those who are willing, how genuine is their experience while they are being observed, while radioisotopes are being injected, and while they are being scanned?

This causes me to consider many questions. What type of glossolalist is willing and able to perform in such an environment? Are they spiritual enough to easily speak in tongues with people staring at them? How much did the IV affect them? How tired were they after having been through the first singing and scanning session? And so on. I don't intend for those questions to sound sarcastic or mean; I'm simply and truly curious. This study was conducted well and produced some very interesting results indeed.

In a later publication, Newberg and Waldman conducted a content analysis of approximately seven hundred descriptions of spiritual experiences. They concluded that there are four core components that seem to be included in spiritual experiences: *unity, intensity, clarity,* and *surrender.*[315]

Unity

Unity is a sense of oneness. Yaden discovered that over seven hundred people felt a deep connection between their sense of self and "something bigger."[316] Non-theists tended to feel connected to things like the universe, universal consciousness, or even nothingness. Theists tended to feel connections to religious figures like God. Everyone felt they became a part of whatever it was that they felt connected to (even the nothingness). From the neurotheological perspective we are using, the parietal lobes, which are located in the posterior superior portion of the brain, process sensory inputs and help to establish one's sense of self within the space in which they are located. The lobes allow us to successfully navigate through the environment. It is likely that the reduction of activity in these lobes is an element that helps to create the feelings of unity and oneness felt during spiritual experiences.

Intensity

The intensity of spiritual events influences the experiencers' ability to recognize them as life-transforming moments. Various components of the brain, such as the limbic system, amygdala, insula, prefrontal cortex, and insula, are involved with emotions and emotional response intensity. In layman's terms, those regions, and some others, help us to recognize events as having different levels of importance. When events vary in importance, so does our perception of the reality of them. Greater intensity equals greater reality.

Clarity

Clarity is often described as one of those "Aha!" moments. We finally *get it*. Those epiphanies can cause us to feel as if we finally understand our relationship to something larger—the universe, for example. Clarity may even be something as simple as a specific sense of purpose and meaning for one's life—a direction. Over 80 percent of the people in the study reported such events. It's not yet clear which brain region, or regions, produce(s) this sense of clarity. The thalamus has been suggested as one possibility.[317] That study demonstrated thalamic changes during intense spiritual events. It also showed long-term thalamic effects in those who had been experiencing intense spiritual experiences for more than fifteen years. The authors opined that thalamic changes might be the reason for the transformation that is a part of those "Aha!" moments.

Surrender

Surrender is the feeling that usually occurs when a speaker begins to feel a sensation of God and submits to the connection. Brain scans indicate a reduction in the prefrontal cortex during these events.[318,319] However, this is in contrast to practices like meditation, which uses intense concentration. Those operations increase prefrontal cortex activity during initial stages of meditation, but prefrontal cortex activity reduces during spiritual experiences.[320,321] It is intriguing that the researchers hypothesized that it may not be the *actual activity level* that causes the surrender sensation. The feeling may be caused by the *speed of the change* and *the amount of change in activity levels*. In other words, practices that start by increasing prefrontal cortex activity may eventually cause that activity to drop below the beginning baseline levels and create a neurophysiological sense of surrender.

Newberg and Waldman propose that these components help to create transformative experiences that last for the remainder of the individual's life.[322] It must be noted that some change for the worse (about 3 to 5 percent), but most changes are positive and can influence areas like occupations, relationships, health, life's meaning, life's purpose, and spiritual or religious beliefs. Neurologically, it seems that the brain is also changed in a permanent way. For example, very skilled meditators' brains show structural differences when compared to those who do not meditate.[323] Some argue that meditators are able to meditate because their brains are different. True, sometimes, but those comments are not always valid because studies show that practice can change our brain to allow us to be better meditators or prayers. This, in turn, can foster heightened levels of unity, intensity, clarity, and a sense of letting go.

In my many years of listening to Pentecostal sermons (not teaching sessions), the vast majority include subliminal themes (not explicitly stated, though some are) of *unity* and *surrender*, in that order of frequency. Subliminal themes of *clarity* and *intensity* are often present too, but they are less common themes. Ultimately, the intricate interplay of *unity, surrender, clarity*, and *intensity* provides a robust framework for understanding how spiritual experiences rewire neural pathways, deepening an individual's sense of purpose, connection, and well-being, and fostering a profoundly enriched, interconnected human existence over time.[324]

Conversations with the Spirit

This transformative interplay of unity, surrender, clarity, and intensity in spiritual experiences naturally extends beyond sermons, inviting individuals into dynamic, two-way conversations with the Divine, as exemplified in biblical narratives. Some people think of the spiritual connection with God or humans as a one-way connection. He tells, and we listen. That may be true at times, but even then we can refuse. Another option we don't often think about is *negotiating* with God. Not everything is negotiable, but He is open to a little bartering on some issues. He is willing to engage in two-way conversation. Several biblical characters come readily to mind: Adam and Eve, Sarah, Abraham, Moses . . . yes, even Satan.

Conversations in the first part of the Bible seem to be relatively basic. In Genesis 2:16-17, God gave Adam some directions regarding what he should and shouldn't eat. He could eat from any tree except one. In Genesis 2:19-20, God had Adam name all of the animals. Later, Adam and Eve heard "the voice of the Lord walking in the garden" after they had eaten from the tree God had said they should not eat from (Genesis 3:8). They were ashamed and hid, so God had to ask, "Where art thou?" Adam responded and explained that he and Eve had hidden because they were ashamed (Genesis 3:9-10). The rest of chapter 3 includes some more conversation and Adam and Eve being banished from the garden. Not a lot of conversational depth here, but conversations do begin to deepen.

In Genesis 18, Abraham was told by some spiritual beings that he and his wife, Sarah, would have a son. Sarah was nearby in the tent and appears to have been eavesdropping because in verse 12 we see that she "laughed within herself." In verse 13 the Lord asked Abraham why Sarah had laughed internally and questioned the possibility that they could have a child at their ages. Verse 15 shows us that Sarah lied when she said she had not laughed. God then "called her out" by saying, "Thou didst laugh."

Soon after, Abraham learned that He would destroy Sodom and Gomorrah. Three of the spiritual beings left after the statement, but Abraham hung around. God didn't ask for a reply, but Abraham offered one anyway. In verse 24 Abraham asked God to spare the city if He could find fifty righteous people. God agreed. Abraham put on his negotiating hat and began to chip away at the fifty. *What about forty-five?* God agreed. The process continued, and the Lord agreed to *ten righteous people.* With the deal established, in verse 33 God left, and Abraham went home.

"*Sarah laughed and thought something internally, but God moved the conversation into the verbal arena when He corrected her.* "

There is a progression of two-way communication in these conversations. Sarah laughed and thought something internally, but God moved the conversation into the verbal arena when He corrected her. Despite her scorning, unbelief, and lying, God still blessed them with a son from which a nation grew. God seemed to be OK with mental and vocal communication.

Abraham negotiated for the lives of humans, some of whom he didn't even know. This shows a deeper level of communication than Sarah's attempt to keep her laughter to herself. In the end they agree on the terms—ten righteous and no destruction. Abraham probably thought his odds of winning were good. (I wonder if he called Las Vegas and made a bet.) In the end, God did not find ten righteous people, but he did spare Abraham's relatives who lived there. God was OK with conversations, or debates, that influenced some of His decisions.

Hundreds of years later, the nation (people of Israel) that had been created from Sarah's promised child found themselves in Egyptian captivity. God wanted to get them out, and, unbeknownst to the cattleman Moses, he was the chosen one. In Exodus chapter 3 Moses saw a burning bush that was not being consumed. Nothing unusual about that, right? The bush talking was normal too. Who hasn't heard one of those? During their conversation, God gave some directions, like, "Take your shoes off." At first, Moses obeyed but began to balk when God's requests grew more complicated. Going back to Egypt to give messages to Pharaoh and the enslaved Israelites required a little more involvement and courage. God didn't ask him to respond, but Moses did anyway. He gave the typical excuses of "I'm nobody" and "They won't listen to me." In other words, Moses began to have a conversation with God about what he (Moses) did not want to do. He didn't want to simply do as he was told. Maybe a little rebellious? In chapter 4, God showed Moses some *tricks* he could use to get Pharaoh and the Israelites to believe that God really did send him, but Moses was still worried.

Moses used the "I'm not good at public speaking" excuse—"I am not eloquent . . . I am slow of speech, and of a slow tongue" (verse 10). In verses 11 and 12 God said He would help Moses speak properly. Still, Moses asked Him to send someone else. In verse 14 we see God's anger was "kindled against Moses," but, as part of the negotiating process, He suggested that Moses take Aaron (his brother) as the spokesperson. Moses accepted those terms, and after a long series of events the Israelites were freed.

Moses could have said "No" and stood by his decision, and God would have found someone else. Instead, Moses provided excuses. But that left the door open for the possibility that God could convince him. Sure, God became aggravated, but that is sometimes a part of normal conversations. In the end, He suggested that someone else go with Moses as his spokesman. God was OK with contentious conversations and with including others in the conversation or processes.

Two elements common to these conversations are the human's engagement with God and God's willingness to return the engagement, even when He didn't appear to be willing. He didn't begin by saying, "Hey, wanna talk about this?" But when the humans responded to His comments (began communicating with Him), He was more than willing to talk. He was open to that two-way communication.

Sarah's initial engagement was mental. We would have been able to claim that God had simply understood her facial expressions if she were visible, but she wasn't. God heard her thoughts. I'm sure she didn't know she would be engaging in conversation when she had those thoughts; she was simply thinking very normally in reaction to the situation. But we need to understand that having thoughts in response to someone else's conversation is still engaging with the conversation.

Abraham's and Moses's engagements with God are more obvious, but the ways they became involved are slightly different. Abraham just jumped right in—"Hey, man, let's talk about this"—but Moses's first invitation was by a visual stimulus (a burning, non-burning bush). Of course, I'm sure their responses were affected by the form of what they were talking to. Abraham spoke to the form of a man, while Moses spoke to a plant. Naturally, their responses would be different.

Another element I find intriguing is God's willingness to include others in the conversations. He extended an invitation for Sarah to join when He asked her about her unbelief. Abraham's conversation included people who did not even know they were being talked about. The city was included without knowing it. With Moses, God's aggravation led to an invitation for Aaron to join the crusade. Only later did Aaron learn of his inclusion in the conversation.

The engagement of humans in conversations with God seems to be important. God could have left Sarah to her thoughts. He could have told Abraham to go away. He could have never set the bush on fire to get Moses's attention. But, once humans engaged, He was willing to talk. Throughout the Bible God seems to grow in His willingness to converse with humans. Just like these examples tend to show a progression from *shallower* to *deeper* conversations, so does the entirety of conversations in the Bible.

There is another broad conversational progression in the Bible. Communication in the Old Testament (some call it the First Testament) tends to be between individuals, though there are some that include small numbers. In the New Testament (Second Testament) the numbers involved in the conversations begin to grow. Jesus spends quite a bit of time with the disciples, but He also speaks to large groups of people. God manifesting as Jesus allowed people to be more comfortable talking with Him. He was just *some carpenter*. A blue-collar guy who became a teacher. I'm sure many were more willing to engage in conversations and to listen to His teachings because He looked like a human. A ghost floating around would not have enticed as many people.

We also have examples of God speaking to non-believers. He even conversed with Satan. There are descriptions of three negotiations between God and Satan—twice in the book of Job (well, one of those was Satan wanting to renegotiate the terms of the first deal) and once in the Gospel of Matthew. Each time Satan approached God and began the conversations. God agreed to the first two deals. I believe one reason is because he trusted Job. God didn't agree to the third deal because it would have given Satan control over the spiritual world.

Jesus also *spoke* with His behaviors. Allowing Himself to be crucified (depicted in Matthew, Mark, Luke, and John) for everyone, even non-believers, continues to speak to people today. Sometime after His resurrection, He returned to heaven. However, He wanted to continue to converse with humans, so He instituted a new form of communication, which was introduced in Acts chapter 2.

With the new method, either God or humans could initiate a conversation. But of course, the one on the other end of the *line* would need to answer the *call*. In Acts chapter 2 we learn that initially one hundred twenty people learned the new language, while others listened and watched flames sitting on top of the speakers' heads. From that initial spiritual experience, the ability to speak directly with God has spread around the world.

An Even More Rare Form of Glossolalia

" Singing in tongues ... can help provide a better understanding of how dissociation can lead to unity. "

While tongues may be uncommon in many settings, it is not uncommon in others. There are even different forms of glossolalia—some more common and some more rare. One of the rarest is singing in tongues. Delving into the phenomenon can help provide a better understanding of how dissociation can lead to unity. Some authors use 1 Samuel 10:1-6 to suggest that singing in tongues can be traced back to early Judaism.[325] Later, in the New Testament, Paul wrote, "I will pray with the spirit, and I will pray with the understanding also: *I will sing with the spirit, and I will sing with the understanding also*" (1 Corinthians 14:15, *emphasis mine*).

Graves shared stories of pastors describing people who normally had absolutely no ability to sing in tune.[326] One described a woman who usually sang out of tune with a harsh, uneven, and dissonant voice experienced a striking change when speaking in tongues—her voice became clear, harmonious, and melodious.

Bartleman wrote that the "spirit of song given from God was like the Aeolian harp, in its spontaneity and sweetness. In fact it was the very breath of God, playing on human heart strings, or human vocal cords. The notes were wonderful in sweetness, volume and duration. In fact they were ofttimes humanly impossible."[327]

Like speaking, singing in tongues is a spiritual experience (though there are also non-religious and pathological versions). Both are viewed as significantly life-changing, and both require a mutual association with God. But if we were to place speaking and glossolalic singing on a spirituality plane, singing would be viewed as more spiritual. Greater or deeper communication. Logically speaking, the concept of a conversation being a two-way communication is easily understood by believers and non-believers alike because it's easier to understand something we do daily in the physical realm. For those who do believe in tongues, the same logical understanding of the communication cycle of the physical realm is easily applied to the supernatural, the main difference being that it happens between the physical and spiritual worlds. However, there is a form of glossolalic singing that defies even this earthly explanation.

One of the most mystical and inexplicable events within the glossolalic tradition is unplanned, spontaneous glossolalic singing. When this happens, individuals sing the same glossolalic *words* while they remain in time, in tune, and in harmony with each other. Even individuals who do not normally have correct pitch obtain and maintain it during these glossolalic events. They lose that ability and return to their typical incorrect pitch after.

McNeil wrote that the experience of corporate glossolalia has retained its appeal within many faith communities, tracing its popularity back to the Apostolic era.[328] He specifically mentions the second-century Montanists, the twelfth-century Albigenses, the thirteenth-century Waldensians, and the eighteenth- and nineteenth-century Mormons and Shakers. In the later-eighteenth century, New England Shakers "rejected the hymns and anthems of the established churches in favor of 'gift' and 'vision' songs." The Azusa Street Revival of the early 1900s provides the most thorough descriptions. Corporate glossolalia was deemed so significant that both spoken and singing glossolalia were typically referenced together. Singing glossolalia was among the most prevalent practices of those baptized in the Spirit and has persisted throughout the twentieth century and is observed globally.[329]

Modern descriptions of this phenomenon frequently use terms that underscore the spontaneous production of beautiful, harmonious melodies, even by individuals who normally have no singing ability at all.[330,331] Duncan portrayed singing glossolalia as a remarkable fusion of tones and harmonious sounds, resembling a sacred musical composition sung by what seemed like angelic voices.[332] In fact, Riss and Riss described wonderfully sophisticated layers of harmony in singing glossolalia, noting that, despite its complexity, the singers maintained precise intonation without any pitch deviation.[333]

Glossolalic Singing Conceptual Model

Like some of you, I tend to be a visual learner, so let's try and get a small sense of some of the connections that are necessary for an unplanned corporate glossolalic singing event to happen by developing an overly simple *sociological connection diagram* (or sociogram) from an actual event. We begin by discussing a few elements of developing the model before exploring actual events.

There are many limitations to presenting such a model here: How do we gauge the *heaviness* of the Spirit? How do the communications differ between individuals? What happens in the spirit world? What are the differing levels of individuals' intensity of connection? We would naturally expect ministers and the choir director to have some of the strongest connections, but is that true? Can someone in the congregation have a stronger connection? What about the individuals in the congregation who may not sing in tongues? Lack of glossolalic singing is not necessarily an indication of a weaker connection— in fact, what if those individuals' connection to God is stronger? They may be more able to commune without the extra neurological and physiological processing necessary for tongues singing. Clearly we could continue with the questions, but you get the point as to why we must try to keep this very basic.

Additionally, we won't consider things like neurological, visual, auditory, or physical connections that occur between humans. Recall my earlier statement that "there are times when we can see . . . more clearly by what we *refuse* to look at rather than what we *choose* to look at." This is one of those times, but it is important to explore a little of why we should struggle to keep this model as simple as possible while still representing some of its complexity. I didn't, and can't, include all connections in the model. For example, considering non-physical relationship elements like spiritual connections, authority, and dissociation (for instance) increases the intricacy, but if we were to try and consider some other connections, like physical ones within our own brains, the model would become even more incomprehensible. For instance, a 1 mm^3 section of the human temporal cortex, roughly the size of half a rice grain, is densely packed with about 57,000 cells, approximately 230 millimeters of blood vessels, and around 150 million synapses, amounting to 1.4 petabytes of data.[334] A petabyte is equal to just over 1,000 terabytes. In other words, that half piece of rice holds about 1,024 terabytes—enough storage to hold enough songs to play non-stop for more than 2,000 years or hold fifty Library of Congresses.

The authors used a *connectomic* approach to study many processes, but one was the connectivity of individual brain cells and their points of communication.[335] The total number of synapses was 149,871,669. Now, take a moment to consider that number of junctions (connections) that transmit electrical or chemical signals between neurons or cells within that 1 mm³ section of brain. Physically connecting those to a different 1 mm³ section increases the complexity, clearly. But how much more difficult will it be to try and comprehend, or include in a conceptual model, the non-physical connections required to have the structures of a 1 mm³ section of Person A communicate with a 1 mm³ section of brain in Person B? If we struggle to understand the connections within and between those two small sections, how can we comprehend the connections within an entire brain, or between the two entire brains of Person A and Person B?

To this point, the study mentioned above is about ten years old, and the dataset is so large that it has not been completely studied. However, images of some brain structures and all of the raw data are available for public viewing and use.[336] The overall goal of the project is to develop complete inventories of brain structures, all the way down to individual cells and their respective "wiring," as a way to further study brain diseases and functions. To that end, researchers are working to map a mouse brain before moving on.

Yes, we went down a rabbit hole (or mouse hole, ha!) during the last few paragraphs, but the main point was to demonstrate the futility of attempting to determine all of the possible connections in, and between, over four hundred beings that needed to function in unity within the glossolalic singing event discussed below. Even the small 1 mm³ sample in the above study is still not completely analyzed. That is why we limit the discussion of connections to simple two-way connections between complete entities. Now, let us return to the non-physical connections of authority and dissociation.

Even the seemingly simple idea of authority added a layer of complexity for the model. For example, the music minister would have the authority to keep such an event from happening. The choir is trained to follow the director's requests and most likely would have stopped singing if directed to do so. The director's association to the Spirit would need to be strong enough for her to understand what was happening and submitted enough to mentally release some control of the choir to the Spirit. But at the same time, the director would need to *walk a tight rope* between the physical and spiritual worlds in order to know when the event was ending so she could reassert an appropriate amount of control so that the choir knew what to do when it ended. Should they return to singing in their native language? Do nothing? Just stop?

> **❝ But even my internal skeptic eventually leads me to conclude that the most obvious and simple conclusion is the best answer. ❞**

Dissociation would increase the complexity of the connections even further. Each individual would need to walk their own *tight rope* between the physical and spiritual domains while maintaining appropriate levels of awareness of the Spirit, choir director, other singers, timing, musicians, harmony, and so on. And the strength of the singers' connections would need to be different from the director's because they would need to be submitted to the director as well as the Spirit. This concept would apply to the musicians too.

Skeptics may say something like this: "Yeah, but the choir spent a lot of time together before the event—maybe even years getting to know each other beforehand. They would have had plenty of time to get to know each other, to learn each other's behaviors, and to anticipate what others might do, so maybe they had great team chemistry and were just responding to each other's previously developed communication avenues." I admit, even as a theist, the skeptical side of my brain has thought something similar. I can understand those thoughts. I sometimes still consider that scenario. But even my internal skeptic eventually leads me to conclude that the most obvious and simple conclusion is the best answer. Occam's Razor (the simplest explanation is usually the best) wins again.

Additionally, the pastor would have his own unique connections because he had authority over the entire service. *Is this from God? Should I let it continue? Should I stop it?* Even other ministers would have a level of authority. We could write an entire book and not cover all of the issues related to the incidents below, but my point is this: we are unable to determine the total number of connections, or the various levels of strength for each connection, that are required for such an event to occur. As you can see, even one relatively small, unplanned, and seemingly simple event that includes trained singers would require an incalculable number of connections. So, let's look at a very basic model.

Each connection between humans and God would need to be two-way communication—everyone must be able to send and receive *messages*. To begin this simple visual understanding, a spiritual association between three beings would result in three connections. But when we adjust for the two-way communication necessary for glossolalic singing, the connections double to six (see Figure 14).

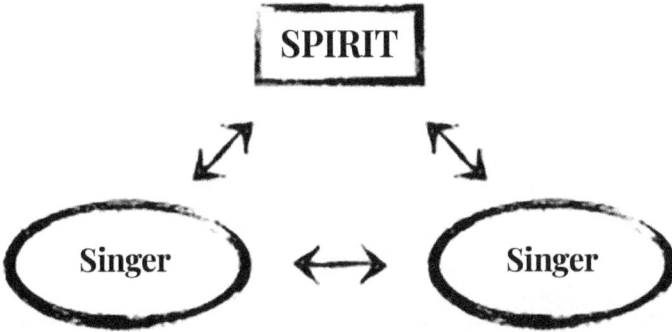

Figure 14. Author's conceptual, simple, triangular representation of two-way communication between three entities.

In the end, the completed "elementary" sociological connection model that includes only these simple two-way connections for the 424 entities described below is far too complex to provide you with any visual clarity, at least in this book—it would only appear as a blob. While the goal was to provide you with a visual representation of the overly simplified connections that would be required between the entities (e.g., God, ministers, choir) for such an event to happen, in the end, I decided that the best demonstration of the level of complexity in the model, at least in this case, is to try and describe some of the complexities in the model (described above) and then provide you with a visual demonstration (toward the end of this chapter) of the results that were produced by the elements of dissociation and unity that can be produced by such an overly complex model. This is one of those times when "what we *choose* to look at [and] what we *refuse* to look at" allows us to see more clearly.

Belfast, Northern Ireland

Reverend Brian Kinsey shared a story in which he witnessed singing in tongues in Belfast, Northern Ireland, in 1979. He was a guest speaker at a church service during a religious conference, and as the choir was singing in their native English language, an unusually *heavy* presence entered the building.

The kind that causes goose bumps, weeping for joy, and a slightly visual haze. Some of the audience sat and cried, some stood and swayed as they cried, some hugged, some simply sat or stood as they enjoyed the feeling. Some laughed with joy, some began speaking in tongues. The feelings of peace and joy were overwhelming. While those behaviors may be common for some Pentecostal services, what made this uncommon was that the presence was more palpable than normal.

Not long after the Spirit began to be felt, the choir switched, as if on cue, to singing in tongues. Once the glossolalia ended, the event was made even more unusual by the choir singing in their native English the interpretation of the spiritual message they had just sung in tongues. A *singing in tongues and interpretation* is very rare indeed.

Since Reverend Kinsey was not familiar with the church, he asked the pastor if the glossolalic singing and the subsequent singing interpretation had been planned. The pastor replied, "No." It had even surprised him. He also confirmed that the choir had never practiced singing in tongues (which would be a sacrilege and not true spiritual glossolalia) nor had they planned to interpret if such an event did happen (again, sacrilege). Besides, if the singing glossolalia were in fact genuine, how could the choir plan to interpret a language they did not understand?

While building the connection model I asked Reverend Kinsey about general numbers. He recalls there being more than thirty choir members, but for skeptical readers I was safe and limited the number to twenty. There was also a choir director, so that is one more. Reverend Kinsey "didn't pay attention" to the musicians so he couldn't give me an exact number, so I just combined them into one group. Also present was the pastor, Reverend Kinsey, the conference director, and other ministers, but again, I kept keep things simple and lumped all the ministers into one group. He also estimated four hundred to five hundred congregants, so I used his lowest number of four hundred. In sum, for the conceptual model we limited our exploration to twenty choir members, one choir director, one group of musicians, one group of ministers, and four hundred congregants for a conservative total of 423 people. Adding the entity of God gave us a total of 424 beings with two-way spiritual connections.

Despite all of the situations that had the potential to create chaos and keep the Belfast event from happening, the potential chaos led to a unified, potent spiritual experience—so potent, in fact, that some of its effects can still be felt decades later. I heard Reverend Kinsey share the Belfast incident shortly after writing the section that follows this one. As he described the events, a palpable feeling entered the building where we were, and some audience members began engaging in emotional behaviors like weeping, speaking in tongues, and saying things like "Hallelujah!" I visited Reverend Kinsey later and interviewed him to get more details.[337]

One of the reasons I shared this story is to try and help us understand that there is no way to comprehend all of the complex processes and connections involved in such situations. But, in the next section we explore how that incomprehensible chaos can unify and create what some call the perfect musical piece. In fact, the dissonance is a vital component of the unity.

Dissonance *and* Unity? Both?

The previous section demonstrated extreme complexity, but it is precisely that complexity that helps clarify the overwhelming importance, and beauty, of unity. It helps us to see that both the chaos and the unity are necessary, and the unity is made more precious by the chaos. The deepest spiritual experiences contain both elements. For the purposes of this book, we need to ask the following questions: Is there a way to explore these spiritual events with secular processes? Can we explore the dissociative and associative elements required for those events? Can such lavish connections still contain discord? The short answer is—yep.

Before the science that follows, we begin by making a few biblical references. Rybarczyk noted that the attractive harmonies found in glossolalic singing also incorporate a certain element of musical dissonance.[338] Some common descriptions (of powerful, spiritual, or group vocal phenomena) include biblical references.[339] Such descriptions come from Bible verses like Revelation 19:6: "Then I heard what seemed to be *the voice of a great multitude,* like *the sound of many waters* and like the *sound of mighty thunder* peals, crying out, 'Hallelujah! For the Lord our God the Almighty reigns'" *(emphasis mine).* The "voice of a great multitude" and "sound of many waters" and "sound of mighty thunder" cause us to automatically feel sensations like power and uncontrollable fury (maybe less so with the "multitude"), but somehow they are used to represent worship for God. How can a multitude, or many waters, or mighty thunder unify to create worship?

This paradox has led some to suggest that the auditory perfection found in singing in tongues is more spiritual than physical. How else can the unity that is heard among the dissonance be explained? Spencer asserted that perfection was attainable in the spiritual domain. He further suggested that singers were not just performing physically but were directed by Divine prompting and a way of hearing supernatural directions.[340] Perfection coming from the spiritual may be true, but is there a way to scientifically discuss this perfection birthed from chaos?

Let's take another short detour. We previously spent some time looking at glossolalia in relation to some pathologies and parsing some of their differences. Doing something similar (though much shorter) at this point will be useful for addressing some of the confusion regarding *dissociation's* relationship to glossolalia. As previously mentioned, I understand why non-glossolalists use the term *dissociation*. Reducing activity in our prefrontal cortex allows for some degree of distancing from reality. Clearly dissociation is there; I agree. It is an important part of the process. But this is one of those situations where being a lifelong, true practitioner provides a deeper understanding. Let me explain.

It's not uncommon for observers to stop when they recognize dissociation. They see it, their presuppositions have been confirmed, so they write up their conclusions. Admittedly, they *are* correct for a small element of the experience; however, they *are not* correct for the majority of the experience. Dissociation must happen before the spiritual connection occurs, but detachment doesn't suddenly stop once the glossolalia begins. After an initial surge, dissociation must be reduced and then maintained at a lower, relatively consistent, level throughout the experience. We don't usually lose complete contact, but keeping 100 percent hold on the physical world doesn't allow for a strong enough spiritual connection. While both earthly dissociation and spiritual association run concurrently, the supernatural is allowed more influence during the process.

Figure 15 (next) is a conceptual, general representation of the process. The medium grey section represents *preparation for, or the beginning stages of, dissociation.* The black sections represent the general path of *dissociation* in relation to glossolalia. There is an increase until the *determination and decision time* is reached (represented by the star at the peak of the pyramid). At that point in time, a potential glossolalists must make a determination and, then, depending on the response to the determination, choose between four general behaviors. *The Determination* (as I call it) is a question: Is the excitement I feel a possible spiritual connection, or is it simply excitement that I built up from activities like meditation, singing, or dancing?

In my experience, and in the experiences of those with whom I have spoken about this process, no one consciously asks themselves the question. Most descriptions indicate that it is more of a subconscious or spiritually suggested/prompted question-and-answer process.

If it is a possible spiritual connection, then one of four general decisions are available:

1. Maintain the current level of dissociation from the physical environment. ("I'm happy where I am.")

2. Increase dissociation from the physical environment but not associate with the Spirit. ("I want less of the physical, but I don't want to connect to, or believe in, the supernatural.")

3. Stop dissociation from the physical environment. ("I want to, or need to, return to normal awareness.")

4. Increase association with the Spirit. ("I want, or need, less of the natural and more of the supernatural.")

If option four is chosen, then the level of dissociation from the physical environment is reduced so that association with the Spirit can be increased and maintained. During this timeframe, the level of dissociation is reduced until it reaches a relatively consistent level of dissociation that is greater than normal, but less than the level of association with the Spirit. The light grey section represents the general "path" of association if one decides to associate with the Spirit. Note that (1) the association is greater than the dissociation, and (2) there is no border between the speaker and the Spirit. It is important to note that the four options above can be fluid. A speaker may make one decision and later change to another.

> **" The levels of association and dissociation do not always remain strictly linear. "**

Of course, the levels of association and dissociation do not always remain strictly linear as represented in the diagram. Often, it is something of a *fluid* situation. For example, an unusual noise could cause a speaker to increase association with the surrounding area and decrease association with the Spirit in an effort to decide if there is an emergency situation in the natural world. Or, a speaker may make a conscious choice to associate with the Spirit more so dissociation from the natural will be affected too.

The large black and light grey dashes at the end of the diagram indicate that either *side* can end the experience. The Spirit may end the communication once the message is sent, or the individual may decide to end the communication by reducing the level of dissociation. Or someone may bump into the speaker. Or the speaker may be tired. Or a friend may say something like, "Hey, wanna go get something to eat?" This understanding that either can end the session is another one of those nuggets that is easily missed.

I spoke with some other tongues speakers to determine if their glossolalic process is similar to what is represented in the model. They were in general agreement. During those conversations, I also asked for input regarding my original model (not provided). The model you see is a combination of those suggestions, and it is more descriptive and more efficient than my original. I am appreciative of them.

As part of that verification process, I asked about the idea of relationships with other humans being improved because of glossolalists' connection to the Spirit. While I didn't specifically ask non-believers or non-practitioners about the model, I did ask about the idea of relationships being improved with everyone (believers and non-believers, glossolalists and non-glossolalists) because of speaking in tongues (represented by the dashed line between the Spirit and others). A general, consistent theme among practitioners, non-practitioners, and non-believers was—*Yes*. One's adamant response was, "Oh, absolutely! I could not be friends with you if you didn't speak in tongues." It appears I need to continue to improve on my *people skills*. Hopefully the general visualization of the glossolalic process helps to explain why researchers easily find dissociation, but practitioners feel that it is more about connection (see Figure 15).

Conceptual model of the glossolalic process

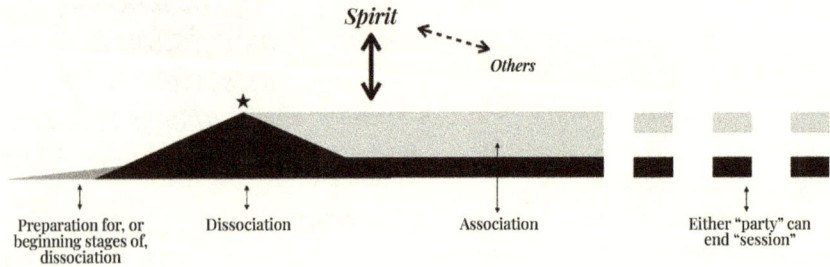

Figure 15. Author's conceptual model of the general process of achieving glossolalia. Development of the model is informed by the author's personal experiences, conversations over a lifetime with other glossolalists, and a survey of research data. The medium grey base represents preparation and initial, increasing dissociation from the physical environment through activities like meditation, prayer, or singing. Black sections show relative levels of dissociation. The star at the peak of the pyramid symbolizes the "determination and decision time," where individuals subconsciously assess if their excitement is spiritual or self-induced. Four potential decision paths follow: maintaining, increasing, stopping dissociation, or associating with the Spirit. The light grey section illustrates the path of spiritual association, where dissociation decreases, and spiritual connection surpasses it, with no barrier between the speaker and the Spirit. Large black and light grey dashes at the end indicate that either the Spirit or the individual can end the experience. A dashed line connects the Spirit to others, showing positive relational impacts because of glossolalia.

As we continue moving toward our goal of viewing coherence among chaos, and in further preparation for the images that follow, and because we use music, we need to define the *dominant chord* and the *tonic chord* for those who may not know what they are. The dominant chord is composed of the perfect fifth, major seventh, and major second notes, while the tonic chord is composed of two or more notes sounded at the same time. When the dominant chord precedes the tonic chord, it produces a sense of tension (coherence, dissonance, dissociation), but that tension needs some form of resolution. That resolution (unity, connection, association) arrives when the music moves to the tonic chord.

Schoenberg wrote that the progression from the dominant to the tonic is known as the most "effective" and "definitive" and "complete" method for ending a musical piece.[341] Musical pieces that do not follow dissonance with unity are perceived as less "effective," "definitive," and "complete." Understanding how this musical flow creates auditory beauty is important, but we are not quite where we need to be for this discussion because the sound of glossolalic singing is more flawless than the standard perfect harmonic progression described above. It also does not quite fit biblical descriptions. The perfect musical piece has unity following dissonance, but the sounds of a "great multitude" or "many waters" or "mighty thunder" contain chaos while also containing a sense of order. They cause readers to feel deeper emotions and have greater visualizations of the events. So we need to take another step in our understanding of what is happening.

Hinck helps us with this next step. Pay attention to my underlined and italicized emphases:

> [T]he sound produced by corporate singing in tongues is highly ordered not only by the presence of consistent tones throughout, but by the mathematical and musical relationships between those tones. Far from being random or chaotic, the tones produced fit into what has long been recognized . . . as a "perfect" harmonic progression, the exception being that *both the chord of tension and chord of resolution are present simultaneously.* This gives the sound produced a great sense of interest rather than feeling overly stable and static. *It is, in essence, the sound of tension that contains its own resolution.*[342] (emphasis mine)

Hinck's understanding that the sound of tension contains "its own resolution" is spot on. He *hit the nail on the head.* It is a terrific description of the concurrent running of dissociation and association, as presented in the model above, that needs to happen as part of the process of both speaking and singing in tongues. Of course, speaking in tongues may not contain harmony (though it does in rare instances), but the concept of dissociation and association happening at the same time applies. Some observers think of the process like an *if-then* statement—*if* they disconnect, *then* they can connect and speak in tongues. In reality, it's more of an *if-then-both-until* statement (yes, I just made that up)—*if* they dissociate from the physical, *then* they can associate with the spiritual, and *both* dissociation and association vary in intensity but are present at the same time *until* the speaker or God ends the communication.

The description Hinck provides of glossolalic singing is perfect. But how did he reach that understanding with the use of science? He began by collecting eight recordings of unplanned, glossolalic singing from the 1970s, 1995, and 2011 from England, Singapore, and the US. He then analyzed the singing. Hinck writes that even though he was separated from the actual events, the voices "raise a thick wall of sound." He also commented that even though "the movement of individual voices can be heard [dissociation], the overall sound itself remains stable [association]."[343]

One area of reflection that resulted from the study is "the presence of order in the midst of a practice that some in the church fear as anarchic." He goes on to discuss the idea that some post-Enlightenment Westerners find it difficult to reduce control of their mental faculties for fear it will lead to chaos. Indeed, a quick survey of the literature since the Azusa Street Revival supports Hinck's argument. As Pentecostal religions have moved toward using rational thoughts on which to build their theological foundations, tongues has reduced or even disappeared. (Ironic, I know; I'm trying to discuss a highly spiritual practice rationally.)

> **" There may, in fact, be an inexplicable sense of order that lies out of sight—'deeper than rationality.' "**

Rybarczyk implied that interactions between the Divine and human go beyond rational understanding, touching on deeper dimensions.[344] I alluded to this earlier when I mentioned we are unable to fully understand all necessary connections. Hinck's study helps to demonstrate that there may, in fact, be an inexplicable sense of order that lies out of sight—"deeper than rationality."[345]

Hinck reflects that in group glossolalic singing, we can hear the "necessity of community." Of course some individuals sing in tongues (not as a group), but the multi-chord structure cannot be produced without a collective of spiritual citizens who set aside a portion of their individual self-consciousness. The releasing of their post-Enlightenment, Western, rational thought processes allows their minds and voices to be open to being guided by the Spirit. The results are musical pieces that are highly interesting yet ordered.

> Only in letting go of the sovereign self and embracing a role as a small part of a greater whole, in continuity rather than

competition with nature, can such harmony be achieved. . . . In sum, *a lack of conscious, self-determined order does not result in chaos.* Rather, a humble recognition that one's own rationality is not the arbiter of reality, that one is in need of community, and that one is a part of the larger created order can yield spectacularly beautiful results.[346] *(emphasis mine)*

Indeed, corporate singing in tongues pushes our limits of rationality far beyond our normal understanding of reality. It also stretches our understanding of our dependence on community and, by extension, our connection to all creation. But maybe, just maybe, we can get a glimpse of that order that is "deeper than rationality."

Below I share, with permission, some of Hinck's visual representations of corporate singing in tongues that helped him reach his conclusions. Sonograms produce a graph that shows the intensity of multiple pitches over time, and those pitches correlate with audio frequencies. The intensity of the differing shades of gray at different points represents the level of the volume of the corresponding frequency at that particular point in time.

Figure 16 is a printout of general crowd noise. It is easy to notice the absence of patterns and the absence of sustained tones. In essence, it is a good example of the noise pollution we may hear in a typical environment. Coffee shop? Mall? Street? Office setting?

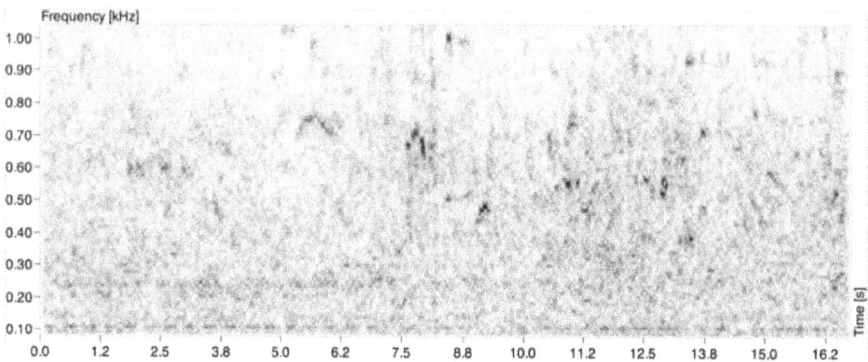

Figure 16. Hinck's sonogram of human vocal disorder in non-ordered environments with noise pollution. Clearly, the auditory frequencies are diffuse with no organization. Used with permission. [347]

Figure 17 is a representation of a harmonizing choir. The darkest spots are the loudest pitches. They are stacked on top of each other because they are forming chords. For example, at time 2.5 we see the most dominant frequencies occur around .20, .40, .60, and .80, respectively, with .80 being the most dominant. At time 10.0 the main ones are approximately .15, .35, .55, .75, and .90, the last four of which make clear drops before rising again. We also see that even though the lower frequencies change slightly, they are more stable and provide something of an auditory foundation.

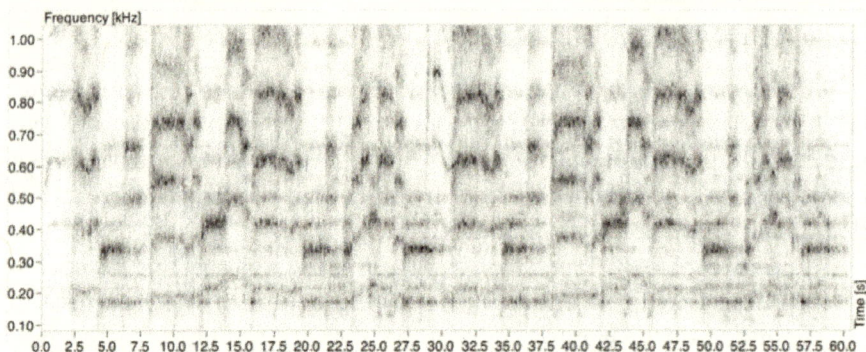

Figure 17. Hinck's sonogram of rehearsed, coordinated human singing. The darkest frequencies are prominent pitches and those pitches are stacked on top of each other to form chords. Clear and more organized auditory patterns are visible. Used with permission. [348]

Figure 18 is a sonogram of a 1977 recording of unplanned, congregational (not only the choir), glossolalic singing in England. The glossolalic singing began shortly after the congregation had finished singing "For His Name Is Exalted." You will notice that despite the movement of some individual voices, the consistency of the frequencies related to the congregational singing is much more consistent than those related to the trained choir in Figure 17.

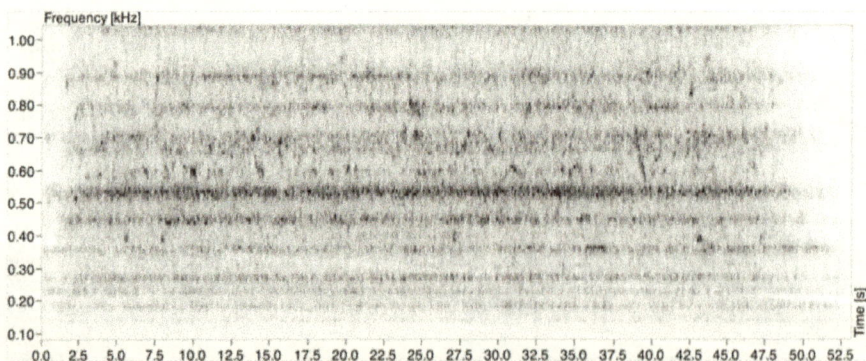

Figure 18. Hinck's sonogram of unrehearsed, unplanned glossolalic singing. This "heavenly choir" is not choral singing as in Figure 17 or crowd noise as in Figure 16. It presents an auditory signature by a congregation that is uniquely its own and highly organized. Used with permission. [349]

Many of the congregants in the above sonogram were probably not trained singers. Others were probably unable to normally maintain pitch, harmony, or timing. Most of us know someone who fits into one or more of those categories. While I can maintain harmony and timing, I'm one who can't seem to get the pitch correct. Yet somehow all of that was corrected during this event.

No matter how we look at Figure 18, it is an amazing feat of harmonic coordination that is made even more impressive when we understand that the untrained congregation was not responding to a visible director. It was their spiritual connections to the Spirit, and to a lesser degree with each other, that allowed them to perceive and respond in a highly coordinated fashion to directions from an unseen, spiritual choir director. Clearly the untrained congregation in Figure 18 produced much greater vocal uniformity than did the trained choir in Figure 17.

When compared to other singing in tongues events, the Belfast event and the Figure 18 event are spectacular in their own rights—Belfast because the choir sang the interpretation after singing in tongues, and Figure 18 because of the untrained congregation's involvement with the singing. Both events required unusually strong spiritual connections. I sometimes try to comprehend the different levels of dissociation from the physical and association with the spiritual required to be able to *perform* without a visible, central human figure (choir director) on whom to focus. Belfast is possibly more impressive because the Spirit-singers' connections had to be strong enough to first sing in tongues before receiving, understanding, and then singing, in their native language, the interpretation given by the Spirit. Then again, the second event included the congregation. Both are impressive in their own right. It reminds me of something I tell both of my children: "You're my favorite."

In Summary

This chapter has been a small attempt to describe why I, and some others, feel that *association* and its synonyms are more correct terms to use when discussing non-pathological glossolalia. Sure, dissociation is necessary for the process to begin and to continue, but it is a small component. An avenue, so to speak, that must be travelled in order to reach a destination—the connection with the supernatural, which is a much larger part of the experience.

The vignette that began this chapter (of Sis. Freeman and I connecting and "talking" without others recognizing) demonstrated how we can communicate on unseen levels without others realizing that we are communicating. A discussion of glossolalia and mental and physical health followed, and we considered how some pathologies are easily, but mistakenly, linked to tongues. Biology allowed us to see that tongues reduces stress and improves health, while brain scans helped us to understand some brain changes related to tongues.

Looking more into the spiritual realm than in past chapters, we considered the possibility that God is open to conversations with us. There seems to be a progression from simple chats with Adam and Eve at the beginning of the Bible to more engaging conversations as we move through the Book.

Toward the end of this chapter we tried to gain a small understanding of the connections required for unplanned glossolalic singing to happen and the unity it produces. We used a small scale sociological connection model and auditory images to try and *see* the unity that those connections with the Spirit can produce. They also helped to demonstrate how dissociation and association can happen at the same time. Both are inherently necessary for that special sound—only healthy dissociation from the physical world allows for such a high level of unity.

Returning to Lynn's quote: "Only those who have experienced the Holy Ghost can make . . . a true phenomenological exegesis."[350] In its most simple terms, *phenomenology* is concerned with studying experiences. Remember James's radical empiricism? *Exegesis* is an attempt to explain or clarify something. Lynn is not the first to understand that non-practitioners who study an event may not make true interpretations of the data. It's not because they don't want to; they just simply miss some of the unobservable connections/communications. Admittedly, I have done something similar in past studies.

Some try to find the truth by asking questions because they know that science can't explain everything. But even that has its limitations—they may not know enough about the experience to ask the correct questions. A good example is of the glossolalists who didn't understand a question that tried to explore the relationship between dissociation and tongues. They were confused by the question because their overall experience with tongues was about connecting. The idea of disconnecting was foreign to them. That is one reason I have tried to weave some science and some autoethnographic data together—to provide my own, personal *phenomenological exegesis* with the use of neurotheology and autoethnography.

This chapter focused on a specific behavior that many believe to be highly spiritual. Though discussions of this specific behavior have been heavily data-driven, my intention has not been to detract from the spiritual nature of such events. So, for the last chapter, let's change our approach and consider spiritual experiences in relation to what can't be scientifically verified. Let's wander down Philosophy Avenue for a while as we consider the glossolalic process.

Introspective Questions for Chapter 9

? **Spiritual Moments In Action:** The author describes skydiving as a "surreal experience" and a "spiritual experience we remember for the rest of our lives." Have you had a moment during an exhilarating activity or in nature that felt spiritually significant? How did it shape your perspective or beliefs?

? **Subtle Communication:** The text notes, "All of this processing . . . was going on between the two of us without the others realizing the communications were happening." Have you experienced a conversation where unspoken cues conveyed more than words? How did you interpret them? What did they reveal about the other person?

? **Truth and Justification:** The author uses "word games" to avoid lying, stating, "I was proud of my word games. . . . I *had* been tied up in my parachute." Where do you draw the line between careful wording and dishonesty in your communication? How do you justify that line?

? **Reality of Spiritual Experiences:** The text asks, "Is glossolalia real? Or is it just made up?" How do you define the "reality" of spiritual experiences? Do you believe they require external validation, or is personal experience sufficient? Why?

? **Distinguishing Experiences:** The text contrasts psychotic and spiritual experiences: "Psychotics use more negative descriptors . . . spiritualists describe . . . clarity, joy, unity." Can a single experience contain elements of both? What criteria (e.g., coherence, social functioning) would you use to differentiate them?

? **Neurological Insights:** The text states, "Reduced blood flow in the frontal lobes . . . is consistent with glossolalists' descriptions of a lack of control." Does learning about neurological correlates of spiritual practices like glossolalia strengthen, weaken, or change your perspective on their validity? Why?

? **Order In Chaos:** The text uses a sports analogy: "Once you understand the rules . . . you can then understand its fluid organization and simplicity." Can you think of an area in your life where understanding deeper patterns transformed your perception of chaos into order? How did this shift affect you?

? **Tension and Resolution:** The text describes glossolalic singing as "the sound of tension that contains its own resolution." Have you experienced a moment where contradictory states (e.g., chaos and peace) coexisted? How did this duality shape your understanding of the experience?

? **Surrender vs. Control:** The text argues, "A lack of conscious, self-determined order does not result in chaos. . . . A humble recognition . . . can yield spectacularly beautiful results." Have you ever let go of control and found unexpected beauty or order? How does this challenge your views on control versus spontaneity?

? **Evaluating Authenticity:** The text suggests assessing spiritual experiences by outcomes: "Observing behaviors to gauge the event. . . . Did they live what they taught?" How do you evaluate the authenticity of someone's spiritual experience? What role do their actions or long-term changes play in your judgment?

CHAPTER 10

Embracing the Embarrassing

Instead of beginning this chapter with a new anecdote, let's return to the beginning of the *Sanctuary Siestas and Synaptic Secrets* chapter, to my childhood experience of sleeping under church pews. I mentioned that as a child, I sensed an undeniable presence, a *something* that grew more potent the nearer I drew to individuals seemingly touched by the supernatural, especially those speaking in tongues. This consistent experience led my young mind to wonder, *If I can perceive such a force externally, what profound sensations must they be experiencing within themselves?* Naturally, I lacked the words for such a question then, but a deep-seated desire to experience that *something* for myself took root in me. Maybe someday I would be the elder that a young child stood next to in order to sense the presence of the something.

However, in my typical contradictory personality, there were times that I felt embarrassed by the glossolalia and my desire to experience it for myself, mostly because I was not able to explain the event to myself or others. Besides, didn't my desire to experience tongues mean I was *weak* and at least *a little bit crazy? What was wrong with me?* (My words from youthful conversations.) How is an adolescent supposed to explain an event that even older, lifelong practitioners struggle to explain? I now have more information and a larger vocabulary with which to attempt explanations, but still, they remain inadequate. Even individuals who are not embarrassed are unable to adequately describe the event. Though I still struggle to describe tongues, I continue to try to bring some clarity to the process.

Through the years I learned that I was not alone. Many of my fellow churchgoers thought similar things (and still do), yet they still chose to seek the supernatural connection. They may not be able to explain the process, but that was not as important as realizing that the association made them better people. Most practitioners realize that glossolalia is an unusual behavior, and with that realization comes an understanding of why others are easily confused by it or why some ridicule it. Two common questions often asked by both practitioners and non-practitioners can be summed up like this: During glossolalia,

- « *How* does the spiritual data flow through the connection in both directions?
- « *What* happens in the non-physical environment that allows spiritual data to flow through the connection in both directions?

The short answer to both questions is, "I don't know, and I don't know anyone who does." All we can do is try and gain some insight into what might be *over there*.

Where's the Data? We Don't Need Philosophy!

As such, for this chapter's inquiry, we move from reliance on science to reliance on philosophy. Despite the use of philosophy, I still think of the process in terms of physical world information. After all, that is what I know best. I sometimes envision supernatural and physical entities as neurons. Those entities may connect with many other entities and communicate by sending messages across open spaces (synapses) to each other. Neurotransmitters are represented by *good* or *bad* data cognitively processed, and those data affect the production of helpful or harmful transmitters. Good spiritual neurotransmitters promote communication between the spiritual neurons (entities) and vice versa. And, like the physical brain, multiple and repeated connections increase the strength and likelihood of spiritual survival, while neurons (entities) with single or few connections quickly fade away.

I know this brief attempt at answering the *how* and *why* may be ineffective for most. Perhaps another example will help some.

My statement that I have felt unease with tongues seems to weaken my argument that glossolalia is more about connection than it is about disconnection. After all, words like *embarrassing* and *unusual behavior* indicate some sort of dissonance and probable mental withdrawal. I have even used those words while teaching in religious settings. Why would I do that? Why would I begin this final chapter with such an admission? My simple answer is this: When the context surrounding my statement is understood, it actually supports this book's overall argument that dissonance can lead to cohesion. Let me explain.

Through my collegiate studies, I learned that we were not alone in our embarrassment. C. S. Lewis also found glossolalia to be a difficult concept to grapple with and said the events evoked a sense of discomfort.[351] How do we know? Because he told us. On May 28th, 1944, during the Feast of Pentecost, Lewis gave a sermon in the Mansfield College Chapel. It must have been difficult for him because after speaking for some time, he paused and left the platform. Naturally, there was a pause in the service. Eventually attendees began singing, and shortly Lewis returned to finish the sermon. It is therefore known as the sermon that he almost did not finish. What could have caused such a theistic defender to hesitate to finish a sermon? Lewis began his sermon by noting that his church observes the Feast of Pentecost to celebrate the Holy Spirit's descent upon the early Christians shortly after Jesus's ascension and he would focus on speaking in tongues because it is one of the spiritual gifts manifested with the Spirit's arrival.

Lewis was Anglican but during his life worked to explain issues that were important to all theists. He did not limit himself to his own denominational beliefs. This is one reason why he was, and still is, respected by people of all belief systems. His unease with glossolalia combined with his willingness to explore topics that were important to other Christians led to his inspiration to explore this topic. In the end, he found an answer to his questions and endorsed the practice—though I haven't found any evidence that he actually participated in tongues.

> **" Though he felt unworthy to directly address the nature of the Holy Spirit or His ways of working, he could approach the topic indirectly. "**

Lewis gave two reasons for working through his apprehension regarding teaching about glossolalia. The first was, though he felt unworthy to directly address the nature of the Holy Spirit or His ways of working, he could approach the topic indirectly, as this provided some mental and theological distance. The second reason was because of his own recurring difficulty in accepting glossolalia. He then pointed out that Saint Paul also seemed to express an unease about it in his first letter to the Corinthians. But it was Lewis's unease and embarrassment that motivated him to explore the phenomenon. In sum, his mental dissonance prompted him to explore the subject.

I truly respect people who can admit that something produces internal turmoil, yet they spend time honestly exploring the topic. That is one of the main purposes of this book, looking at some topics (e.g., medications, media, near-death experiences) that may cause us some unease. Another of Lewis's reasons for his unease was tongues' connection to pathologies. However, after a short discussion, he concluded that glossolalia was the actual event the Lord had instructed the Church to look for. Because of that understanding, and in spite of his own unease with the practice, he decided he would endeavor to make the topic a little less troubling for others, if he could.

Transposition

Lewis's sermon was titled "Transposition." As he defined it, transposition is an *adaptation of something from a higher-level medium to a lower-level medium* and it *allows the lower to participate in the process and reflect the higher, even if imperfectly.* This interface between the physical and the spirit worlds provides us with a framework to explore their connections and communications. We are able to explore somewhat "below the surface" of the physical, behavioral expressions (glossolalia) of a supernatural connection. How might the higher supernatural adapt to work within the lower physical? Answering this question is important because tongues without the Spirit is pathological, mockery, or demonic. Transposition also places a focus on the Divine and helps to move theistic glossolalia further away from the pathological and closer to the holy.

To illustrate transposition, C. S. Lewis used the example of a common physical sensation, such as the internal stirrings felt in the stomach. In the experience of love, this internal stirring is felt as pleasant, while in seasickness, the same feeling is felt as anguish. On a more positive note, spiritual joy (higher reality) may be transposed into a physical sensation like a tickle (lower one). While a higher reality may cause a sensation, that sensation often directly embodies the quality of that higher reality within the lower physical experience. The point is that a limited physical sensation can serve as the medium for connection to, and communication with, richer higher-order experiences. The senses must, in a way, play nice and share with each other.

> **" Tongues without the Spirit is pathological, mockery, or demonic. "**

Even after grasping this concept, some mistakenly assume that sensations from higher emotions directly correspond to those from lower ones, expecting, for instance, that *A* in the higher system aligns precisely with *a* in the lower. The problem is that such a direct correspondence is impossible when one system is significantly richer than the other. To represent the richer system (A) in the poorer one (a), each element in the poorer system must carry multiple meanings. Translating the richer into the poorer requires an algebraic approach, not a simple arithmetic one.

Later, Lewis used drawings (lower) to help explain the transposition of the higher onto the page. How can we represent a three-dimensional world with a pencil on a flat sheet of paper? The answer is that it comes down to our perspective. In order to create the correct three-dimensional perspective, the artist must use two-dimensional shapes that can represent more than one thing. For example, an acute angle (less than ninety degrees) could be used to represent a spear point, but it could also be used to draw a cube or a road extending into the distance. Even though we recognize the acute angle as a road, that recognition is dependent upon our understanding of our three-dimensional world and the context of the art.

For example, when an element in a drawing represents something from the physical world, like a sun, its sketched qualities, such as appearing to shine, are dependent on the actual source (sun) it represents. Lewis noted that the suns and lamps in pictures or drawings appear to shine only because actual suns or lamps shed light on them; they (lower) would not seem to glow brightly without the reflected light of their real counterparts (higher). These insights can shed light on how transposition occurs between the mind and body, as well as in the relationship between God and humanity.

Recognizing that boundless higher sensations must rely on limited physical sensations offers deeper insight into how this process functions. It also clarifies why many experiences of speaking in tongues are so expressive. If we consider the spiritual realm to be inherently more emotionally *rich* than the physical world, such unrestrained physical manifestations are entirely consistent with what one would predict when spiritual realities are translated into physical expressions. Those profound transposed spiritual sensations may be most effectively conveyed through ecstatic physical behaviors.

This is a good explanation for why unusual church behaviors like shouting, running, jumping, and crying for joy can be typical behaviors in some churches. The flood of positive emotions coming from the spirit world overwhelm the physical senses. Senses have to share and share alike. However, that sharing may produce unusual behaviors because the little a is trying to express the immense feelings of being connected to the big A. So yes, we can be exuberant because our physical senses are not able to effectively process the joyful data.

I no longer sleep under pews during the sermons; that would be weird. At least until I live a few more years. For now, I sit and live vicariously through the children sleeping under the pews.

One day, as I watched my oldest daughter sleeping, I began to look at some of the other children doing the same. My *behaviorist lens* kicked in, and I began to notice that the interactions between adults and children were similar to the ones I had in my childhood. As they went under the pews to nap, the adults in the vicinity changed their behaviors. Some adults moved items to give the kids space, gave them candy, and ensured that the children had a comfortable and safe place to sleep. Essentially, the behaviors of those involved were the same as when I was young.

Those observations gave me a little better understanding of transposition. As a child, my perspective had been limited to my small *purse-and leg-walled* arena under the pew. I could see very little, and my mind could not comprehend even the tiny bit that I saw and heard while I was down there. But, as an adult sitting in the pew, I could see, hear, and understand so much more. I could look down and see things on the floor. I could look around and see other adults. I could look up a little and see the platform and those on it. I could turn around and see what was behind and to the sides. I could look up and see the ceiling. I was able to see and comprehend more things and behaviors than I could as a child. I also understood more of what had happened to get us to the point where those church services could occur.

As a former ironworker and carpenter, I knew what it had taken to get those walls built and those steel rafters and purlins up there. I could listen to the preacher and make mental connections to previously learned academic and professional information. I could sing and have an idea of some of the physical and mental processes required to do so. I could shake someone's hand and have an idea of the neurological and biological connections being formed. I could hug a brother (but not for twenty seconds, ha!) and understand that there was much more to it than just a hug. I could pray, and maybe speak in tongues, and understand some of the physical and spiritual behaviors necessary for those experiences. The point of this rambling is that as an adult (higher), I had a much greater understanding of the things and behaviors around me than I did as a child (lower). Life was much simpler as a child, but I also observed and understood so much less. Even if someone had tried to share all of that information with me as a child, I would not have been able to comprehend it.

I don't claim to know intimate details of the metallurgy of the steel in the rafters, or the metal in the tools I use to make a desk, or the metal that composes the tiny screws in my glasses, or the minute details of synaptic functions. Any one of those topics would require a long time to master. What I am claiming is that my perspectives have sufficiently broadened to the point that I know I will never understand everything. Knowing that I know very little is beneficial. I will never know everything. There simply isn't enough time in this life, and I don't have the mental capabilities.

This book relies heavily on behaviorism and neurology to explore connections within and through contrasting situations. Though I have various levels of knowledge and experience in each of those areas, I would be a fool to claim I know everything about any one of those specialty areas. Even subject matter experts have more to learn about their craft.

Occasionally someone may get to the absolute rock bottom of a topic, but that creates a problem of its own if the individual stops there. Informational silos produce individuals that others often pity or dislike. Let's put this in terms of gifted athletes. How many times have we seen players with far greater natural abilities than anyone else, but they were lazy, complained about practice, wasted their bodies on drugs, were not good teammates, or did stupid end zone dances after they scored? Personally, I never wanted to be around people like that. I never could understand why they felt it was their abilities alone that caused them to score—"Forget my teammate who passed me the ball!" "Forget my teammate who blocked for me!" "I did this! Me! Alone!" I have no time for such people. Even writing about them agitates me. There is nothing wrong with being excited, but when an individual performs well, the celebration should be more about the ones who helped with the performance.

Here's an old-school thought: what ever happened to being humble? When I scored, I'd give some high-fives or fist bumps (no keister slaps; still don't understand that), maybe jump excitedly a few times, then jog to my position and get ready for the match to continue. I had a job to do. I had to fulfill *my role* as a team member. After the match, win or lose, visiting with the opposing team was fun. This is an important point too—opponents (conflict) make your scoring efforts worth the strife. Think about this: I could grab my rugby ball and go in the backyard and score as much as I wanted, but I don't because I would be bored. I would not have an opponent. I would need an appropriate level of opposition (a child would not suffice) in order to feel the excitement of scoring. It is the contrasting of our wills-to-win-and-stop-the-other-from-scoring that actually causes a bond (connection) to form between opponents. He feels elated when he keeps me from scoring, and I feel elated when I score, and we build a relationship through that contest.

I apologize for the digression of a psychological tour of sports, but it helps me make my point: *athlete silos,* like informational silos or belief system silos, are harmful, and they do not last. Such individuals are either pushed away by teammates or left alone to simply fade away. When they (we) understand that opposition helps us to become more complete, we will be more open to looking at many things from many angles. So those rare know-it-alls who may actually know everything about a topic should look for ways to connect their knowledge to other informational sources. They should seek to understand viewpoints of others or broaden their perspective by looking for other informational silos that they can connect to theirs, and then another, and so on. Or simply ask a friend or colleague what he or she thinks about a topic. And actually listen. Try to understand the opposing view, and, like sports, the opposition will create a connection between the two. Those examples apply to theological silos too.

All of this to say, individuals who refuse to learn about views outside of their silos will eventually fade away. Those few who do manage to survive within their silo often adopt corrupted views. Even the Bible instructs us to be aware of the times, so we must continue to learn. The only way to grow into an individual that others will want to connect with is through the healthy interaction of both supportive and oppositional views.

As Lewis comments, we waste our time trying to talk with others who look only at the natural. Effective conversations will require all of us (yes: theists, agnostics, and atheists) to repeatedly ask questions of ourselves and others. *Is there a supernatural world? If there is not a supernatural, is there something else beyond the natural? Does Satan exist? Does God exist? If He (or Satan) does exist, is He (or Satan) involved in the physical world? If so, to what degree? Why are we here? Where do we go, if anywhere, after death? If there is not a God, how do we exist?*

I have asked those questions and others like them. As an agnostic and atheist, I asked them. As a theist, I still ask them—quite often. Why would I do that? Because I have learned that keeping myself from getting stuck in an informational silo widens and solidifies my theological foundation. Are you surprised that I sometimes rationally reconsider agnosticism or atheism? Don't be because data from other silos makes my silo more stable. Also, if I fail to continue to ask such questions as a theist, I make myself a hypocrite because I want others to ask questions. I also continue to ask questions because I believe that if I have found the true path, my footing will become surer and the path clearer. Failing to continue to clear the path will allow it to become overgrown, unstable, and impassable. I have been alive long enough to watch some become so secure in their faith that they became stuck in a theological silo before eventually fading away or adopting a twisted theology. When handled appropriately, a small amount of insecurity leads to greater security.

Don't think that I'm suggesting you need to switch your belief system. I'm not here to proselytize. What I am suggesting is that all of us be confident enough in our beliefs to have a look around. I'm not asking atheists to become theists or agnostics. I'm only suggesting we have a look around. I'm asking my theist brothers and sisters to have enough faith in their respective theologies to look at atheistic and agnostic systems as well as other theistic systems. Oneness believers explore Trinitarian theology and vice versa. Only by honestly and consistently exploring other areas will we find the truth. The honest sharing of dissociated views will help promote associations that allow for greater communications on a level that will easily fit within James's definition of a spiritual experience.

" When handled appropriately, a small amount of insecurity leads to greater security. "

Here is a statement that might cause some theists to feel slightly offended: As a youth leader, I consistently asked theistic students the questions above, and others like them. Some might think such exercises are inappropriate for youth classes in a religious environment. I often respond with something like, "They are berated with questions and statements like that in almost every non-religious setting. And they only get one-sided answers. Don't you want your child to see how I and their peers in the classroom think about and process those questions and answers?" My wife and I purposely structured our classes to be discussion focused so that students would be able to see multiple applications to the lives of others. Sure, there were classes that were more traditional. At times that is the most effective way to teach, but we always followed up with *processing* times where we explored how the students had applied what had been previously taught. Such teaching methodologies are just sound educational practices.

As we climb out of this rabbit hole and return to Lewis's transposition, we should now have a clearer understanding of the importance of glimpsing the supernatural world that lies just beyond our physical perceptual abilities. When we approach this discussion from above, everything looks different.

As I write this, I am reminded of Flew's reframing of the theistic/atheistic debate. Lewis and Flew had some debates, and Lewis's transposition was presented before Flew's 1973 *Presumption of Atheism*. I sometimes wonder if Flew adapted Lewis's transposition to atheism as a way to reframe debates. I mean no discredit toward Flew. His argument was original, effective, and highly influential, and I don't mean to imply otherwise. I just wonder if Lewis's thoughts prompted Flew's thoughts. If so, it is even greater support for my claim that the sharing of different ideas is important for the progression of our understandings.

Lewis concluded his sermon by addressing four areas related to transposition: development, incarnation, judgmental errors, and resurrection. I summarize them because they may help to further clarify some of the processes associated with glossolalia. Understandably, it can be a difficult process for us to comprehend. Following Lewis's four areas (development, incarnation, judgmental errors, resurrection), I add one—eschatology.

Development

Physical things don't inherently become otherworldly through some random automatic process. Drawings don't eventually grow into actual trees or grass. There's no unguided evolution at play in transposition. Lewis clarified that his point was not to suggest that a simple, natural act like eating could, over millions of years, somehow organically develop into a sacred Christian ceremony (Communion). He argued that a pre-existing Spiritual Reality—which was present even before creatures—is what bestows (transposes) new, higher meaning upon such natural (lower) behaviors as eating. However, in certain circumstances, the Spiritual Reality effectively redefines the natural act, making it into something different and imbued with deeper significance.

Lewis makes a clear distinction between the spiritual and the natural. Art and rituals can be meaningful and even life-changing, but they belong in their own separate realms. The pictures we take or draw remind us of the physical world, but they can't become reality. Similarly, the natural act of eating doesn't automatically become a religious symbol just because we repeat it many times. However, eating can become sacred if we apply the Spirit. The Christian practice of Communion is the application of the Spirit to the natural act of eating that gives it a deeper, spiritual meaning. In other words, divinity elevates ordinary actions to the realm of the sacred through spiritual meaning and purpose.

Incarnation

The Incarnation may be the greatest example of transposition. The Bible tells us that God transposed into an earthly form so that humans could comprehend Him and be more open communicating with Him. To use organizational terminology, this is often viewed as a *top-down model*. But it can also be viewed as a *bottom-up model*—those who want to communicate with Him may do so. He developed a closer relationship (connection) with humans so that they could communicate with Him more effectively.

Jesus's ascension did not end the movement toward deeper unity between humans and God; instead, humanity, while remaining distinct, is brought into closer communion with the Divine. This concept allows for further recognition of how contrasting elements such as the spiritual and the physical can converge into an interaction that is both top-down *and* bottom-up. The relationship is not limited to *either/or* interactions; it is *both/and*. Jesus is a good example of that. He was *both* fully God *and* fully man. He was a physical representation of the spiritual two-way relationship.

Judgmental Errors

Lewis's third point was that examining transposition solely from a lower (physical) perspective leads to flawed judgments. He pointed out that the effectiveness of skeptics' arguments often hinges on diminishing terms like *only* or *nothing more than*. In a narrow sense, their conclusions are true for them because they genuinely do not perceive anything beyond physical realities. They accurately claim to have observed all the tangible evidence and assert that nothing else is present. They grasp all the facts but miss their deeper meaning, genuinely believing they've seen everything, unaware of the ultimate significance beneath the surface.

> **Contrasting elements such as the spiritual and the physical can converge into an interaction that is both top-down and bottom-up. The relationship is not limited to either/or interactions; it is both/and.**

This example helps to shed some light on our previous discussion of non-glossolalists who research tongues. As I said, most are respectful and are genuinely seeking to understand the practice. Their conclusions are usually correct for the information they have. From their *lower* viewpoint they are correct when they find an element of dissociation, but they miss the *higher* meaning—the all-pervasive *association*.

Even those who have been glossolalists for long periods of time are not able to auditorily or visually explain the experience. I still struggle. In fact, similar to Lewis, this book has been something of a deeper learning process for me, but still, there is absolutely no way to express it using physical means. Ask anyone to describe it, and they will be unable. They will look up and to the right as they try to find some way. Most will stutter as they search for words and metaphors. I do this too, and that used to annoy me until one day it occurred to me that maybe it is not supposed to be describable. Maybe it is supposed to remain largely in the mystical so that we need to exercise faith.

How can we truly describe such a deep spiritual experience? One in which God is communicating with a human using an unknown language? Our minds experience information overload at trying to comprehend the limitless information being transposed from the higher world to the lower. We have no human way to represent the experience with our finite minds or limited senses, so we try and use multiple senses to explain, but we have no words. We have no art. We have no comprehensible actions that can represent the experience. The best we have are emotional and ecstatic, seemingly pathological, expressions.

I have mentioned that being a true member of a group affords greater insights into group experiences. My experiences provide a deeper understanding than a researcher who was simply involved in ethnographic participant-observation. Sure, researchers might gain some insight, but think back to my example of sleeping under the pew. My perceptions were very limited, but my perspectives have gotten *higher* and are continually on a journey to increasingly higher planes so I will know more tomorrow (hopefully) than I do now. I am not a theologian nor am I a particularly spiritual person, and those spiritually *higher* than I might be able to provide you with a better analysis of glossolalia than I can. However, my point regarding researchers is made: researching spiritual experiences, or having one in order to simply learn about it, will not provide the same level of understanding as a true practitioner.

Don't suppose from any of my comments that I am suggesting all glossolalic researchers should be practitioners. Far from it. This book has been about the connections that can be created by sharing respectful, differing views. As a whole, the current state of glossolalic research focuses on the dissonance stage of glossolalia, but I see unity becoming more evident in the future and suggest that the focus should move further into the association "arena." Researchers of all belief systems (including atheists) who conduct honest research into this area will help that unity to arrive. The more we learn about the views of others the more unified we can become. Like the perfect musical piece that is created from the unity that follows the dissonance, tongues exploration is headed in that direction, and a foundation that is created from multiple views will produce one that is solid. The dissonance that is created by current glossolalic research will help to create depth and beauty when it unifies.

Resurrection

Lewis proposes that transposition offers fresh insights into the Resurrection. God descended into human form as Jesus and later ascended. Scripture suggests that His ascension aims to draw humanity into the supernatural. This process started with God taking on human form and will culminate with humanity rising (ascending, being drawn) into the supernatural realm.

Initially, this might seem unremarkable, but transposition can have profound effects on simple processes. Lewis illustrated the remarkability of this process by pointing out the vast differences that exist between an actual *thing* and its portrayal in a picture. He used the example of an artist working with only white paper to illustrate a variety of things like the sun, clouds, snow, water, and even human skin. From one standpoint, using such a plain medium for so many different things appears drastically insufficient. Yet, from another perspective, it achieves a kind of perfection. Lewis explained that if artistic techniques, such as shading, are executed skillfully, that plain white paper with its careful shading can brilliantly resemble glaring sunlight. Despite the vast gap between spirit and nature, or a thing and its illustration, a drawing uses mere white paper and skillful technique to bring things to life. Though this seems woefully inadequate, it's also remarkably effective. Yes, we can almost feel cold while gazing at paper snow or warm our hands at a paper fire.

Further exploring how, as Lewis illustrated, simple drawings can evoke profound effects, we see that their power often stems from the skillful interplay of contrasts. The most striking drawings likely owe their impact to this dynamic. The ability to almost feel cold from paper snow or warmth from a paper fire, as Lewis described, relies on these contrasts creating a vivid, tangible response. This principle extends beyond art to life, where our differences—cultural, personal, or emotional—blend to form beautiful, meaningful lives. For those who believe in an afterlife, these contrasts may also guide us toward the ultimate connection we anticipate there, harmonizing our diverse experiences into a transcendent whole. Speaking of the afterlife. . . .

Eschatology (added)

Lewis ended his sermon by talking about the Resurrection, but that leads me, and others such as Richie, to add eschatological (end result) considerations to the fate of glossolalia after the Resurrection.[352] If tongues is about a connection between the Divine and physical, and both entities are seeking to draw closer together, what happens to glossolalia when those entities eventually combine? First Corinthians 13:8 informs us that the phenomenon of tongues will eventually cease. Why? Why would such a profound spiritual experience come to an end? Some theologians argue that glossolalia serves as a temporary *bridge* for communication between the physical and supernatural realms. Others suggest that it will transform into the universal mode of communication, understood by all. Thus, it will *cease* to be a specialized phenomenon because it will be universally understood. Everyone will speak and comprehend it. If God truly desires humans to experience preliminary glimpses of heaven, as Lewis proposes, glossolalia may actually be the language of the Divine kingdom, offering a preview of the future age. If so, then this concept also helps to explain present-day miracles when we read Revelation 21:4, which tells us that there will no longer be illness. There will no longer be a need for miracles. The same can be said of everlasting peace. It is those glimpses into the higher world that work to draw participants closer to the supernatural.

In the end we see that glossolalia is more about unity, with others and with the supernatural, than it is about dissociating. Sure, as we have discussed, dissociation is necessary to create the perfect musical piece, and that process relates to humans needing to slightly dissociate from their surroundings (prefrontal cortex) in order to achieve the unity produced by tongues. It also happens when we engage with others. The same general process creates a dynamic unity between individuals and between individuals and the Divine.

> **" Glossolalia is more about unity, with others and with the supernatural, than it is about dissociating. "**

There's an intellectual beauty in C. S. Lewis's thoughtful approach to difficult topics, showing how his blend of rational inquiry and spiritual openness can transform an initial aversion to an unsettling phenomenon (glossolalia) into a possible, remarkable shift in perspective. What may initially seem humiliating or deeply uncomfortable, even causing a sense of alienation, can lead to a dramatic reorientation of views. For our purposes, glossolalia may be revealed as a Divine dialogue and unity with God. Indeed, exploration of an Achilles' heel may lead to profound insights.

Moving Back to James's Spiritual Experiences

As we have moved through this book, we have gradually focused on a specific spiritual experience within a specific group, but as we work toward its conclusion, let us re-widen our focus to include wider spiritual experiences that can be a part of James's definition. After all, James has been a guide throughout, and it would be improper to exclude him now.

Hopefully this concept of transposition helps you to envision one way the supernatural and the natural may interface. It may also provide greater understanding for why I chose to focus on the brain throughout this work: the mind is the filter through which the supernatural attempts to communicate with us. The mind is important for the transposition process, and it is an element that we all possess. There may be additional *filters* for humans, and some filters on the supernatural side as well. The Bible does give some indication that there are contentions between angels, so that can be considered one type of filter, but our purpose here is with the human side and the area in which they meet. Recall James's spiritual definition uses positive human behaviors as a gauge to determine if an event was in fact a spiritual experience.[353] This book included vocal and physical forms of communication (facial expressions, behaviors, and so on) within that definition because they are also forms of human behavior and can produce positive, lasting change.

The idea of the human mind as a filter within Lewis's process of transposition also makes some of the information presented regarding sound, vision, behaviors, and the brain much more important. Though Lewis focused on tongues, his concept has implications for James's much broader definition of spiritual experiences. I mentioned earlier that my time in Alaska was one of the most spiritually and psychologically healing for me, but I didn't give a lot of reasons why. Allow me to provide a very brief summary.

I slept in my classroom when I first arrived in Alaska because I didn't have a place to stay. It's not uncommon in places with such limited housing. I went to the school gym and pulled one of the track high jump mats into my room to sleep on. During the day I stood it up against the wall. At night it was like having a mansion to myself. I cooked in the home economics classroom. I had the gym and weight room to myself. I rode my mountain bike through the halls. I eventually stayed in a fishing lodge for the winter after it closed for the season. Mostly I just had to pay the power bill and keep the pipes from freezing. My first night there I was sleeping with the window open, and I was awakened by the sound of a horse trotting on the dirt road outside. It suddenly hit me, *Wait, there ain't no horses here.* I jumped up to see the tail end of a moose trotting toward town.

The town had no doctors. We dealt with our aches and pains and relied on others when necessary. There were no radio stations. No satellite radio. I had a few CDs in my truck. No TV. Some people had some of those old six-foot satellite dishes. No newspapers. No cell phones. No fast food. During fishing season there might be two or three places to get some food. Except for a few staples like milk, butter, bread, and rice, I caught or shot what I ate each night. Most days I pulled crab pots after work. On the way back to shore, I would fill a large pot with salt water from the Gulf of Alaska and use that to cook the crabs and the rice.

When other teachers and families flew home for Christmas holidays, I stayed behind to pull their crab pots and clean and store their crabs for them. I kayaked when I felt like it. I put my mattress on the floor in front of the fireplace in the living room and slept there for the two-week holiday. My daily routine included various forms of exercise, spirituality, healthy food, and a very small number of good people. I even enjoyed going to the post office to visit with the workers. We jokingly called our time visiting "going postal." (The old timers will get that reference.) When I walked in, I'd say something like, "Let's go postal." My point is that there were few things to clog my mental filters.

The lack of interference from music, media, and social strife helped to clear my filters. My senses became more attuned to things happening within my own body, within nature around me, and to the supernatural. I was, and still am, amazed at the spirituality I felt during Tlingit native dances. Of time spent in nature. When I went to Harlequin Lake for my private Sunday *church* services, it was easy for me to have spiritual experiences. I didn't have to clear my mental filters before connecting with the Spirit. It was easy to access the spiritual realm because I was in an almost constant state of spiritual awareness. It was not necessarily because I was in Alaska; it was because of the lack of man-made inferences clogging my spiritual filters. The transposition of the spiritual into my environment was much easier. I had lived a lot of life before I moved there, and I had not realized how clogged those filters were with earthly experiences until I had been in Yakutat for quite a while.

When I left to pursue my PhD, I was *punched in the face* with the realization of how much sensory overload our brains must manage and how that hindered transposition. That realization has influenced my studies and occupation since. When I picked my truck up at the Seattle docks, I felt I would explode because of the Seattle traffic. Talk about road rage. I had it. Later, I thought I would enjoy a meal from a fast-food restaurant but soon needed to stop somewhere on Interstate 90 to throw up. I was unaccustomed to the junk they put in the food. I had difficulty sleeping at night because of the noise and light pollution. No more moose trotting down the street, no wolves howling, no bear prowling outside my tent, no Northern Lights as a night-light. My senses were not accustomed to the onslaught of unnatural stimulation.

In the many years since leaving Alaska, my filters have often gotten clogged with junk that doesn't need to be there. At times it was because of work. There were times I had to look at things and do things at work that I was not necessarily comfortable with. It might be things I heard in a store. It might be something I saw on the internet (I still don't do social media). Some things were from my PhD studies. It might be something on the magazine cover in the store. But one of my tricks to help unclog those filters is to dwell on my time in Yakutat. I utilize other methods, but mental imagery of those times is pretty effective. It provides me with a focal point that continually reminds me of how much my senses were, and are, overloaded. It also provides me with a gauge that helps to keep me aware of when I need to unclog my senses so that I am better at connecting with the Divine and with those around me.

Throughout this book, we have spent a considerable amount of time looking at how elements of vision and hearing can clog our mental filters, create dissonance, and limit our abilities to connect to both the physical and spiritual realms. But that was done to show that we can use those stressful, filter-clogging situations to promote stronger connections than we would have been able to without the conflict. That's not to say that strong connections cannot be made without quarrels, only that they can be highly beneficial if we can find and use the "tools" found in those situations to promote cohesion. Recalling Wyatt and his tube socks is just one example.

Over the last few years, my wife has occasionally made comments similar to this: "You've changed a lot for the better since we were married. You're much more calm." It's nice to know that I've matured, at least a little, after six decades of living. Joking aside, I know what she means. In my early teens I was often told I had that "laid-back surfer attitude." Unfortunately, I can point to several specific instances that created major, negative changes to that attitude. Most of my crazy life experiences happened before she and I met, but I carried a lot of that baggage into our marriage. I also carried it into other aspects of my life, like careers and ministry.

I often reacted, and sometimes still do, too quickly. It's what I had been trained to do since I was seventeen, and some behaviors can be difficult to unlearn when they have been subconsciously engrained—you see a problem, you deal with it, you move on to the next problem. But that doesn't always work well in family or ministry. Many times I wish I would have reacted with more patience, but on the positive side, I learned to apologize for my actions. And honestly, there were times when my impatient reactions were absolutely necessary. Somewhere along this journey of life, I have learned that what I allow into my mind can either help me to become a better person (coherence), or it can hinder my personal development and social interactions (dissociation). It can clog my filters.

This helps bring me to the point of why I felt it was important to share such a broad amount of information throughout this book. In the last few chapters we looked at a specific, non-pathological religious experience that requires a slight degree of dissociation, which allows for a high degree of association. Prior to that, in chapters 7, 6, 5, and 4 we explored how what we hear and see can affect the correct and incorrect neurological processing of data and how that can affect our behaviors and abilities to connect. Chapter

3 explored spiritual experiences from a very broad perspective that included theistic, atheistic, evolutionary, chemical, and near-death experiences, to name a few. My general journey through theism, agnosticism, atheism, then back to theism, along with some relatively well-known personalities who had travelled similar paths, were presented in chapter 2. Chapter 1 provided an overview of the historically fluid, and sometimes contentious, connection between science and religion. Finally, the introduction presented neurotheology and James's spiritual argument as some guiding principles. And lastly, or firstly, this book started with a brief explanation of autoethnography and some of my early years that related to religion and education. All of that was done to help you begin to understand the depths to which what we see, hear, and speak affect us as individuals and, by extension, others, and to provide a few personal examples of some of those effects. It was also to point out that although our spiritual filters become clogged, we can still learn to clear them or set those issues aside so that we can connect with the spiritual world—however we view that world.

I am sure you noticed that I summarized this book in reverse order. That was intentional. I wanted to end by reviewing some of my first comments. My main theme has been about connecting. One of the *colors* we used to explore connections was to clarify that *what we allow into our minds affects our behaviors, with the end result being either dissociation, association, or some combination of the two.* Good *in* tends to equal good *out*; bad *in*, tends to equal bad *out*. We also spent significant real estate discussing how differences can lead to positive relationships. Our differences can become a solid foundation. The theistic spiritual experience of glossolalia was used as an example of how dissociation can lead to association. I also clarified that researchers who end a study when they find dissociation in glossolalia unintentionally miss the unity that follows. Along the way, I hope I have allowed opposing belief systems (atheists, agnostics, theists) to see into the world of others in a manner that provides some respectful, conversational material.

I hope my stream of consciousness style reflections on some of my own behavioral conditioning, struggles, mistakes, and successes has allowed you to find something to which you can connect. Though this was not intended to be a theistic or an atheistic work, it seemed to become heavily theistic during the discussion regarding glossolalia. But even with glossolalia, I attempted to let the secular quantitative and qualitative data speak for itself, except when I presented personal experiences. In the end, this information can be beneficial in both secular and religious settings. As we create more positive connections from our contrasts, we create stronger and healthier human and spiritual (whatever form of spirituality you choose) relationships.

Hopefully you have paused to consider at least one topic in relation to your current beliefs. While I have attempted to ease your stress in some sections, such as medications and strictly evolutionary ideas and heavily theistic discussions, the reality is that many deal with those issues each day, and caring theists and atheists alike should try to understand the struggles of the others. Avoiding topics that might offend only leads to long-term inability to deal with conflict. As previously mentioned, I don't always view conflict as a bad thing — it can be a great place to find "tools"

66 Avoiding topics that might offend only leads to long-term inability to deal with conflict. 99

to improve relationships. It can be a great teacher and unifier, and I have presented multiple examples of individuals who developed wonderful lives and works from conflict and dissociation. I summarize three that exemplify the beauty that can result from contrasts.

1. David struggled with his leadership at personal, familial, and national levels, but what would have happened to the Jewish nation if David had simply given up? Had not learned from his mistakes? How might the Jewish nation look now if he had been a one-trick pony? Just a warrior and not a poet or musician? We wouldn't have the psalms. There would be one less nation, or at least it would look very different. Even secular leadership methods would be lacking because some of the most effective and modern methods are based on some of David's teachings.

2. James struggled with mental and physical illnesses for a large portion of his life, but where would the field of psychology be if he had simply given up? His weaknesses became a driving force. He based much of psychology's foundation in spirituality. The field currently has a lot of negativity associated with it, but that often results from the removal of spirituality from the field. James also made significant contributions to the field of philosophy. Without him we might not have solid psychological or philosophical foundations from which to discuss spiritual experiences.

3. Lewis struggled with religious issues. He went from theism to atheism, then back to theism, though he still had some theological struggles (don't we all?). But it was his path that led him to becoming one of the greatest philosophers, and one of the most effective Christian defenders, of all time. In relation to the later portions of this book, he provided a great example of how

theists can approach theistic topics that cause "embarrassment." Through his study he found answers that continue to unify people decades later.

I ask, *What conflicts are in our lives that have the potential to create unity and beauty in such a way that it will have positive results for years to come?* Let's revisit Lewis's drawing analogy that real-world items, such as landscapes, can be transposed into pictures: the pictures themselves will not undergo a natural transformation and grow into actual trees and grass. He elaborated that while there is a vast gap between the Divine and nature, these drawings demonstrate how the lower can still reflect the higher, even when the medium seems woefully inadequate. Yet, still, when shadows are skillfully rendered, a mere piece of white paper can convincingly convey the brilliance of intense sunshine. Similarly, viewers might almost experience a chill when looking at snow depicted on paper or feel a semblance of warmth from a drawn fire.

Our lives may seem simple and boring, seemingly consisting of only white paper and lead. We seem inadequate. We behave in ways that harm us and others. We seem *not beautiful*. But when properly done, the tapestry of the lives we draw will allow others to see and feel the opposing forces of *cold* (dissociation) while they *warm* their hands at the *paper fire* of unity (association). Our Achilles' heel becomes a beacon.

A Brief Explanation of the Title (Part 2)

Just as I began this book in an unusual manner, I end it in an unusual manner—with a rewording of the explanation of the title.

Finding *coherence* within *chaos* was the general flow of this book, and that is the *paradox*. *Dissonance* was represented by other words like *stress, disagreement, dissociation, struggle, animosity*, and so on. Likewise, *coherence* was represented by multiple synonyms.

Some of the themes explored were between religion and science, religion and religion, person to person, and person to *something*. We used the relatively new field of neurotheology to converge various research fields. Later chapters surveyed information that argues that what we see and hear is cognitively processed and then affects how we speak, both vocally and visually. Visual communication included both intended (i.e., sign language, wink of an eye) and unintended (i.e., facial expressions, immediate reactions) behaviors.

The focus on mental processes, sensory experiences, and self-analysis influenced me to write large portions in a non-academic manner. However, some sections required some academic structure and citations. Sections that relate to relatively recent research concerning media's effects on the brain are a good example. Such inclusions are acceptable because they are a part of my autoethnographic mental processes, and it will help provide you with greater confidence in my conclusions.

The ellipsis at the end of the title is important. An ". . ." may be used for multiple reasons. Most important for this book, it indicates (1) a trailing off of a thought, (2) that something is not quite complete, or (3) a process is continuing. It is also important for the ending of this work. I use it to indicate that there is a lot of information we were unable to explore, but mostly, I use it to indicate that our *journeys* are not complete. Our *odysseys* continue. . . .

In Summary

In this chapter, we moved away from scientific analysis and into philosophy. C. S. Lewis's concept of *transposition* was used to explore a "bridge" between spiritual and physical realms. Transposition posits that "higher" realities (e.g., spiritual insights) adapt to "lower" mediums (e.g., human senses), and because our senses often share multiple meanings, the framework provides a means to consider some of glossolalia's ecstatic behaviors as physical expressions of overwhelming spiritual input. Despite the potential to appear pathological or "embarrassing," like both Lewis and I, and some others, initially found it, many have learned that glossolalia can be an "organ of the Holy Ghost" that promotes unity with the spiritual world and with the physical world.

A central idea has been that dissonance—whether from glossolalia's strangeness, personal discomfort, or intellectual conflict—can foster unity. We critiqued "informational silos" that isolate beliefs and advocated for dialogue across theistic, atheistic, and agnostic perspectives to help prevent stagnation and to build stronger connections. Conflict, likened to sports rivalries, was used as an example of a potential unifier, creating bonds through opposition. Alaska's minimal distractions, at least in my situation, were contrasted with "civilization's" sensory overload to illustrate that spiritual connections can be hindered when our "cognitive filters" become clogged by modern noise (media, stress). But, clearing these filters enhances awareness and increases our appreciation for healthy connections. Along the way, I also demonstrated, and called for, humility ("knowing that I know very little is beneficial") and openness to mystery because of their importance in understanding complex subjects that remain elusive ("I don't know, and I don't know anyone who does"), like glossolalia's mechanics.

Transposition was considered in light of the Incarnation and Resurrection of Jesus as an example of a divine entity transposing into human form, before extending it to the possible eschatological role of tongues. We wondered if, even though it is considered Divine speech, it will cease to exist or be the universal language of the afterlife. We also included a tapestry metaphor: life's contrasts—struggle and joy, dissociation and association—can create beauty and unity, like warming our hands at the paper fire. Embracing these tensions, appropriately questioning assumptions, and respectfully engaging diverse perspectives are essential for personal and spiritual growth and opening doors for connections. Despite containing dissociation, glossolalia is a profound symbol of association between ethereal and physical worlds.

Introspective Questions for Chapter 10

? **Beyond Scientific Explanations:** When have you encountered a question (e.g., about spirituality, consciousness, or purpose) where scientific explanations felt incomplete? How did you, or might you, use philosophical or introspective methods to seek deeper understanding, similar to how the text shifts to philosophy for further explanation of glossolalia?

? **Discomfort as Motivation:** C. S. Lewis found glossolalia embarrassing, yet this discomfort drove exploration. Reflect on a time when unease or confusion about a belief or practice (like glossolalia) motivated you to understand it better. What insights or growth resulted from this process?

? **Transposition's Limits:** Lewis's transposition involves expressing a higher reality (e.g., spiritual insight) through a lower medium (e.g., words, behaviors, drawings). Where do you feel the limitations of language or physical expression most acutely when sharing profound experiences? How does this shape your understanding of spiritual communication?

? **Perspective and Humility:** The author contrasts a child's limited view under the pew with an adult's broader perspective, noting, "Knowing that I know very little is beneficial." How does acknowledging your perspective's limits influence your engagement with those holding different beliefs? What challenges or benefits arise from this humility?

? **Judgmental Errors:** Lewis warns that viewing phenomena only from below misses deeper meaning, leading to incorrect conclusions. Have you ever focused solely on observable facts and misunderstood a situation's significance? How might considering a higher perspective (e.g., spiritual or emotional) alter your understanding?

? **Breaking Informational Silos:** The author cautions, "Informational silos produce individuals that others often pity or dislike." Where might you be susceptible to staying in a comfortable intellectual or theological silo? What steps could you take to respectfully engage with opposing viewpoints to foster growth?

? **Conflict and Connection:** The author argues, "It is the contrasting of our wills . . . that actually causes a bond." When has a disagreement or challenge (e.g., in relationships, debates, or sports) led to a stronger connection or insight? What factors enabled this unity? How do you balance conviction with openness?

? **Mental Filters and Clarity:** The author found spiritual clarity in Alaska's simplicity, where "mental filters" were unclogged. What sources (e.g., media, stress) clog your mental filters today? What practices (e.g., nature, solitude) help clear them to enhance connection with yourself, others, or the spiritual?

? **Mystical and Ineffable:** The text suggests glossolalia's indescribability may be intentional, enhancing its mystical nature. How do you approach experiences or concepts that defy logical explanation? Does their ineffability deepen their meaning or prompt skepticism? How does this shape your spiritual perspective?

? **Adversity and Beauty:** The text highlights how struggles (e.g., David's, Lewis's) create beauty, concluding, "The tapestry of the lives we draw" uses contrasts to inspire. How have adversities or contrasts in your life shaped a meaningful outcome? How can you use life's shadows and white paper to create unity or impact?

MIC DROP . . . OH WAIT . . .

I t is my interest in the *contrasting quirks* evident in the lives of others like King David and William James, and the rich insights their lives offer about the human condition, that fuels my inquiry into complex behaviors. My own contrasts and those of others I know continue to stoke the flames. This drive to understand the multifaceted nature of our physical and spiritual experiences underpins the question I now present: *Why have we invested so much time exploring a deeply spiritual phenomenon like glossolalia, especially when I naturally look for physical explanations over spiritual ones?*

The answer lies in the wealth of insights it provides for unraveling some of the *hows* and *whys* of human behavior. We began by examining how *sight* and *sound* subconsciously shape our actions, for better or worse. This led to a discussion on why negative behaviors might hold hidden positive potential. Though sometimes viewed skeptically, non-pathological speaking in tongues positively influences conscious and subconscious processing. Even tongues' ecstatic behaviors were explored through the lens of Lewis's transposition.

Glossolalia's value extends beyond the spiritual, as its patterns resonate with everyday life. The Conceptual Model of the Glossolalic Process (Figure 15) offers a versatile framework for understanding behavior. For example, when our children frustrate us, eventually reaching the "determination and decision time"—that pivotal moment marked by the star at the dissociation triangle's peak. Here, we choose, consciously or subconsciously, to redirect the raw emotions or continue to allow them to grow. Ideally our choice fosters reconnection with our child (symbolizing connecting with the Spirit), despite our lingering frustration (lower level of dissociation). The tragic Mustang-Hyundai accident, where one driver's actions severely injured another, illustrated this dynamic vividly. While we all face this cycle throughout each day, high-stress environments often require more frequent navigation through the model's stages.

Dissociation and our progression through the stages may even last for a long time. The dissonance of feeling like a high school "quitter" fueled my drive to pursue education—after mentors planted the seeds—but I had to be the one who chose to act and to persist. Along the way, and in life in general, I have also learned to evaluate my unwise choices so that each bad decision teaches me something that will help me make better ones next time (hopefully).

I've seen students face similar "determination and decision time" moments with profound consequences. Some made destructive choices—gang involvement, drug use, attempted murder—while others simply chose to fall into negative patterns because, as one student said, "It's easy," despite knowing better. Yet, many chose paths to become good parents, social workers, carpenters, or teachers. Daniel* is a good example of a student who embodies this positive transformation.

Daniel's stubbornness, which I warned him could either harm or help him, mirrored my own youthful defiance. Though I rarely suggested military service, I urged Daniel to look toward the Army or Marines to learn how to channel his doggedness constructively. Years later, as I walked out of my classroom, I was surprised to see him walking toward me in his Marine uniform. He came to attention and saluted me. After I returned the salute, the first thing he said was, "I was a jerk." The first thing I said was, "Yep." Both of us smiled and teared a little at the same time. As we talked, he shared how his stubbornness sustained him through many tough times, especially during the Battle of Fallujah. But more importantly for him, during the chaos of combat, his "pigheadedness" helped him to save fellow Marines. He transitioned "from a hellion to a hero" (my words, not his).

Daniel's story highlights the interplay between physical and spiritual realms (recall my previous universal definition of spirituality: *healthy behaviors that result from activities that help humans to connect*). His initial misuse of stubbornness (dissociation) laid the foundation for a life now admired for its positive impact on the community in which he now lives (association). Reflect on your own life, and you'll likely find moments where adversity, when positively redirected, fostered resilience and purpose.

Our conceptual framework bridges observable actions (physical) with inner thoughts (spiritual) and reveals how people navigate complex emotional and moral landscapes. Patterns in one domain, like glossolalia, illuminate others. For instance, my unspoken "conversation" with Sis. Freeman, better understood as a mental connection rather than visible or audible, supports this insight.

Our deep dive into glossolalia, therefore, was not merely an academic look at a niche spiritual phenomenon; it was an exploration of a human psychological *and* spiritual process that has broad behavioral applicability. With its discernible stages and clear parallels to decision-making in everyday life, it acts as a bridge between the two realms and allows us to investigate those *how* and *why* questions with both empirical and existential data and depth. For instance, after completing the conceptual model, I recognized that it loosely mirrors cognitive processes identified in behavioral psychology, where individuals reach a critical "tipping point" between ingrained habitual responses and deliberate, intentional change for the better.

Ultimately, I hope to have shown that my natural inclination toward physical explanations doesn't negate spirituality; it roots it in academic data, tangible examples, and conversational material that make spiritual aspects more relatable and accessible.

Introspective Questions for Mic Drop

? **Reflecting on Contrasts In Your Life:** Think about a time when you faced a personal contrast, such as a struggle between a negative trait (e.g., stubbornness) and a positive outcome (e.g., perseverance). How did the tension shape your decisions or growth? What parallels do you see with Daniel's journey from defiance to heroism?

? **Navigating "Determination and Decision Time":** The conceptual model highlights a pivotal moment—"determination and decision time"— where we choose to redirect emotions or let them escalate (e.g., a parent reconnecting with a child despite frustration). Can you recall a moment when you faced such a choice? What influenced your decision? How did it impact your relationships or actions?

? **The Role of Stubbornness:** Stubbornness, or tenacity, can be both a barrier and a strength, as seen in Daniel's story. In what ways has your own doggedness held you back or propelled you forward? How might you channel this trait constructively in future challenges?

? **Physical and Spiritual Connections:** The author defines spirituality as healthy behaviors that foster connection. Can you identify a moment when a physical action (e.g., a conversation, a task) led to a deeper sense of connection with yourself, others, or something greater? How does this relate to the idea that glossolalia's patterns mirror everyday decision-making?

? **Learning from Adversity:** The author shares how feeling like a high school "quitter" fueled his pursuit of education, much like Daniel's obstinacy became heroism. Reflect on a setback or adversity in your life. How did you redirect it into resilience or purpose? What lessons did you learn?

? **Choices and Consequences:** The Mustang-Hyundai accident illustrates the consequences of failing to navigate critical decision points. Think of a high-stakes decision you've made. How did your choice reflect your values? What might have happened if you'd chosen differently?

? **Mentorship and Transformation:** The author's guidance helped Daniel channel his bad behaviors into a constructive path. Who has been a mentor or guide in your life, planting seeds for positive change? How have you, in turn, influenced someone else's "determination and decision time"?

? **Applying the Conceptual Model:** The conceptual model of the glossolalic process applies to everyday scenarios, like managing frustration or making moral choices. Consider a recent challenge (e.g., a conflict, a career decision). How might the model's stages—dissociation, decision, reconnection—help you analyze your response and make better choices in the future?

? **Patterns Across Domains:** Glossolalia's patterns resonate with broader human experiences, like the unspoken "conversation" with Sis. Freeman. Can you identify a nonverbal or subconscious moment in your life that felt profoundly meaningful? How does it connect to your understanding of your own behavior?

? **Bridging Physical and Spiritual Realms:** The author's inquiry shows how physical explanations (e.g., behavioral psychology) can complement spiritual insights. In your own life, how do you balance rational, observable explanations with deeper, less tangible experiences? How might exploring both enhance your understanding of yourself or others?

MIC DROP . . .
FOR REAL THIS TIME

Some Grades

Because so much of my career was in education, and to not be hypocritical, I feel like I should be an example and give myself grades regarding how I manage three of the large areas addressed in this book: (1) the physical world, (2) the spiritual world, and (3) how I combine the two. Maybe something similar might be helpful for you.

Physical World: "C"

I am only average at managing my day-to-day life. I have made, and continue to make, a lot of mistakes. When I was younger I didn't see the value of learning from them. I didn't want to admit I had failed, so I swept my mistakes under the rug. That led to making the same ones many times with ever-increasing consequences. But I now look for what I can do to stop making mistakes and improve on them when I do make them. Within the physical world, I can do much better, but I can also do much worse. I'm *average*.

Spiritual World: "D+"

Not quite failing. Barely good enough to pass the *test*. It's not that I don't want to be more spiritual—I do. I wish I were better at getting past my logical thought processes. I envy (healthily, of course) those who are able to interpret glossolalic messages, meet someone (person *A*) for the first time and receive Divine messages that will help *A*, help others feel the Spirit through song, simply be more compassionate, and so on. But, though I strive to be a more spiritual person, I am learning to accept and have confidence in my *not super spiritual* role. In fact, I now cherish my limitations in this area because the few successes I have had are made more precious to me. However, that does not mean that I have given up on improving in this area, but I feel that I remain *below average*.

Combining the Physical and Spiritual Worlds: "B+"

It might seem that I made a mistake by giving myself a B+ when the previous grades were a C and a D+, but this grade is not about the average of the two. The B+ is about how well I feel I *combine* the worlds. This is, after all, possibly the most important of the areas because we are both physical and spiritual beings. Denying one world harms the other world, or at least limits it in some way. Can I do better? Absolutely. I'm working on it. Can I do worse? Yep, much worse.

I continue to work to accept and to value my calling to meld the two worlds. This is my role for now. Maybe it will change, maybe it won't. But one thing I have noticed is that the more confident I become with this role, the more I am able to help others be more comfortable in their roles—whether they excel in the physical world, excel in the spiritual world, or excel in combining the two. After all, all three are important, and they provide us with more stable grounds from which to have beneficial discussions. While the role of others, believers and non-believers alike, is to add to our knowledge base by honestly sharing information from their respective secular or spiritual fields, maybe, just maybe, my purpose is to add to our conversational foundation by attempting to intertwine the two. I'm a little *above average*.

Introspective Questions for Mic Drop #2

? **Self-Assessment:** The author uses grades (C, D+, B+) to evaluate his physical, spiritual, and integrative efforts. How would you assess your own management of these areas, using grades, metaphors, or another method? What insights emerge from this reflection?

? **Emotions of Evaluation:** What feelings or resistances arise when you consider evaluating your practical and spiritual life? How do these compare to your experiences with evaluation in other contexts? How does the book influence your approach?

? **Learning from Mistakes:** The author learned to face mistakes rather than hide them. How has your relationship with mistakes in your daily life (e.g., work, relationships) evolved? What book-inspired strategy could help you learn from them now?

? **Defining Success In the Physical World:** What does "doing well" in managing your day-to-day life mean to you? How do the book's insights about the physical world align with or challenge your standards?

? **Your Spiritual Dimension:** How do you define or experience the "spiritual" in your life? How does the author's perspective (e.g., his D+ self-assessment) resonate with or differ from your own sense of spiritual growth?

? **Cherishing Limitations:** The author finds value in "cherishing limitations" because he highlights successes. Are there areas where you feel limited?

How might reframing these, as suggested by the book, reveal strengths or deepen your appreciation for achievements?

? **Balancing Acceptance and Growth:** Where do you feel tension between accepting yourself as you are and striving for spiritual or personal growth? How does the book help you navigate this balance?

? **Integrating Key Aspects:** The author emphasizes integrating the physical and spiritual worlds. What major aspects of your life (e.g., work/family, action/reflection) require integration? How well do you balance them? What book insight could improve this?

? **Your Unique Role:** The author sees his role as melding worlds to foster connection. What unique role or contribution feels authentic to you in the physical, spiritual, or integrative space? How does the book clarify your sense of purpose, if it does?

? **Fostering Connection:** How might growing confident in your own path—whether in practical, spiritual, or integrative efforts—help you support others, as the author does through conversation? What book idea inspires you to build these connections?

GLOSSARY

This glossary offers definitions of key terms as they are used in this book, reflecting the author's professional knowledge, personal experiences, and the specific contexts of psychology, neuroscience, religion, music, and philosophy. Tailored to the book's interdisciplinary themes, these definitions may differ from broader uses and serve as a reference to enhance reader understanding.

Action observant treatment (AOT): A therapeutic approach emphasizing mindful observation of actions and their consequences to promote behavioral change.

Active listening: Fully concentrating, understanding, and responding to a speaker, showing engagement through verbal and non-verbal cues.

Affective system: The brain's neural network responsible for processing emotions and emotional responses.

Age of Reason: A historical period (17th–18th centuries) emphasizing rational thought and science; also, the developmental stage (around age seven) when children develop logical reasoning.

Agnosticism: The belief that the existence of God or the supernatural is unknown or unknowable.

Altered state of consciousness (ASC): A mental state differing from normal wakefulness, often induced by meditation, drugs, or trance.

Alternation (in music): The technique of switching between contrasting musical sections or themes.

Amygdala: A brain structure involved in processing emotions, fear, and memory.

α-Amylase (alpha-amylase): An enzyme in saliva, used as a biomarker for stress or arousal.

Aphasia: A disorder impairing the ability to understand or produce language, often due to brain damage.

Apologist (Christian): A person who defends Christian beliefs through reasoned arguments.

Apostolic Pentecostals (Apostolics): A Christian denomination emphasizing baptism in Jesus' name, speaking in tongues, and strict holiness standards.

Artificial intelligence (AI): Computer systems designed to perform tasks requiring human-like intelligence, such as learning or problem-solving.

Glossary

Association/associative: The mental process of linking ideas, memories, or stimuli based on experience or similarity.

Atheism: The lack of belief in the existence of gods or deities.

Attentional capacity: The brain's ability to focus on and process a limited amount of information at once.

Attentional filtering: The process of selectively focusing on relevant stimuli while ignoring distractions.

Auditory behaviors: Actions or responses triggered by sound, such as listening or reacting to music.

Auditory cortex: The brain region responsible for processing sound and auditory information.

Auditory imagery: The mental ability to recreate or imagine sounds without external stimuli.

Auditory mirror neurons: Neurons that activate when hearing sounds associated with actions, mirroring the action's neural response.

Auditory prism: A metaphorical concept describing how the brain separates and processes different auditory components.

Audiovisual mirror neurons: Neurons that respond to both visual and auditory cues related to actions, aiding in imitation and understanding.

Autoethnography: A research method combining autobiography and ethnography to study personal and cultural experiences.

Avatar: A digital or virtual representation of a person, often used in gaming or online environments.

Aversion to killing: A psychological or moral reluctance to take life, often studied in military or ethical contexts.

Azusa Street Revival: A historic Pentecostal revival (1906–1915) in Los Angeles, sparking the global Pentecostal movement.

Basal ganglia: Brain structures involved in coordinating movement, reward processing, and habit formation.

Behaviorism: A psychological theory focusing on observable behaviors and their conditioning, ignoring internal mental states.

Behaviorist: A proponent of behaviorism, studying behavior through stimulus-response relationships.

Belief checks: Cognitive processes to evaluate the validity or consistency of one's beliefs.

Belladonna: A toxic plant (Atropa belladonna) used historically in medicine and rituals for its psychoactive effects.

Bicycle Day: April 19, 1943, when Albert Hofmann ingested LSD, marking its first recreational use.

Big Bang: The scientific theory describing the universe's origin from a rapid expansion approximately 14 billion years ago.

Binocular rivalry: A phenomenon where conflicting visual inputs from each eye cause alternating perceptions.

Biocultural: The interplay between biological and cultural factors in shaping human behavior or evolution.

Blind spot (visual): An area in the retina lacking photoreceptors, resulting in a gap in the visual field.

Blindsight: The ability to respond to visual stimuli without conscious awareness, often due to brain damage.

Bounce rate: The percentage of website visitors who leave after viewing only one page, used in web analytics.

Brain: The organ responsible for thought, emotion, memory, and bodily functions, central to the nervous system.

Brain-Computer Interface (BCI): Technology enabling direct communication between the brain and external devices.

Brain-Derived Neurotrophic Factor (BDNF): A protein promoting neuron growth, survival, and plasticity in the brain.

Brodmann Area 44 (BA44): A brain region in the frontal cortex, part of Broca's area, involved in language production.

Broca's Aphasia: A language disorder caused by damage to Broca's area, impairing speech production but not comprehension.

Call-and-response: A musical or communicative pattern where one party responds to another's call, common in music and dialogue.

Card catalog: A traditional library system using cards to index books by author, title, or subject.

Charismatic experience: Intense spiritual or emotional experiences, often associated with Pentecostal or charismatic Christianity.

Child sexual abuse material (CSAM): Illegal content depicting sexual abuse of minors, also called child pornography.

Chladni figures: Patterns formed by vibrating surfaces sprinkled with powder, revealing nodal lines, studied in acoustics.

Cochlea: A spiral-shaped inner ear structure converting sound vibrations into neural signals.

Cognitive abilities: Mental skills like reasoning, memory, problem-solving, and attention.

Cognitive filters: Mental processes that prioritize or exclude information based on relevance or bias.

Cognitive functioning/processes: The brain's activities, including perception, memory, and decision-making.

Cognitive load capacity: The amount of mental effort a person can handle before performance declines.

Cognitive system: The brain's network of processes for acquiring, processing, and using information.

Coherence: The logical consistency or clarity of thoughts, arguments, or sensory experiences.

Communal singing: Group singing, often fostering social bonding or spiritual connection.

Compression of meaning: Condensing complex ideas or emotions into concise symbols or expressions.

Compulsive Sexual Behavior Disorder: A condition involving uncontrollable sexual urges causing distress or impairment.

Conditioning (classical and operant): Learning processes where behaviors are shaped by associations (classical) or consequences (operant).

Conditioning responses: Learned reactions to specific stimuli due to prior conditioning.

Confinement (philosophical problem): The metaphysical issue of whether free will is limited by determinism or physical constraints.

Connections: Neural or conceptual links between ideas, memories, or brain regions.

Connectomic approach: Studying the brain's neural connections (connectome) to understand its functions.

Conscious mind: The part of the mind aware of thoughts, sensations, and experiences.

Consciousness: The state of being aware of oneself and one's environment.

Conscious: Being awake and aware, capable of thought and perception.

Constructive memory: The process where memories are reconstructed, often influenced by biases or new information.

Contentious relationships: Interactions marked by conflict, disagreement, or tension.

Contrast: The difference between elements (e.g., in music or visuals), enhancing perception or meaning.

Conversion Disorder: A condition where psychological stress manifests as physical symptoms without medical cause.

Corporate glossolalia/corporate singing: Collective speaking or singing in tongues during religious services, often in unison.

Corticospinal motor movements: Motor actions controlled by the corticospinal tract, connecting the brain to muscles.

Cortisol: A stress hormone regulating metabolism, immune response, and stress reactions.

Creationism (biblical): The belief that the universe and life were created by God as described in the Bible.

Cultural neurophenomenological perspective: A framework combining neuroscience and phenomenology to study cultural influences on consciousness.

Cymatics: The study of visible sound vibrations, often creating patterns in materials like sand or water.

Deaf listening: The experience of deaf individuals perceiving music or sound through vibrations or visual cues.

Declarative learning: Acquiring knowledge that can be consciously recalled, like facts or events.

Deep reading: Engaged, focused reading that promotes critical thinking and comprehension.

Dehumanization: Treating individuals or groups as less than human, often to justify mistreatment.

Deism: The belief in a Creator God who does not intervene in the universe after Creation.

Delusions: False beliefs held despite evidence, often associated with mental disorders.

Demonic possession: The belief that an evil spirit controls a person's body or behavior.

Denial defense: A psychological mechanism where one refuses to acknowledge uncomfortable truths.

Dependence potential: The likelihood a substance or behavior will lead to addiction.

Depersonalization: Feeling detached from one's body or self, as if observing oneself externally.

Depersonalization/Derealization Disorder: A condition involving persistent depersonalization and/or derealization.

Derealization: Feeling that the external world is unreal or dreamlike.

Desensitization: Reduced emotional or physiological response to stimuli after repeated exposure.

Dewey Decimal System: A library classification system organizing books by subject using numerical codes.

Digital immigrants: People who adapted to digital technology later in life, as opposed to those born into it.

Digital natives: Individuals born in the digital age, naturally familiar with technology.

Dissociation: A disconnection between thoughts, identity, or reality, often a coping mechanism.

Dissociative amnesia: Memory loss for specific events or periods, often linked to trauma.

Dissociative disorders: Conditions involving disruptions in memory, identity, or consciousness.

Dissociative Identity Disorder (DID): A condition where a person has multiple distinct identities or personalities.

Dissociative Neurological Symptom Disorder: Neurological symptoms (e.g., paralysis) caused by psychological factors, not medical issues.

Dissonance: In music, clashing sounds; in psychology, conflicting thoughts causing discomfort.

Dominant chord: In music, the fifth chord in a key, creating tension resolved by the tonic.

Dopamine: A neurotransmitter linked to reward, motivation, and pleasure.

DSM-5-TR: The Diagnostic and Statistical Manual of Mental Disorders, 5th Edition, Text Revision, used for diagnosing mental disorders.

Dualism: The philosophical view that mind and body (or matter and spirit) are distinct entities.

Dysphasia: A milder form of aphasia, impairing language comprehension or production.

$E = MC^2$: Einstein's equation relating energy (E) to mass (M) and the speed of light (C), fundamental to relativity.

Earworms: Catchy tunes or melodies that replay involuntarily in the mind.

Ecstatic physical behaviors: Intense physical expressions (e.g., dancing, shaking) during religious or emotional experiences.

Endorphins: Hormones released during exercise or stress, producing feelings of euphoria.

Energy suckers: Informal term for people or situations that drain one's emotional or mental energy.

Enlightenment Period: An intellectual movement (17th–18th centuries) emphasizing reason, science, and individualism.

Epileptic events/temporal lobe epilepsy: Seizures originating in the temporal lobe, sometimes linked to mystical experiences.

Ernst Chladni: An 18th-century physicist who pioneered the study of acoustics and vibrating plates (Chladni figures).

Eschatology: The study of end times or ultimate destiny in religious or philosophical contexts.

Ethnographic participant-observation: A research method involving immersive observation within a cultural group.

Eyeless sight: The claimed ability to perceive without using eyes, often studied in parapsychology.

Faith: Belief in something (often religious) without empirical evidence.

False memories/changed memories: Recollections altered or fabricated due to suggestion or bias.

Feast of Pentecost: A Christian holiday celebrating the Holy Spirit's descent, linked to glossolalia in Acts 2.

Fetal Alcohol Syndrome: A condition caused by prenatal alcohol exposure, leading to developmental and cognitive impairments.

First Amendment: U.S. Constitutional amendment protecting freedom of speech, religion, press, assembly, and petition.

FOXP2 gene: A gene linked to speech and language development in humans.

Frequencies (audio): The rate of sound wave vibrations, measured in Hertz, determining pitch.

Frontal lobe: Brain regions involved in decision-making, planning, and impulse control.

Frontoparietal networks: Neural networks linking frontal and parietal lobes, critical for attention and problem-solving.

Galvanic skin response (GSR): Changes in skin's electrical conductivity due to emotional arousal, used in lie detection.

Gaming Disorder: A condition involving excessive video gaming, impairing daily life, recognized in ICD-11.

Gifford Lectures: A prestigious lecture series on natural theology and religion, established in 1888.

Glossolalia: Speaking in tongues, producing unintelligible speech, often in religious contexts.

Good Friday Experiment: A 1962 study where psilocybin induced mystical experiences in divinity students.

Hans Jenny: A 20th-century scientist who advanced cymatics, studying wave patterns and vibrations.

Harmonic progression: A sequence of chords creating musical flow and resolution.

Harmony: The combination of musical notes to create pleasing sounds or chords.

Hertz (Hz): The unit of frequency, measuring cycles per second, used for sound or brain waves.

Hippocampus: A brain structure critical for memory formation and spatial navigation.

Holy Ghost (Holy Spirit): In Christianity, associated with divine presence and power.

Holy Ghost glossolalia (HGG): Speaking in tongues attributed to the Holy Spirit in Pentecostal worship.

Holy rollers: A colloquial term for Pentecostals exhibiting ecstatic behaviors during worship.

Holographic life review: A near-death experience phenomenon where one vividly recalls their life in detail.

Human Genome Project: A global research effort (1990–2003) to map all human genes.

Humanities: Academic disciplines studying human culture, such as literature, history, and philosophy.

Hypocrisy: Pretending to hold beliefs or virtues one does not practice.

Hypofrontal syndromes: Conditions involving reduced frontal lobe activity, linked to impulsivity or apathy.

Hysteria: A historical term for emotional or physical symptoms attributed to psychological distress, now outdated.

ICD-11: The International Classification of Diseases, 11th edition, used for diagnosing health conditions.

Ideology: A set of beliefs or principles shaping a group's worldview or actions.

Immunoglobulin A: An antibody in mucosal areas, linked to immune response and stress regulation.

Impulse control: The ability to resist urges or immediate reactions in favor of long-term goals.

Incarnation: In Christianity, God becoming human in the form of Jesus Christ.

Information workers/knowledge workers: Professionals whose primary tasks involve handling or generating information.

Informational silos: Isolated data or knowledge systems that hinder communication or collaboration.

Institutionalized brain: The brain as shaped by societal structures, norms, or education.

Insula: A brain region involved in emotion, self-awareness, and interoception.

Intelligent Design: The belief that life's complexity indicates a purposeful intelligent cause, often religious.

Intensity: The strength or magnitude of a stimulus, emotion, or experience.

Internal vibrations: Sensations of trembling or energy within the body, often linked to spiritual or physiological states.

Internet Watch Foundation (IWF): A UK organization combating online child sexual abuse material.

Jamesian Approach: A perspective based on William James, emphasizing subjective experience in psychology and religion.

James's Criteria: William James's standards for evaluating religious experiences, focusing on immediacy, passivity, and ineffability.

Jezebel: A biblical figure symbolizing seduction or rebellion; used metaphorically in religious contexts.

Jinn: Supernatural beings in Islamic tradition, capable of influencing humans.

Judgmental errors: Cognitive mistakes in evaluating situations or people, often due to biases.

Jump master: A military role overseeing parachute jumps.

Knowledge songs: Songs conveying cultural, spiritual, or educational information.

Laterality Index: A measure of brain hemisphere dominance, often for language or motor functions.

Legitimate authority: Power recognized as valid by those subject to it, based on law or tradition.

Limbic and paralimbic regions: Brain areas involved in emotion, memory, and motivation, including the amygdala and insula.

Limbic system: A set of brain structures regulating emotions, memory, and survival behaviors.

LSD (Lysergic Acid Diethylamide): A psychedelic drug inducing altered consciousness and perceptions.

Lyrical diet: The consumption of music lyrics to influence mood or mindset.

Marksmanship training: Training to improve firearm accuracy, often involving focus and motor skills.

Mechanical disturbances: Physical disruptions, like vibrations or noise, affecting systems or perception.

Meditation: A practice of focused attention or contemplation to achieve mental clarity or spiritual insight.

Medication-assisted treatments (MAT): Therapies combining medications and counseling for addiction, like opioid dependence.

Melody: A sequence of musical notes perceived as a single, cohesive line.

Mental filters: Cognitive biases or frameworks shaping how information is perceived or prioritized.

Mental hiccup: A brief disruption in thought or perception, often due to stress or distraction.

Mental justifications: Rationalizations created to defend beliefs or actions, often unconsciously.

Meta-analysis: A statistical method combining results from multiple studies to draw broader conclusions.

Microcephalin: A gene linked to brain development and size, studied in human evolution.

Microsaccades: Tiny, involuntary eye movements aiding visual perception.

Mind: The seat of consciousness, thought, and emotion, encompassing cognitive and emotional processes.

Mirror neurons: Neurons that fire when performing or observing an action, aiding empathy and imitation.

Monotheism: Belief in a single deity, as in Christianity, Islam, or Judaism.

Moral Law Argument: A philosophical argument that universal moral laws suggest a divine lawgiver.

Motor action plan: The brain's strategy for coordinating movements to achieve a goal.

Motor cortex: The brain region controlling voluntary muscle movements.

Motor learning: The process of acquiring and refining movement skills through practice.

Motor mirroring: The neural process where mirror neurons mimic observed actions, aiding learning.

Multitasking: Performing multiple tasks simultaneously, often reducing efficiency due to divided attention.

Mystical: Relating to spiritual experiences that transcend ordinary understanding, often ineffable.

Naloxone: A medication used to reverse opioid overdoses by blocking opioid receptors.

Near-death experience (NDE): Profound psychological events during life-threatening situations, often involving visions or peace.

Neural circuitry: The network of interconnected neurons enabling brain functions.

Neural pathways: Routes formed by neuron connections, facilitating communication in the brain.

Neurochemicals: Chemicals like neurotransmitters or hormones regulating brain activity.

Neurogenesis: The formation of new neurons, primarily in the hippocampus, aiding learning and memory.

Neurological bonds: Emotional or cognitive connections facilitated by neural processes.

Neurological clutch: A metaphorical term for the brain's ability to shift focus or adapt under pressure.

Neurological filing error: Mis-processing or mis-storage of information in the brain, leading to errors.

Neurological malfunctions: Disruptions in brain function, causing cognitive or behavioral issues.

Neurological pathways: Specific routes of neural communication, similar to neural pathways.

Neurological processing: The brain's handling of sensory, cognitive, or motor information.

Neuromodulation: Techniques or processes altering neural activity, like brain stimulation or drugs.

Neuronal excitability: The tendency of neurons to fire in response to stimuli, influencing brain activity.

Neurophysiological: Relating to the physiological processes of the nervous system.

Neurotheology: The study of the neural basis of religious and spiritual experiences.

Neurotransmitters: Chemicals transmitting signals between neurons, like dopamine or serotonin.

Niacin: A B vitamin (B3) used in metabolism, sometimes studied for mental health effects.

No-touch torture: Psychological or sensory techniques causing distress without physical contact.

Norepinephrine/epinephrine: Neurotransmitters/hormones involved in arousal, stress, and fight-or-flight responses.

Occam's Razor: The principle favoring simpler explanations when multiple hypotheses are possible.

Glossary

Organ of the Holy Ghost: A metaphorical term in some Christian contexts for the body or mind as a vessel for the Holy Spirit.

Organum: An early form of polyphonic music in medieval Europe, using parallel melodies.

Otago exercise program: A physical therapy program to prevent falls in older adults.

Out-of-body experience (OBE): A sensation of floating outside one's body, often during trauma or meditation.

Oxytocin: A hormone linked to bonding, trust, and social interactions, often called the "love hormone."

Pantheism: The belief that the universe and God are identical, equating nature with divinity.

Parietal lobes (superior parietal lobe): Brain regions involved in spatial awareness, attention, and sensory integration.

Partial Dissociative Identity Disorder: A milder form of DID with less distinct alternate identities.

Participatory music: Music involving active engagement, like singing or playing, rather than passive listening.

Passive listening: Hearing music or sounds without active engagement or focus.

Pathological: Relating to or caused by disease or abnormal processes, often in psychology.

Pathologies: Abnormal conditions or diseases, physical or mental.

Peak experience: A profound, euphoric moment of insight or transcendence, per Maslow's psychology.

Pentatonic scale: A five-note musical scale common across cultures, used in folk and popular music.

Pentecostal: A Christian movement emphasizing direct experience of the Holy Spirit, including glossolalia and healing.

Pepsi paradox: The phenomenon where blind taste tests favor Pepsi, but Coca-Cola dominates market preference.

Peripheral vision: The outer edges of the visual field, less detailed but sensitive to motion.

Perspective-taking: The ability to understand another's viewpoint or emotions.

Perspective: A particular way of viewing or interpreting events, shaped by experience or belief.

Petabytes/terabytes: Units of digital data storage, with petabytes larger than terabytes (roughly 1,000 terabytes in one petabyte).

Phenomenological exegesis: Interpreting experiences or texts by focusing on subjective, lived perspectives.

Philosophy: The study of existence, knowledge, ethics, and reality through reasoned inquiry.

Phonemic restoration: The brain's ability to fill in missing speech sounds based on context.

Physiology: The study of biological functions and processes in living organisms.

Plant Acoustic Frequency Technology (PAFT): Experimental technology using sound frequencies to influence plant growth.

Polyphony: Music with multiple independent melody lines performed simultaneously.

Pornography: Material depicting explicit sexual content, often debated for its psychological and social impacts.

Possession trance (PT): A state where an individual believes they are controlled by a spirit or entity.

Possession Trance Disorder: A condition where possession trances cause distress or impairment, per ICD-11.

Post-Enlightenment: The period after the Enlightenment, marked by skepticism toward rationalism and new philosophies.

Post-Traumatic Stress Disorder (PTSD): A mental health condition triggered by trauma, causing flashbacks and anxiety.

Predictive Algorithms: Computational models forecasting outcomes based on patterns in data.

Prefrontal cortex (PFC): The frontal brain region governing executive functions like planning and impulse control.

Presentational music: Music performed to convey emotion or meaning, often in ritual or theater.

Presumption of atheism: The philosophical stance that atheism is the default until theism is proven.

Primary auditory cortex: The brain area first processing auditory information from the cochlea.

Primitive neural circuitry: Evolutionarily older brain systems governing basic survival functions.

Probability (argument from): A philosophical argument using probability to support claims, like the existence of God.

Problematic pornography use (PPU): Excessive or compulsive pornography consumption causing distress or harm.

Problematic usage of the internet (PUI): Maladaptive internet use impairing daily life, per ICD-11.

Procedural learning: Acquiring skills through practice, like riding a bike, often unconscious.

Prolactin: A hormone involved in lactation and regulating stress responses.

Psychoactive drugs: Substances altering mood, perception, or cognition, like LSD or caffeine.

Psychoneuroimmunology: The study of interactions between psychological factors, the nervous system, and immune function.

Psychopathology: The study of mental disorders and abnormal behaviors.

Psychotic experiences/psychosis: Severe mental states involving delusions, hallucinations, or disorganized thinking.

Psychology: The scientific study of behavior, cognition, and emotion.

Psychotropic medications: Drugs affecting mental states, used to treat disorders like depression or schizophrenia.

PubMed: A database of biomedical and life sciences literature, maintained by the NIH.

Quark confinement: A quantum physics principle where quarks are permanently bound within particles like protons.

Radical Empiricism: William James's philosophy emphasizing experience as the sole basis for knowledge.

Radioisotope (radioactive isotope tracer): A radioactive substance used to track biological or chemical processes.

Rearrangement: In music, altering the structure or elements of a composition; in psychology, cognitive restructuring.

Reductionism: Explaining complex phenomena by reducing them to simpler components.

Religion: A system of beliefs and practices concerning the Divine or supernatural.

Religious songs: Music with spiritual or worship themes, often used in religious services.

Repetition (in music): Reusing musical phrases or motifs to create structure or emphasis.

Representation: The mental or symbolic depiction of ideas, objects, or experiences.

Repression: Unconsciously blocking distressing thoughts or memories from awareness.

Resurrection: In Christianity, Jesus' rising from the dead; broadly, revival or rebirth.

Reward centers: Brain regions, like the nucleus accumbens, activated by pleasurable stimuli.

Rhythm: The pattern of beats or time in music or movement.

Rostral anterior cingulate cortex (rACC): A brain region involved in emotion regulation and conflict monitoring.

Sacrilege: Disrespect or violation of something sacred.

Sanctuary: A sacred or safe place, often a religious site.

Schizophrenia/schizophrenics: A mental disorder involving psychosis, disorganized thinking, and social withdrawal.

Schizotypy: A personality trait involving mild psychotic-like experiences, like unusual beliefs.

Science: The systematic study of the natural world through observation and experimentation.

Scientific Method: A process of hypothesis testing, experimentation, and analysis to gain knowledge.

Scientific revolution: A 16th-to-17th-century shift toward empirical science, led by figures like Galileo and Newton.

Second Law of Thermodynamics: A principle stating that entropy (disorder) in a closed system increases over time.

Secondary Dissociative Syndrome: Dissociation caused by external factors like trauma or drugs, not a primary disorder.

Secular study/secular data: Research or information free from religious or spiritual influence.

Secular: Non-religious or worldly, independent of spiritual beliefs.

Sidgwick Question: A philosophical inquiry into the origins of moral norms, posed by Henry Sidgwick.

Selective serotonin reuptake inhibitors (SSRIs): Antidepressants increasing serotonin levels, like Prozac.

Self-generated CSAM: Child sexual abuse material created by minors, often via sexting.

Sensory domain transference: The crossover of sensory experiences, like hearing colors in synesthesia.

Sensory input/systems: The body's mechanisms for receiving and processing environmental stimuli.

Sensory overload: Overwhelm caused by excessive sensory stimulation, leading to stress or disorientation.

SERE (survival, evasion, resistance, and escape): Military training for surviving and resisting in hostile environments.

Serotonin: A neurotransmitter regulating mood, sleep, and appetite.

Severely emotionally/behaviorally disturbed: A clinical term for significant emotional or behavioral issues.

Sexual coercion: Pressuring or forcing someone into sexual activity against their will.

Sexual conditioning: Learned sexual responses shaped by experiences or stimuli.

Shamanic practices/trances: Spiritual rituals involving altered states to communicate with spirits or heal.

Sharenting: Parents sharing children's personal information or images online, often on social media.

Singing in tongues (glossolalic singing): Singing unintelligible, spirit-inspired sounds in religious worship.

Smartphone: A mobile device combining phone, internet, and computing functions.

Social learning: Acquiring behaviors or knowledge by observing others.

Socialization: The process of learning societal norms, values, and behaviors.

Sociological connection model: A theoretical framework in sociology that examines how social relationships and networks link individuals, groups, or institutions, influencing behaviors, norms, and societal structures; focuses on nodes (actors), ties (relationships), and network structures to analyze the flow of resources, information, and influence, often using concepts like social capital and network theory.

Society for Psychical Research: An organization studying paranormal phenomena, founded in 1882.

Sonograms: Visual representations of sound waves, used in audio analysis or medical imaging.

Soundboard: A device or software mixing and controlling audio signals in music or events.

Sovereign self: The concept of an autonomous, self-governing individual identity.

Spectrum analyzer: A device measuring the frequency components of audio or electromagnetic signals.

Spirit baptism: A Pentecostal experience of being filled with the Holy Spirit, often marked by glossolalia.

Spirituality: Personal beliefs or practices concerning the Divine or transcendent, often distinct from organized religion.

Spiritual data: Information derived from subjective religious or mystical experiences.

Strict synchrony: Precise alignment of actions or rhythms, often in music or group behavior.

Subconscious/unconscious mind: Mental processes operating below conscious awareness, influencing behavior.

Subjective experience: Personal, internal perceptions or feelings, unique to the individual.

Supernatural: Phenomena beyond natural laws, often attributed to divine or mystical forces.

Suppression: Consciously ignoring or restraining thoughts, emotions, or impulses.

Suzuki Method: A music education approach emphasizing early learning and imitation, like language acquisition.

Synapse: The junction between neurons where signals are transmitted via neurotransmitters.

Synesthesia: A condition where one sensory input triggers another, like seeing colors when hearing sounds.

Tarrying at the altar: A Pentecostal practice of prolonged prayer or waiting for spiritual experiences.

Task switching: Shifting attention between different tasks, often incurring a cognitive cost.

Task-switch cost: The time or efficiency loss when alternating between tasks.

Technology integration (in education): Incorporating digital tools into teaching and learning processes.

Temporal lobe: A brain region involved in memory, language, and auditory processing.

Thalamus: A brain structure relaying sensory and motor signals to the cortex.

The Knowledge: The detailed mental map of London streets mastered by taxi drivers.

The Varieties of Religious Experience: A 1902 book by William James analyzing religious and mystical experiences.

Theism: Belief in one or more gods, often with personal attributes.

Theist: A person who believes in the existence of a god or gods.

Theological silos: Isolated religious belief systems that limit broader theological dialogue.

Glossary

Time Dilation Theory: A relativity concept where time passes slower in stronger gravitational fields or at higher speeds.

Tone: The quality or character of a sound, determined by its frequency and timbre.

Tonic chord: The primary chord in a musical key, providing resolution and stability.

Torah: The first five books of the Hebrew Bible, central to Jewish law and tradition.

Transference (sensory): The redirection of sensory experiences across modalities, similar to synesthesia.

Trance Disorder: A condition where trance states cause distress or impairment, per ICD-11.

Transposition: Shifting a musical piece to a different key or pitch.

Triple A (addiction): A model of addiction involving accessibility, affordability, and anonymity.

Trustees: Individuals entrusted with managing assets or responsibilities for others.

Two-tiered system: A structure with two distinct levels, often in social, economic, or cognitive contexts.

Ultrasound: High-frequency sound waves used in medical imaging or industrial applications.

Unity: The state of being whole or cohesive, often in spiritual or social contexts.

Unspecified Dissociative Disorder: A dissociative condition not fitting specific diagnostic criteria.

Upanishads: Ancient Hindu texts exploring philosophical and spiritual concepts.

Usurpation of free will: The overriding or manipulation of an individual's autonomy.

Vagal tone: The activity level of the vagus nerve, linked to stress regulation and emotional health.

Vagus nerve: A cranial nerve regulating autonomic functions like heart rate and digestion.

Vague lyrics: Song lyrics that are ambiguous or open to interpretation, often enhancing emotional impact.

Ventral system: Brain pathways, like the ventral visual stream, processing object recognition.

Ventromedial prefrontal cortex (VMPFC): A brain region involved in decision-making and emotional regulation.

Vibrational quality: The perceived texture or resonance of sound or energy, often in music or spirituality.

Vignette: A brief, evocative description or scenario, often used in research or storytelling.

Virtual reality (VR): A simulated environment experienced through digital interfaces, often immersive.

Voice-figures: Patterns created by vocal vibrations, similar to Chladni figures, used in acoustic studies.

Voodoo: A syncretic religion combining African, Catholic, and indigenous beliefs, often involving rituals.

Xenoglossy/xenolalia: Speaking a language one has not learned, often attributed to supernatural causes.

Zār: A trance-based ritual in some African and Middle Eastern cultures to appease spirits.

INDEX

Index

ENDNOTES

Introduction

1   James W. 1890. *The Principles of Psychology*. Henry Holt and Company.

2   James W. 1902. *The Varieties of Religious Experience: A Study in Human Nature*. Longmans, Green, and Co.

Chapter 1

3   Kant I. 1781. *The Critique of Pure Reason*. CreateSpace Independent Publishing Platform.

4   Schiller FCS. 1891. *Riddles of the Sphinx: A Study in the Philosophy of Evolution*. London: S. Sonnenschein. Pages xxvii, 468.

5   James W. 1898. *Human Immortality: Two Supposed Objections to the Doctrine*. Houghton, Mifflin.

6   Baker MC, Goetz S. 2010. *The Soul Hypothesis: Investigations into the Existence of the Soul*. Bloomsbury Publishing.

7   Eccles JC. 1994. *How the Self Controls Its Brain*. Springer-Verlag.

8   Snow CP. 1959. *The Two Cultures and the Scientific Revolution*. Cambridge University Press.

9   Maslow AH. 1964. *Religions, Values, and Peak-Experiences*. Ohio State University Press.

10 Sciences NAo, Medicine Io. 2008. *Science, Evolution, and Creationism*. Washington, DC: The National Academies Press. Page 88.

11 Wachowski L, Wachowski L. 1999. *The Matrix*.

Chapter 2

12 Zee A. 1989. *Fearful Symmetry: The Search for Beauty in Modern Physics*. Collier Books.

13 Quoted in Chidambaram RS. 2011. *Law of Love and the Mathematics of Spirituality*. AuthorHouse.

14 Downing DC. 2012. *C. S. Lewis as Atheist Turned Apostle*.

15 Flew A. "Theology and Falsification." 1950. Presented at Socratic Club, Oxford University.

16 Flew A. "Theology and Falsification." 1950–51. *University*.

17 Flew A. 1966. *God and Philosophy*. Hutchinson.

18 Flew A. 1976. *The Presumption of Atheism and Other Philosophical Essays on God, Freedom, and Immortality*. Barnes and Noble.

19 Flew A, Varghese RA. 2007. *There Is a God: How the World's Most Notorious Atheist Changed His Mind*. HarperCollins.

20   Collins FS. 2006. *The Language of God: A Scientist Presents Evidence for Belief.*
      Free Press.

21   Lewis CS. 1952. *Mere Christianity.* Macmillan.

22   Collins 2006

23   Hawking S. 1998. *A Brief History of Time.* Random House Publishing Group.

24   Schroeder GL. 2009. *God According to God: A Physicist Proves We've Been Wrong
      About God All Along.* HarperCollins.

Chapter 3

25   Stanley AQ. 2006a. *Teacher Efficacy in Educators of Students Identified as
      Emotionally or Behaviorally Disturbed at Separate, Self-Contained, Public Day
      Schools.*

26   Stanley AQ. 2011. Benefits of Teacher 'Connections' in Stressful Educational
      Settings. *International Journal of Children's Spirituality* 16: 47–58.

27   James 1890

28   James 1902

29   James 1902

30   Hamer DH. 2004. *The God Gene: How Faith Is Hardwired into Our Genes.* New
      York: Doubleday.

31   Miller KR. 2007. *Finding Darwin's God: A Scientist's Search for Common Ground
      Between God and Evolution.* New York: Harper Perennial.

32   Newberg A, Waldman M. 2007. *Born to Believe: God, Science, and the Origin of
      Ordinary and Extraordinary Beliefs.* New York: Free Press.

33   Santomauro DF. November 6, 2021. Global Prevalence and Burden of
      Depressive and Anxiety Disorders in 204 Countries and Territories in 2020 due
      to the COVID-19 Pandemic. *Lancet* 398(10312): 1700–1712. doi:10.1016/
      s0140-6736(21)02143-7.

34   Gable RS. June 2004. Comparison of Acute Lethal Toxicity of Commonly
      Abused Psychoactive Substances. *Addiction* 99(6): 686–96. doi:10.1111/j.1360-
      0443.2004.00744.x.

35   James 1902

36   Maslow 1964

37   Roberts TB, Jesse RN. 1997. Recollections of the Good Friday Experiment: An
      Interview with Huston Smith. *The Journal of Transpersonal Psychology* 29: 6.

38   Griffiths RR, Richards WA, McCann U, Jesse R. 2006. Psilocybin Can
      Occasion Mystical-Type Experiences Having Substantial and Sustained Personal
      Meaning and Spiritual Significance. *Psychopharmacology (Berl)* 187: 268-83;
      discussion 84–92.

39   Kurtz E. 1988. *A.A.: The Story.* Harper & Row.

40   Sidgwick H, Johnson A, Myers FWH, Podmore F, Sidgwick EM. 1894. Report
      on the Census on Hallucinations. Vol. X. 1894: 33. *Proceedings of the Society for
      Psychical Research.*

41   Moody RA. 1975. *Life After Life: The Investigation of a Phenomenon—Survival of
      Bodily Death.* Mockingbird Books.

42   Sabom MB. 1998. *Light and Death: One Doctor's Fascinating Account of Near-Death Experiences.* Zondervan.

43   Reinee-Pasarow. 1981. A Personal Account of an NDE. *Vital Signs* 1: 4–7.

44   Clark K. 1984. Clinical Interventions with Near-Death Experiencers in *The Near-Death Experience: Problems, Prospects, Perspectives,* ed. B Greyson, CP Flynn: Charles C Thomas Publishing Limited.

45   Cook EW, Greyson B, Stevenson I. 1998. Can Any Near-Death Experiences Provide Evidence for the Survival of Human Personality after Death? Relevant Features and Illustrative Case Reports. *Society for Scientific Exploration* 12: 377–406.

46   van Lommel P, van Wees R, Meyers V, Elfferich I. 2001. Near-Death Experience in Survivors of Cardiac Arrest: A Prospective Study in the Netherlands. *Lancet* 358: 2039–45.

47   Ring K, Cooper S. 1997. Near-Death and Out-of-Body Experiences in the Blind: A Study of Apparent Eyeless Vision. *Journal of Near-Death Studies* 16: 101–47.

48   Ring & Cooper 1997

49   Grossman N. 2002. Guest Editorial: Who's Afraid of Life After Death? *Journal of Near-Death Studies* 21(1): 5-24. doi:10.1023/A:1020408011319.

50   Peniston EG, Kulkosky PJ. 1991. Alpha-Theta Brainwave Neuro-Feedback for Vietnam Veterans with CombatRelated Post-Traumatic Stress Disorder. *Medical Psychotherapy* 4: 47–60.

51   Maguire EA, Woollett K, Spiers HJ. 2006. London Taxi Drivers and Bus Drivers: A Structural MRI and Neuropsychological Analysis. *Hippocampus* 16: 1091–101.

Chapter 4

52   Marshall SLA. 2000. *Men Against Fire: The Problem of Battle Command.* University of Oklahoma Press.

53   Lord FA. 1995. *Civil War Collector's Encyclopedia: Volumes I & II.* Book Sales.

54   Carpenter WB. 1874. Principles of Mental Physiology. *Nature* 10: 40–42.

55   Miller NS, Katz JL. March–April 1989. The Neurological Legacy of Psychoanalysis: Freud as a Neurologist. *Comprehensive Psychiatry* 30(2): 128–34.

56   Galbis-Reig D. 2003. Sigmund Freud, MD: Forgotten Contributions to Neurology, Neuropathology, and Anesthesia. *The Internet Journal of Neurology* 3(1).

57   Jung CG, Read H, Fordham M, Adler G. 1979. *Freud and Psychoanalysis,* vol 4. Princeton University Press.

58   Pegna AJ, Khateb A, Lazeyras F, Seghier ML. 2005. Discriminating Emotional Faces Without Primary Visual Cortices Involves the Right Amygdala. *Nature Neuroscience* 8: 24–25.

59   de Gelder B, Tamietto M, van Boxtel G, Goebel R, Sahraie A, van den Stock J, Stienen B, Weiskrantz L, Pegna A. 2008. Intact Navigation Skills after Bilateral Loss of Striate Cortex. Pages R1128–R29.

60   Yi J, Costello P, Fang F, Huang M, Sheng H. 2006. A Gender- and Sexual Orientation-Dependent Spatial Attentional Effect of Invisible Images. *Proceedings of the National Academy of Sciences of the United States of America* 103: 17048–52.

61   McClure SM, Li J, Tomlin D, Cypert KS, Montague LM, Montague P. 2004. Neural Correlates of Behavioral Preference for Culturally Familiar Drinks. *Neuron* 44: 379–87.

62   Cunningham MR. 1979. Weather, Mood, and Helping Behavior: Quasi Experiments with the Sunshine Samaritan. *Journal of Personality and Social Psychology* 37: 1947–56.

63   Rind B. 1996. Effects of Beliefs About Weather Conditions on Tipping. *Journal of Applied Social Psychology* 26: 137–47.

64   Saunders EM. 1993. Stock Prices and Wall Street Weather. *The American Economic Review* 83: 1337–45.

65   Hirshleifer D, Shumway T. 2003. Good Day Sunshine: Stock Returns and the Weather. *The Journal of Finance* 58: 1009–32.

66   Wade KA, Garry M, Read JD, Lindsay DS. 2002. A Picture Is Worth a Thousand Lies: Using False Photographs to Create False Childhood Memories. *Psychonomic Bulletin & Review* 9: 597–603.

67   Braun KA, Ellis R, Loftus EF. 2002. Make My Memory: How Advertising Can Change Our Memories of the Past. *Psychology & Marketing* 19: 1–23.

68   Cialdini RB, Demaine LJ, Sagarin BJ, Barrett DW, Rhoads K, Winter PL. 2006. Managing Social Norms for Persuasive Impact. *Social Influence* 1: 3–15.

69   di Pellegrino G, Fadiga L, Fogassi L, Gallese V, Rizzolatti G. 1992. Understanding Motor Events: A Neurophysiological Study. *Experimental Brain Research* 91: 176–80.

70   Rizzolatti G, Fadiga L, Gallese V, Fogassi L. 1996. Premotor Cortex and the Recognition of Motor Actions. *Cognitive Brain Research* 3: 131–41.

71   Bellelli G, Buccino G, Bernardini B, Padovani A, Trabucchi M. 2010. Action Observation Treatment Improves Recovery of Postsurgical Orthopedic Patients: Evidence for a Top-Down Effect? *Archives of Physical Medicine and Rehabilitation* 91: 1489–94.

72   Jackson RC, Warren S, Abernethy B. 2006. Anticipation Skill and Susceptibility to Deceptive Movement. *Acta Psychologica* 123: 355–71.

73   Liu-Ambrose T, Donaldson MG, Ahamed Y, Graf P, Cook WL, Close J, Lord SR, Khan KM. 2008. Otago Home-Based Strength and Balance Retraining Improves Executive Functioning in Older Fallers: A Randomized Controlled Trial. *Journal of the American Geriatrics Society* 56: 1821–30.

74   Kawasaki T, Tozawa R, Aramaki H. 2018. Effectiveness of Using an Unskilled Model in Action Observation Combined with Motor Imagery Training for Early Motor Learning in Elderly People: A Preliminary Study. *Somatosensory & Motor Research* 35: 204–11.

75   Li Z, Han X-G, Sheng J, Ma S-J. May 1, 2016. Virtual Reality for Improving Balance in Patients After Stroke: A Systematic Review and Meta-Analysis. *Clinical Rehabilitation* 30(5): 432–440. doi:10.1177/0269215515593611.

76   Golomb MR, Warden SJ, Fess E, et al. 2011. Maintained Hand Function and Forearm Bone Health 14 Months After an In-Home Virtual-Reality

Videogame Hand Telerehabilitation Intervention in an Adolescent With Hemiplegic Cerebral Palsy. *Journal of Child Neurology* 26(3): 389–393. doi:10.1177/0883073810394847.

77 Golomb MR, McDonald BC, Warden SJ, et al. January 2010. In-home Virtual Reality Videogame Telerehabilitation in Adolescents with Hemiplegic Cerebral Palsy. *Archives of Physical Medicine and Rehabilitation* 91(1): 1–8.e1. doi:10.1016/j.apmr.2009.08.153.

78 Grossman DA. 2009. *On Killing: The Psychological Cost of Learning to Kill in War and Society*. Little, Brown.

79 Dye DA. 1985. Chuck Cramer: IDF's Master Sniper. *Soldier of Fortune* 60.

80 Grossman 2009

81 Swank RL, Marchand WE. 1946. Combat Neuroses: Development of Combat Exhaustion. *Archives of Neurology & Psychiatry* 55: 236–47.

82 Grossman 2009

83 Rupcic T. December 4, 2023. Techno-Religion and Cyberspace Spirituality in Dystopian Video Games. *Religions* 14(2): 247. doi:https://doi.org/10.3390/rel14020247.

84 Thorold A. 1925. "The Dialogue of the Seraphic Virgin, Catherine of Siena: Dictated by Her, While in a State of Ecstasy, to Her Secretaries, and Completed in the Year of Our Lord 1370. Together with an Account of Her Death by an Eyewitness; Translated from the Original Italian, and Preceded by an Introductory Essay on the Life and Times of the Saint." Burns, Oates & Washbourne Limited.

85 Watson P. 1978. *War On The Mind: The Military Uses and Abuses of Psychology*. Basic Books.

86 Grossman DA, Christensen LW. 2008. On Combat: The Psychology and Physiology of Deadly Conflict in War and in Peace. *Warrior Science Publications*.

87 Grossman 2009

Chapter 5

88 Carr N. 2008. Is Google Making Us Stupid? What the Internet Is Doing to Our Brains. *The Atlantic*.

89 Carr N. 2010. *The Shallows: What the Internet Is Doing to Our Brains*. WW Norton.

90 Marino S. 2023. What Happens in an Internet Minute: 90+ Fascinating Online Stats.

91 Carr 2010

92 Small G, Vorgan G. 2008. *iBrain: Surviving the Technological Alteration of the Modern Mind*. HarperCollins.

93 Rideout VJ, Foehr UG, Roberts DF. January 20, 2010. Generation M2: Media in the Lives of 8- to 18-Year-Olds, Kaiser Family Foundation.

94 Common Sense Media. 2015. Landmark Report: U.S. Teens Use an Average of Nine Hours of Media Per Day, Tweens Use Six Hours. https://www.commonsensemedia.org/press-releases/landmark-report-us-teens-use-an-average-of-nine-hours-of-media-per-day-tweens-use-six-hours.

95   PBS. December 1, 2009. Interview with Clifford Nass. https://www.pbs.org/wgbh/pages/frontline/digitalnation/interviews/nass.html.

96   ScienceDaily. July 26, 2006. Multi-Tasking Adversely Affects Brain's Learning, UCLA Psychologists Report. https://www.sciencedaily.com/releases/2006/07/060726083302.htm.

97   Mark G, Gonzalez V. 2004. Proceedings of the SIGCHI Conference on Human Factors in Computing Systems. Vienna, Austria. ACM Digital Library.

98   Mark G, Gonzalez V, Harris J. 2005. Proceedings of the SIGCHI Conference on Human Factors in Computing Systems. Vienna, Austria, 321–30. ACM Digital Library.

99   Wilmer HH, Sherman LE, Chein JM. 2017. Smartphones and Cognition: A Review of Research Exploring the Links between Mobile Technology Habits and Cognitive Functioning. *Frontiers in Psychology* 8: 605.

100 Mark G, Gudith D, Klocke U. 2008. *The Cost of Interrupted Work: More Speed and Stress.* University of California.

101 Sapolsky RM. *Stress, the Aging Brain, and the Mechanisms of Neuron Death.* 1992. MIT Press.

102 Richtel M. July 28, 2009. In Study, Texting Lifts Crash Risk by Large Margin. *New York Times.*

103 Center PR. April 7, 2021. Mobile Fact Sheet.

104 Fineberg NA, Menchón JM, Hall N, Dell'Osso B, Brand M, Dell'Osso B, Brand M, Potenza MN, Chamberlain SR, Cirnigliaro G, Lochner C, Billieux J, Demetrovics Z, Rumpf HJ, Müller A, Castro-Calvo J, Hollander E, Burkauskas J, Grünblatt E, Walitza S, Corazza O, King DL, Stein DJ, Grant JE, Pallanti S, Bowden-Jones H, Ameringen MV, Ioannidis K, Carmi L, Sales CMD, Jones J, Gjoneska B, Király O, Benatti B, Vismara M, Pellegrini L, Conti D, Cataldo I, Riva GM, Yücel M, Flayelle M, Hall T, Griffiths M, Zohar J. 2022. Advances in Problematic Usage of the Internet Research—A Narrative Review by Experts from the European Network for Problematic Usage of the Internet. *Comprehensive Psychiatry* 118: 152346.

105 Tang CSK, Wu AMS, Yan ECW, Ko J HC, Kwon JH, Yogo M, Gan YQ, Koh YYW. 2018. Relative Risks of Internet-Related Addictions and Mood Disturbances Among College Students: A 7-Country/Region Comparison. *Public Health (Elsevier)* 165: 16–25.

106 Cheng H, Liu J. 2020. Alterations in Amygdala Connectivity in Internet Addiction Disorder. *Scientific Reports* 10: 2370.

107 Stavropoulos V, Frost TMJ, Brown T, Gill P, Footitt TA, Kannis-Dymand L. 2021. Internet Gaming Disorder Behaviours: A Preliminary Exploration of Individualism and Collectivism Profiles. *BMC Psychiatry* 21: 262.

108 Lochner C, Albertella L, Kidd M, Kilic Z, Ioannidis K, Grant JE, Yücel M, Stein DJ, Chamberlain SR. 2022. The COVID-19 Pandemic and Problematic Usage of the Internet: Findings from a Diverse Adult Sample in South Africa. *Journal of Psychiatric Research* 153: 229–35.

109 Ouvrein G, Verswijvel K. 2019. Sharenting: Parental Adoration or Public Humiliation? A Focus Group Study on Adolescents' Experiences with Sharenting Against the Background of Their Own Impression Management. *Children and Youth Services Review* 99: 319–27.

110 Delacroix S. 2020. Social Media Manipulation, Autonomy and Capabilities.

111 Supervisor EDP. 2018. Opinion 3/2018: EDPS Opinion on Online Manipulation and Personal Data.

112 Nemorin S. 2017. Neuromarketing and the "Poor in World" Consumer: How the Animalization of Thinking Underpins Contemporary Market Research Discourses. *Consumption Markets & Culture* 20: 59–80.

113 Pizzolato G, Mandat T. 2012. Deep Brain Stimulation for Movement Disorders. *Frontiers in Integrative Neuroscience* 6.

114 Bonaci T, Calo R, Chizeck HJ. 2015. App Stores for the Brain: Privacy and Security in Brain-Computer Interfaces. *IEEE Technology and Society Magazine* 34: 32–39.

115 Takabi H. 2016. IEEE Conference on Communications and Network Security (CNS): 370–71.

116 Chiuzbaian A, Jakobsen J, Puthusserypady S. 2019. 7th International Winter Conference on Brain-Computer Interface (BCI): 1–5.

117 Onuora S. 2021. Implanted 'Smart' Cells Release Biologic Drugs on Demand. *Nature Reviews Rheumatology* 17: 643–43.

118 Wright PJ. 2023. But Do Porn Sites Get More Traffic than TikTok, OpenAI, and Zoom? *The Journal of Sex Research* 60(6): 763. doi:10.1080/00224499.2023.2220690.

119 Irizarry R, Gallaher H, Samuel S, Soares J, Villela J. June 2023. How the Rise of Problematic Pornography Consumption and the COVID-19 Pandemic Has Led to a Decrease in Physical Sexual Interactions and Relationships and an Increase in Addictive Behaviors and Cluster B Personality Traits: A Meta-Analysis. *Cureus* 15(6): e40539. doi:10.7759/cureus.40539.

120 Rose K. April 3, 2025. Watching Porn at Work? The Consequences of Risky Browsing. CovenantEyes. https://www.covenanteyes.com/blog/watching-porn-at-work-the-consequences-of-risky-browsing/.

121 Mecham NW, Lewis-Western MF, Wood DA. January 1, 2021. The Effects of Pornography on Unethical Behavior in Business. *Journal of Business Ethics* 168(1): 37-54. doi:10.1007/s10551-019-04230-8.

122 Wolak J, Mitchell K, Finkelhor D. 2007. Unwanted and Wanted Exposure to Online Pornography in a National Sample of Youth Internet Users. *Pediatrics* 119(2): 247–257. doi:10.1542/peds.2006-1891.

123 Sun C, Bridges A, Johnson JA, Ezzell MB. May 1, 2016. Pornography and the Male Sexual Script: An Analysis of Consumption and Sexual Relations. *Archives of Sexual Behavior* 45(4): 983–994. doi:10.1007/s10508-014-0391-2.

124 Wright PJ, Debby H, Paul B. November 9, 2020. Adolescent Condom Use, Parent-Adolescent Sexual Health Communication, and Pornography: Findings from a U.S. Probability Sample. *Health Communication* 35(13): 1576–1582. doi:10.1080/10410236.2019.1652392.

125 IWF. https://www.iwf.org.uk/annual-report-2023/trends-and-data/reports-analysis/.

126 IWF. https://www.iwf.org.uk/annual-report-2023/trends-and-data/self-generated-child-sex-abuse/.

127 IWF "self-generated" 2023

128   IWF. https://www.iwf.org.uk/annual-report-2023/case-studies/sexual-recordings-of-3-6-year-olds-via-online-devices/.

129   Foundation IW. 2024. *What has Changed in the AI CSAM Landscape?: AI CSAM Report Update.* https://www.iwf.org.uk/media/nadlcb1z/iwf-ai-csam-report_update-public-jul24v13.pdf.

130   Zattoni F, Gül M, Soligo M, Morlacco A, Motterle G, Collavino J, Barneschi AC, Moschini M, Moro FD. 2021. The Impact of COVID-19 Pandemic on Pornography Habits: A Global Analysis of Google Trends. *International Journal of Impotence Research* 33: 824–31.

131   Hilton DL, Watts C. February 2011. Pornography Addiction: A Neuroscience Perspective. *Surgical Neurology International* 2: 4.

132   Fineberg et al. 2022

133   Cooper A, Scherer CR, Boies SC, Gordon BL. 1999. Sexuality on the Internet: From Sexual Exploration to Pathological Expression. *Professional Psychology: Research and Practice* 30: 154–64.

134   McIlhaney JS, Bush FM. 2008. *Hooked: New Science on How Casual Sex Is Affecting Our Children.* Moody Publishers.

135   Basile KC, Smith SG, Breiding M, Black MC, Mahendra RR. 2014. Sexual Violence Surveillance: Uniform Definitions and Recommended Data Elements, Version 2.0., National Center for Injury Prevention and Control, Centers for Disease Control and Prevention, Atlanta, GA.

136   Rao P. April 5, 2025. 50 Years of Video Game Industry Revenues, by Platform. Internet. Visual Capitalist. https://www.visualcapitalist.com/video-game-industry-revenues-by-platform/.

137   Association ES. 2022b. 2022 Essential Facts About the Video Game Industry.

138   Schusste M. 2000–2003. "Video Gaming Industry Evolution in the US." https://bestgamingtips.com/video-game-industry-statistics-us/.

139   Statista. 2025. "Games - Worldwide." Accessed April 5, 2025. https://www.statista.com/outlook/amo/media/games/worldwide?currency=USD.

140   Clement J. 2025. "Video Game Industry - Statistics & Facts." Statista. Accessed April 5, 2025. https://www.statista.com/topics/868/video-games/.

141   Statista 2025

142   Statista 2025

143   Association AP. 2025. "Teens Say Video Gaming has Social and Mental Health Benefits, but Some Downsides as Well: Problems Include Loss of Sleep, Bullying, and Harassment, Especially for Boys." American Psychological Association. Accessed April 5, 2025. https://www.apa.org/monitor/2025/03/teen-video-gaming-benefits-downsides.

144   Association 2022b

145   Organization WH. 2019. International Classification of Diseases, Eleventh Revision (ICD-11).

146   von Deneen KM, Hussain H, Waheed J, Xinwen W, Yu D, Yuan K. 2022. Comparison of Frontostriatal Circuits in Adolescent Nicotine Addiction and Internet Gaming Disorder. *Journal of Behavioral Addictions* 11: 26–39.

147   Brizendine L. 2006. *The Female Brain.* New York: Morgan Road Books. Pages xix, 279.

Chapter 6

148   Mlodinow L. 2013. *Subliminal: How Your Unconscious Mind Rules Your Behavior*. Vintage Books.

149   Schlaug G. 2015. Chapter 3: Musicians and Music Making as a Model for the Study of Brain Plasticity, in *Progress in Brain Research*, ed. E Altenmüller, S Finger, F Boller, pp. 37–55: Elsevier.

150   Keysers C, Kohler E, Umiltà MA, Nanetti L, Fogassi L, Gallese V. 2003. Audiovisual Mirror Neurons and Action Recognition. *Experimental Brain Research* 153: 628–36.

151   Kohler E, Keysers C, Umiltà MA, Fogassi L, Gallese V, Rizzolatti G. 2002. Hearing Sounds, Understanding Actions: Action Representation in Mirror Neurons. *Science* 297: 846–48.

152   Kohler et al. 2002

153   Haueisen J, Knösche TR. 2001. Involuntary Motor Activity in Pianists Evoked by Music Perception. *Journal of Cognitive Neuroscience* 13: 786–92.

154   Bangert M, Peschel T, Schlaug G, Rotte M, Drescher D, Hinrichs H, Heinze HJ, Altenmüller E. 2006. Shared Networks for Auditory and Motor Processing in Professional Pianists: Evidence from fMRI Conjunction. *NeuroImage* 30: 917–26.

155   Baumann S, Koeneke S, Schmidt CF, Meyer M, Lutz K, Jancke L. 2007. A Network for Audio–Motor Coordination in Skilled Pianists and Non-Musicians. *Brain Research* 1161: 65–78.

156   D'Ausilio A, Altenmüller E, Olivetti Belardinelli M, Lotze M. 2006. Cross-Modal Plasticity of the Motor Cortex While Listening to a Rehearsed Musical Piece. *European Journal of Neuroscience* 24: 955–58.

157   Wu CC, Hamm JP, Lim VK, Kirk IJ. 2016. Mu Rhythm Suppression Demonstrates Action Representation in Pianists During Passive Listening of Piano Melodies. *Experimental Brain Research* 234: 2133–39.

158   Haslinger B, Erhard P, Altenmüller E, Schroeder U, Boecker H, Ceballos-Baumann AO. 2005. Transmodal Sensorimotor Networks During Action Observation in Professional Pianists. *Journal of Cognitive Neuroscience* 17: 282–93.

159   Fitzpatrick F. 2021. *Amplified: Unleash Your Potential Through the Power of Music*. Amplified Media.

160   Jourdain R. 1997. *Music, the Brain, and Ecstasy: How Music Captures Our Imagination*. New York: W. Morrow. Pages xvii, 377.

161   Jourdain 1997

162   Jourdain 1997

163   Jourdain 1997

164   Jourdain 1997

165   Mlodinow 2013

166   Mlodinow 2013

167   Khan HI. 1996. *The Mysticism of Sound and Music: The Sufi Teaching of Hazrat Inayat Khan*. Shambhala.

168   Cusick S. 2008. "'You Are in a Place that Is Out of the World. . .' Music in the Detention Camps of the 'Global War on Terror.'" *Journal of the Society for American Music* 2: 1–26.

169   Mayer J. 2008. *The Dark Side: The Inside Story of How the War on Terror Turned into a War on American Ideals.* New York: Doubleday.

170   Sacks O. 2008. *Musicophilia: Tales of Music and the Brain.* New York: Vintage Books. Page 425.

171   Medina J. 2008. *Brain Rules: 12 Principles for Surviving and Thriving at Work, Home, and School.* Seattle, WA: Pear Press. Page 301.

172   Levitin DJ. 2009. *The World in Six Songs: How the Musical Brain Created Human Nature.* Penguin Publishing Group.

173   Levitin 2009

174   Huron D. 2011. Why Is Sad Music Pleasurable? A Possible Role for Prolactin. *Musicae Scientiae* 15: 146–58.

175   Sacks 2008

176   Beeli G, Esslen M, Jäncke L. 2005. When Coloured Sounds Taste Sweet. *Nature* 434: 38–38.

177   Beeli 2005

178   Mlodinow 2013

179   McFerrin B. 2009. Notes and Neurons: In Search of the Common Chorus. World Science Festival.

Chapter 7

180   Zatorre RJ, Salimpoor VN. 2013. From Perception to Pleasure: Music and Its Neural Substrates. *Proceedings of the National Academy of Sciences of the United States of America* 110 Suppl 2: 10430–7.

181   Newberg A, Waldman MR. 2012. *Words Can Change Your Brain: 12 Conversation Strategies to Build Trust, Resolve Conflict, and Increase Intimacy.* Penguin Publishing Group.

182   DeBartolo T. 2005. *How to Kill a Rock Star: A Novel.* Naperville, Ill.: Sourcebooks Landmark.

183   Freud S. 1971. The Complete Introductory Lectures on Psychoanalysis. London, Allen & Unwin, Strachey J, ed.

184   Hawthorne N. 1932. *The American Notebooks.* Ohio State University Press.

185   Fitzpatrick F. 2021. *Amplified: Unleash Your Potential Through the Power of Music.* Amplified Media.

186   Pereira CS, Teixeira J, Figueiredo P, Xavier J, Castro SL, Brattico E. 2011. Music and Emotions in the Brain: Familiarity Matters. *Public Library of Science ONE* 6: e27241.

187   Margulis EH. 2014. *On Repeat: How Music Plays the Mind.* New York, NY: Oxford University Press. Pages xi, 204.

188   Kraemer DJM, Macrae CN, Green AE, Kelley WM. 2005. Musical Imagery: Sound of Silence Activates Auditory Cortex. *Nature* 434: 158–58.

189   Janata P. 2009. The Neural Architecture of Music-Evoked Autobiographical Memories. *Cerebral Cortex* 19: 2579–94.

190   Fitzpatrick 2021

191   Margulis 2014

192   Twain M. 1876. A Literary Nightmare. *The Atlantic.*

193   Turino T. 2008. *Music as Social Life: The Politics of Participation.* University of Chicago Press.

194   Cramer JG. March 30, 2013. The Sound of the Big Bang. University of Washington. http://faculty.washington.edu/jcramer/BBSound.html.

195   Rayleigh L. 1877/2011. *The Theory of Sound.*

196   Watts-Hughes M. 1904. *The Eidophone; Voice Figures: Geometrical and Natural Forms Produced by Vibrations of the Human Voice.*

197   Waller MD, Chladni EFF. 1961. *Chladni Figures: A Study in Symmetry.*

198   Jenny H. 1967. *Cymatics: A Study of Wave Phenomena and Vibration.*

199   Lauterwasser A. 2007. *Water Sound Images: The Creative Music of the Universe.* MACROmedia.

200   Stuart J, Reid AS. 1997. Cymatics Experiment in the Great Pyramid. Token Rock.

201   Schroeder GL. 1997. *The Science of God: The Convergence of Scientific and Biblical Wisdom.* New York, NY: Broadway Books.

Chapter 8

202   American Psychiatric Association. 2013. *Diagnostic and Statistical Manual of Mental Disorders: DSM-5, 5th ed.* Arlington, VA, US: American Psychiatric Publishing, Inc. Pages xliv, 947.

203   Affairs USDoV. Dissociative Subtype of PTSD.

204   Lanius RA, Brand B, Vermetten E, Frewen PA, Spiegel D. 2012. The Dissociative Subtype of Posttraumatic Stress Disorder: Rationale, Clinical and Neurobiological Evidence, and Implications. *Depression and Anxiety* 29: 701–8.

205   Lanius RA, Vermetten E, Loewenstein RJ, Brand B, Schmahl C, Bremner JD, Spiegel D. 2010. Emotion Modulation in PTSD: Clinical and Neurobiological Evidence for a Dissociative Subtype. *American Journal of Psychiatry* 167: 640–7.

206   American Psychiatric Association. 2022. *Diagnostic and Statistical Manual of Mental Disorders, Fifth Edition, Text Revision.* American Psychiatric Publishers.

207   Organization WH. 2019/2021. International Classification of Diseases, Eleventh Revision (ICD-11). Licensing agreement: https://creativecommons.org/licenses/by-nd/4.0/deed.en.

208   Johnson N. 1957. *The Three Faces of Eve.*

209   Petrie D. 1976. *Sybil.*

210   Hoblit G. 1996. *Primal Fear.*

211   Fincher D. 1999. *Fight Club.*

212   Shyamalan MN. 2016. *Split.*

213   Bourguignon E. 1976. *Possession.* Prospect Heights, IL: Waveland Press.

Endnotes

214 Friedkin W. 1973. *The Exorcist.*

215 Church of Satan. F.A.Q. Demonic Possession, Strange Dreams, and/or Diabolical Destiny. Accessed April 23, 2025. https://churchofsatan.com/faq-possession-dreams-destiny/; The Satanic Temple, Frequently Asked Questions: Do You Worship Satan? Accessed April 23, 2025. https://thesatanictemple.com/pages/faq; Church of Satan. F.A.Q. Fundamental Beliefs. Accessed April 23, 2025. https://churchofsatan.com/faq-fundamental-beliefs/.

216 Becker J. 2004. *Deep Listeners: Music, Emotion, and Trancing.* Indiana University Press.

217 Goodman FD. 1988. *How about Demons?: Possession and Exorcism in the Modern World.* Indiana University Press.

218 Brown KM. 2001. *Mama Lola: A Vodou Priestess in Brooklyn.* University of California Press.

219 Vitebsky P. 1995. *The Shaman.* Macmillan.

220 Boddy J. 1989. *Wombs and Alien Spirits: Women, Men, and the Zār Cult in Northern Sudan.* University of Wisconsin Press.

221 Suryani LK, Jensen G. 1993. *Trance and Possession in Bali: A Window Into Multiple Personality, Possession Disorder, and Suicide.* New York: Oxford University Press.

222 Ward CA. 1989. Possession and Exorcism: Psychopathology and Psychotherapy in a Magico-Religious Context, in *Altered States of Consciousness and Mental Health: A Cross-Cultural Perspective.* Thousand Oaks, CA, US: Sage Publications, Inc. Pages 125–44.

223 Kehoe AB, Giletti DH. 1981. Women's Preponderance in Possession Cults: The Calcium-Deficiency Hypothesis Extended. *American Anthropologist* 83: 549–61.

224 Guillaume A. 1938. *Prophecy and Divination: Among the Hebrews and Other Semites.* Hodder and Stoughton Limited.

225 Sullivan CA. 2025. A History of Glossolalia: Did it Exist Before 1879? Accessed April 14, 2025. https://charlesasullivan.com/1904/glossolalia-ecstasy-tongues/#easy-footnote-4-1904.

226 Erman A. 1894. *Life in Ancient Egypt.* Macmillian.

227 May LC. 1956. A Survey of Glossolalia and Related Phenomena in Non-Christian Religions. *American Anthropologist* 58(1): 75-96.

228 Jennings GJ. August 1967. An Ethnological Study of Glossolalia. Presented at: American Scientific Affiliation. Stanford University, Stanford, CA.

229 May LC. 1956. A Survey of Glossolalia and Related Phenomena in Non-Christian Religions. *American Anthropologist* 58(1): 75–96.

230 Dillon S. 1998. *Glossolalia: An Ethnographic Study of the Rhetorical Role of Speaking in Tongues in the Creation of the Pentecostal Religious Culture.* Wayne State University. https://digitalcommons.wayne.edu/oa_dissertations/1262.

231 McDonnell K. 1970. Catholic Pentecostalism: Problems in Evaluation. *Dialog* 9(4): 35–54. doi:https://doi.org/10.1111/j.1540-6385.1970.tb00560.x.

232 Smith J. March 1, 1842. Our Epitome of Faith. *Times and Seasons,* p. 709. The Joseph Smith Papers.

233 Rose S. 1996. *Orthodoxy and the Religion of the Future.* 4th ed. Saint Herman of Alaska Brotherhood.

234 Lynn CD. 2013. "The Wrong Holy Ghost": Discerning the Apostolic Gift of Discernment Using a Signaling and Systems Theoretical Approach. *Ethos* 41(2): 223–247.

235 May 1956

236 Dillon 1998

237 Samarin WJ. 1979. Making Sense of Glossolalic Nonsense. *Social Research* 46: 88–105.

238 Samarin WJ. 1972. *Tongues of Men and Angels: The Religious Language of Pentecostalism*. Macmillan.

239 Goodman FD. 1972. *Speaking in Tongues: A Cross-Cultural Study of Glossolalia*. Chicago, Illinois: University of Chicago Press.

240 Samarin 1979

241 Goodman 1972

242 Cutten GB. 1927. *Speaking with Tongues: Historically and Psychologically Considered*. Vol 9. Yale University Press.

243 Hine VH. 1969. Pentecostal Glossolalia toward a Functional Interpretation. *Journal for the Scientific Study of Religion* 8: 211–26.

244 Malony HN, Lovekin AA. 1985. *Glossolalia: Behavioral Science Perspectives on Speaking in Tongues*. Oxford University Press.

245 Martínez-Taboas A. 1999. A Case of Spirit Possession and Glossolalia. *Culture, Medicine and Psychiatry* 23: 333–48.

246 Jung CG. 1969. *Psychology and Religion: West and East*. Princeton University Press.

247 Brende JO, Rinsley DB. 1979. Borderline Disorder, Altered States of Consciousness, and Glossolalia. *Journal of American Academy of Psychoanalysis* 7: 165–88.

248 Castelein JD. 1984. Glossolalia and the Psychology of the Self and Narcissism. *Journal of Religion and Health* 23: 47–62.

249 Dawkins R. 2006. *The God Delusion*. Houghton Mifflin Company.

250 Cutten 1927

251 Reeves RR, Kose S, Abubakr A. 2014. Temporal Lobe Discharges and Glossolalia. *Neurocase* 20: 236–40.

252 Samarin WJ. 1973. Glossolalia as Regressive Speech. *Language and Speech* 16: 77–89.

253 Goodman FD. 1973. Glossolalia and Hallucination in Pentecostal Congregations. *Psychopathology* 6: 97–103.

254 Kavan H. 2004. Glossolalia and Altered States of Consciousness in Two New Zealand Religious Movements. *Journal of Contemporary Religion* 19: 171–84.

255 Johnson KD. 2009. A Neuropastoral Care and Counseling Assessment of Glossolalia: A Theosocial Cognitive Study. *Journal of Health Care Chaplaincy* 16: 161–71.

256 Kildahl JP. 1972. The Psychology of Speaking in Tongues.

257 Devereux G. 1961. Shamans as Neurotics. *American Anthropologist* 63: 1088–90.

258 Hollan D. 2000. Culture and Dissociation in Toraja. *Transcultural Psychiatry* 37: 545–59.

259 Hempel AG, Meloy JR, Stern R, Ozone SJ, Gray BT. 2002. Fiery Tongues and Mystical Motivations: Glossolalia in a Forensic Population Is Associated with Mania and Sexual/Religious Delusions. *Journal of Forensic Sciences* 47(2): 305–12.

260 Junginger J. 1990. Predicting Compliance with Command Hallucinations. *The American Journal of Psychiatry* 147: 245–47.

261 American Psychiatric Association 2022

262 Cohn W. 1967. A Movie of Experimentally-Produced Glossolalia. *Journal for the Scientific Study of Religion* 6: 278–78.

263 Holm NG. 1991. Pentecostalism: Conversion and Charismata. *The International Journal for the Psychology of Religion* 1: 135–51.

264 Williamson WP, Hood Jr. RW. 2011. Spirit Baptism: A Phenomenological Study of Religious Experience. *Mental Health, Religion, Culture* 14.

265 Spanos NP, Cross WP, Lepage M, Coristine M. 1986. Glossolalia as Learned Behavior: An Experimental Demonstration. *Journal of Abnormal Psychology* 95: 21–3.

266 Alland A. 1962. "Possession" in a Revivalistic Negro Church. *Journal for the Scientific Study of Religion* 1: 204–13.

267 Williamson and Hood Jr. 2011

268 Holm 1991

269 Lopes D, Vala J, Garcia-Marques L. 2007. Social Validation of Everyday Knowledge: Heterogeneity and Consensus Functionality. *Group Dynamics: Theory, Research, and Practice* 11: 223–39.

270 Goodman FD. 1969. Goodman FD. Glossolalia: Speaking in Tongues in Four Cultural Settings. *Confinia Psychiatrica* 12(2): 113–29.

271 Synan V. 2004. The Pentecostal Movement in North America and Beyond. *Journal of Beliefs and Values* 25: 153–65.

272 Synan 2004

273 Goodman 1988

274 Warfield BB. 1930. *Studies in Tertullian and Augustine*. Oxford University Press.

275 NobelPrize.org. Charles Richet – Facts. The Nobel Prize. Accessed April 19, 2025. https://www.nobelprize.org/prizes/medicine/1913/richet/facts/.

276 Richet C. 1933. *Thirty Years of Psychological Research: A Treatise on Metaphysics*. De Brath S. The MacMillian Company.

277 Evrard R. 2020. Charles Richet and the Emancipation of Metapsychics. *Journal of the Society for Psychical Research* 84(2): 93–109.

278 Goodman 1988

279 Spiegel H. 1963. The Dissociation-Association Continuum. *Journal of Nervous and Mental Disease* 136: 374–8.

280 Wier DR. 1996. *Trance: From Magic to Technology*. Trans Media.

281 Spiegel 1963

282 Spiegel 1963

Chapter 9

283 James W, Perry RB. 1912. *Essays in Radical Empiricism*. Longmans, Green, and Company.

284 Chakrabarty D. 2000. *Provincializing Europe: Postcolonial Thought and Historical Difference*. Princeton University Press.

285 Greeley A. 1987. Mysticism Goes Mainstream. *American Health*.

286 Saver JL, Rabin J. 1997. The Neural Substrates of Religious Experience. *Journal of Neuropsychiatry and Clinical Neurosciences* 9: 498–510.

287 James 1902

288 Koenig HG, Cohen HJ. 2002. *The Link between Religion and Health: Psychoneuroimmunology and the Faith Factor*. Oxford University Press.

289 Koenig H, Koenig HG, King D, Carson VB. 2012. *Handbook of Religion and Health*. Oxford University Press, USA.

290 Koenig HG, McCullough ME, Larson DB. 2001. *Handbook of Religion and Health*. Oxford University Press.

291 Cutten 1927

292 Boisen AT. 1939. Economic Distress and Religious Experience: A Study of the Holy Rollers. *Psychiatry MMC* 2: 185–94.

293 Alland 1962

294 Kiev A. 1964a. *Magic, Faith, and Healing: Studies in Primitive Psychiatry Today*. London: Glencoe Free Press. Pages 3–35.

295 Kiev A. 1964b. Psychotherapeutic Aspects of Pentecostal Sects among West Indian Immigrants to England. *Transcultural Psychiatric Research Review and Newsletter* 15: 129–38.

296 Stagg F, Hinson EG, Oates WE. 1967. *Glossolalia: Tongue Speaking in Biblical, Historical, and Psychological Perspective*. Abingdon Press.

297 Pattison EM, Casey RL. 1969. Glossolalia: A Contemporary Mystical Experience. *International Psychiatry Clinics* 5: 133–48.

298 Hine 1969

299 Samarin 1972

300 Kildahl 1972

301 Goodman FD. 1972. *Speaking in Tongues: A Cross-Cultural Study of Glossolalia*. Chicago, Illinois: University of Chicago Press.

302 Spanos NP, Hewitt EC. 1979. Glossolalia: A Test of the "Trance" and Psychopathology Hypotheses. *Journal of Abnormal Psychology* 88: 427.

303 Grady B, Loewenthal KM. 1997. Features Associated with Speaking in Tongues (Glossolalia). *British Journal of Medical Psychology* 70: 185–91.

304 Francis LJ, Kay WK. 1995. Personality, Mental Health and Glossolalia. *Pneuma* 17: 253–63.

305 Francis LJ, Jones SH. 1997. Personality and Charismatic Experience among Adult Christians. *Pastoral Psychology* 45: 421–28.

306 Johnson 2009

Endnotes

307 Francis LJ, Robbins M. 2003. Personality and Glossolalia: A Study Among Male Evangelical Clergy. *Pastoral Psychology* 51: 391–96.

308 First MB, Williams JB, Karg RS, Spitzer RL. 2016. *SCID-5-CV: Structured Clinical Interview for DSM-5 Disorders: Clinician Version.* Arlington, VA: American Psychiatric Association Publishing.

309 Kéri S, Kállai I, Csigó K. Attribution of Mental States in Glossolalia: A Direct Comparison With Schizophrenia. *Frontiers in Psychology.*

310 Kéri S, Kállai I, Csigó K. 2020. Enhanced Verbal Statistical Learning in Glossolalia. *Cognitive Science* 44: e12865.

311 Chouiter L, Annoni J-M. 2018. Glossolalia and Aphasia: Related but Different Worlds. *Neurologic-Psychiatric Syndromes in Focus—Part II* 42: 96–105.

312 Stanley AQ. 2006b. *Teacher Efficacy in Educators of Students Identified as Emotionally or Behaviorally Disturbed at Separate, Self-Contained, Public Day Schools.* The University of Iowa, Iowa City, Iowa. Page 218.

313 Lynn CD. 2009. *Glossolalia Influences on Stress Response among Apostolic Pentecostals.* University at Albany, State University of New York. Page 358.

314 Newberg A, Waldman M. 2006. *Born to Believe: God, Science, and the Origin of Ordinary and Extraordinary Beliefs.* New York: Free Press.

315 Newberg A, Waldman MR. 2016. *How Enlightenment Changes Your Brain: The New Science of Transformation.* Hay House.

316 Yaden DB, Le Nguyen KD, Kern ML, Belser AB, Eichstaedt JC, Iwry J, Smith ME, Wintering NA, Hood RW, Newberg AB. 2017. Of Roots and Fruits: A Comparison of Psychedelic and Nonpsychedelic Mystical Experiences. *Journal of Humanistic Psychology* 57: 338–53.

317 Newberg AB, Wintering N, Waldman MR, Amen D, Khalsa DS, Alavi A. 2010. Cerebral Blood Flow Differences Between Long-Term Meditators and Non-Meditators. *Consciousness and Cognition: An International Journal* 19: 899–905.

318 Newberg AB, Wintering NA, Morgan D, Waldman MR. 2006. The Measurement of Regional Cerebral Blood Flow During Glossolalia: A Preliminary SPECT Study. *Psychiatry Research: Neuroimaging* 148: 67–71.

319 Newberg AB, Wintering NA, Yaden DB, Waldman MR, Reddin J, Alavi A. 2015. A Case Series Study of the Neurophysiological Effects of Altered States of Mind during Intense Islamic Prayer. *Journal of Physiology* 109: 214–20.

320 Newberg A, D'Aquili E, Rause V. 2001. *Why God Won't Go Away: Brain Science and the Biology of Belief.* New York, NY: Ballantine.

321 Newberg A, Pourdehnad M, Alavi A, d'Aquili EG. 2003. Cerebral Blood Flow during Meditative Prayer: Preliminary Findings and Methodological Issues. *Perceptual and Motor Skills* 97: 625–30.

322 Newberg and Waldman 2016

323 Newberg et al. 2010

324 Sherrill S. 2023. "Open Wide: Inviting God's Presence."

325 Hustad DP. 1987. The Historical Roots of Music in the Pentecostal and Neo-Pentecostal Movements. *The Hymn* 38.

326 Graves R. 2017. *Praying in the Spirit.* Harrison House Publishers.

327 Bartleman F. 1925. *How Pentecost Came to Los Angeles: As It Was in the Beginning.*

328 McNeil WK. 2005. Singing in Tongues. In *Encyclopedia of American Gospel Music.* New York: Routledge.

329 Alexander KE. 2016. Heavenly Choirs In Earthy Spaces: The Significance of Corporate Spiritual Singing In Early Pentecostal Experience. *Journal of Pentecostal Theology* 25: 254–68.

330 Alexander 2016

331 Riss RM, Riss KJ. 1997. *Images of Revival: Another Wave Rolls In.* Destiny Image Publishers.

332 Duncan LT. 1987. Music Among Early Pentecostals. *The Hymn* 38.

333 Riss and Riss 1997

334 Shapson-Coe A, Januszewski M, Berger DR, Pope A, Wu Y, Blakely T, Schalek RL, Li PH, Wang S, Maitin-Shepard J, Karlupia N, Dorkenwald S, Sjostedt E, Leavitt L, Lee D, Troidl J, Collman F, Bailey L, Fitzmaurice A, Kar R, Field B, Wu H, Wagner-Carena J, Aley D, Lau J, Lin Z, Wei D, Pfister H, Peleg A, Jain V, Lichtman JW. 2024. A Petavoxel Fragment of Human Cerebral Cortex Reconstructed at Nanoscale Resolution. *Science (American Association for the Advancement of Science)* 384(6696): eadk4858. doi:10.1126/science.adk4858.

335 Shapson-Coe et al. 2024

336 https://h01-release.storage.googleapis.com/landing.html

337 Stanley AQ. 2022. Interview with Rev. Brian Kinsey regarding his experience of witnessing glossolalic singing at a church conference in Belfast, Northern Ireland, in 1979.

338 Rybarczyk EJ. 2005. Reframing Tongues: Apophaticism and Postmodernism. *Pneuma* 27: 83–104.

339 Alexander 2016

340 Spencer JM. 1990. *Protest and Praise: Sacred Music of Black Religion.* Fortress Press.

341 Schoenberg A. 1983. *Theory of Harmony.* University of California Press.

342 Hinck J. 2018. Heavenly Harmony: An Audio Analysis of Corporate Singing in Tongues. *Pneuma* 40: 167–91.

343 Hinck 2018

344 Rybarczyk 2005

345 Hinck 2018

346 Hinck 2018

347 Stanley AQ. Permissions to use images from Joel Hinck glossolalic singing article, email ed: Hinck, Joel; March 6 & 7, 2023.

348 Stanley AQ. Permissions to use images from Joel Hinck glossolalic singing article, email ed: Hinck, Joel; March 6 & 7, 2023.

349 Stanley AQ. Permissions to use images from Joel Hinck glossolalic singing article, email ed: Hinck, Joel; March 6 & 7, 2023.

350 Lynn 2009

Chapter 10

351 All C. S. Lewis references in this chapter refer to the following: Lewis CS. 1949. *Transposition, and Other Addresses.* Samizdat University Press Quebec.

352 Richie T. 2004. Transposition and Tongues: Pentecostalizing an Important Insight of C. S. Lewis. *Journal of Pentecostal Theology* 13: 117–37.

353 James 1902